D0098292

The International Development Association

A NEW APPROACH TO FOREIGN AID

The International Development Association

A NEW APPROACH TO FOREIGN AID

JAMES H. WEAVER

FREDERICK A. PRAEGER, Publishers
New York · Washington · London

The purpose of the Praeger Special Studies is to make specialized research monographs in international economics and politics available to the academic, business, and government communities. For further information, write to the Special Projects Division, Frederick A. Praeger, Publishers, 111 Fourth Avenue, New York, N.Y. 10003.

FREDERICK A. PRAEGER, *Publishers*
111 Fourth Avenue, New York 3, N.Y., U.S.A.
77-79 Charlotte Street, London W.1, England

Published in the United States of America in 1965
by Frederick A. Praeger, Inc., Publishers

Library of Congress Catalog Card Number: 65-19792

Printed in the United States of America

ACKNOWLEDGMENT

I would like to acknowledge the assistance given me in this study by the faculty of the Economics Department of the University of Oklahoma, where the research was originally undertaken as a dissertation for the Ph. D. degree. Professors Alexander J. Kondonassis and Paul D. Dickens read the entire manuscript and made many constructive suggestions. Other faculty members also made helpful comments.

The staff of the International Development Association has been extremely cooperative. Officials in the United States Treasury Department, in the State Department, and in the Congress have also provided much useful information. Diplomats of member countries of the International Development Association granted me an enormous amount of time. I am grateful for this assistance.

I wish to extend my thanks to all the persons who granted me interviews during the preparation of this study. A number of those who were interviewed preferred anonymity and their wishes have been respected. However, I do wish to extend my deepest thanks to all of them. I would also like to thank the economists who expressed their views concerning the International Development Association in personal letters.

During the course of this research I was provided funds from the National Defense Education Act Fellowship Program in International Studies and the Woodrow Wilson Fellowship Subvention at the University of Oklahoma. Funds were also provided by the American University. Such assistance was very much appreciated. Research assistance, typing, and proofreading were done by Mrs. Diane Hadwiger, Mrs. Claire Heath, and Mrs. Sue Priestland. And finally, I would wish to acknowledge the fact that my wife, Mary Carver Weaver, through her patience and encouragement, has contributed as much to the successful completion of this study as have any efforts of my own.

CONTENTS

LIST OF TABLES

The International Development Association

A NEW APPROACH TO FOREIGN AID

CHAPTER 1 INTRODUCTION

BACKGROUND

Is economic development necessary? Must we change the economic relationships that have bound men together during the millions of years the earth has been inhabited? Oh, we know that people have called for changes in these relationships almost since the beginning of recorded history. We recall Hosea and Jeremiah denouncing society for ignoring the widows and orphans at the gate. We recall the questions they posed. "How can you call yourselves religious people when you do nothing to clothe the naked and feed the hungry?" Or again we recall the venom with which Karl Marx indicted the capitalists of the 19th century for the condition of the working class. But, despite prophets and profits, most of the billions of people born into this world have lived lives that were nasty, brutish, and short. Most still do.

The question that concerns us is whether this condition should be altered. Economists are materialists and would argue that people who live in dry houses, have adequate clothing, eat balanced meals, drive Buick cars, and occasionally get to attend a performance of the Metropolitan Opera are better off than people who live in mud huts, wear rags, eat rice, walk, and have no visible means of entertainment. Nevertheless, there is little agreement that members of an affluent society are really happier than people who wear loin cloths and climb cocoanut trees for their dinner. Why, then should these people suddenly stop climbing cocoanut trees?

The advocates of economic development give two reasons. First, they argue that with the advent of modern communications, people in Africa, Asia, Latin America and even Polynesia know that it is possible to have something more than a life lived in a thatched hut. Once this knowledge has been widely disseminated there is pressure to change. And this pressure seems to mount as the disparities between the well-fed and the ill-fed increase. According to the best estimates, people in the United States of America enjoyed per capita incomes of $2,691 in 1962. Per capita income in India in that same year was $73. If we extrapolate the trends in per capita income that existed during the recent past--that is, if Indian per capita income continues to grow at its present rate of 1.4 per cent and if United States per capita income continues to grow at its present rate of 1.1 per cent per year; by the year 2000 the U. S. citizen will have a per capita income of $4,105 and the Indian will have a per capita income of $126. Thus, although the absolute difference between U. S. and Indian incomes today is $2,618, by 2000 the absolute difference will be $3,979.[1] Thus Marx' prediction is coming true on the international scene--that is, the rich are getting richer and the poor poorer. As this disparity grows it can be expected that the poor will become more zealous for economic development and may exercise their one opportunity--the opportunity to be dangerous.

The second reason that is given for rapid economic change is that it is now possible. For the first time in history it is unnecessary for large numbers of people to go hungry. We have the technical capacity to provide everyone in the world with enough to eat. Thus, hunger in the world becomes an anachronism--some people starving while those who live in the rich countries wrestle with the problem of obesity. Persons in the United States and Western Europe--well-fed, well-educated, well-dressed--seldom think of the fact that half the people in the world are hungry. They never contemplate the curious unevenness of blessings throughout the world and that is the truly odd part about life in the mid-twentieth century. Those who do think about it know that world-wide poverty is dangerous and that its elimination calls for sweeping economic change.

How is this change to be brought about? We can, perhaps, see two different patterns it might follow. One would be a do-it-yourself type of development. This was the path followed by the Soviet Union. The U.S.S.R. had little, if any, outside capital during its period of rapid industrialization and yet from 1913 to 1964, it went from the position of sixth or seventh largest industrial power in the world to its present position as the second largest industrial power. Industrial output in 1913 was between 11 and 12 per cent of that of the United States. Soviet industrial output was approximately 48 per cent of United States output in 1962.[2] A jump from 11 to 12 per cent to 48 per cent of U. S. output in 49 years indicates that the do-it-yourself method does work.

However, a second pattern is also discernible. That is the pattern followed by the United States and it entails massive injections of credit from abroad. The United States was, after all, the first new nation to go to the developed countries of the world begging for help. And by the end of the nineteenth century it is estimated that European investors had plowed $3.7 billion into the United States.[3] In addition to this investment, done with a goal of profit, the United States was also the recipient of the largest foreign aid program in history. We refer to the millions of immigrants who came to the United States after Europe had paid the cost of their unproductive childhood years. In many cases Europe paid the cost of their training, also. And many immigrants brought capital with them when they came.

It is necessary at this point to call attention to my own bias in this matter. I have come to feel that the United States pattern of development was preferable to that followed by the Soviet Union. But, having made allowance for this bias, it is possible to discern a fairly general agreement that the pattern followed by the United States was less painful for the people concerned. Lest we be accused of contributing to the myths that surround the economic development of the United States, let us hasten to add that the differences between the lives of the people in 19th century America and 20th century Russia were less than popular folklore has it. Most accounts of life in the United States during the nineteenth century were written by members of the middle and upper classes who were benefitting from the process of economic development. Therefore, they saw economic development as an essentially beneficent process.[4] Most members of the working class did not come home from their 12 hours in the mines and factories to write of the wonders of industrialization.

It is necessary to remind ourselves that the United States was settled through a policy of genocide. It is also necessary to remember that the economy was built up through the use of millions of steerage immigrants and human slaves.[5] However, having pointed this out, it is still an arguable point that the quality of economic change in the United States was less harsh than in the Soviet Union. And one of the main reasons that it was less harsh was the fact that the United States was able to get credit from Europe to finance a large part of the necessary investment.

So, the alternatives facing the underdeveloped countries today are essentially those of using credit to develop or of developing without it. An analogy to the domestic economy might be illuminating. Should we wait until we have the cash to purchase motor cars, houses, or refrigerators? Or are there advantages in being able to borrow the funds for these purchases? Would the United States gross national product be valued at more than half a trillion dollars today if we did not rely on credit? The answer is obvious because the function of credit on the domestic scene has long been understood. The reason people borrow money is to purchase assets; so that the creation of debt is matched by an increase in national wealth. The same is true in the international economy. Every person who studies the international economy today will have to agree that the process of economic development could be greatly accelerated by extending credit to the developing countries. But, once the point concerning the wisdom of credit is granted, then the question of terms on which to extend the credit arises.

Is aid necessary? This is the question which finally arouses controversy. There is little difference of opinion concerning the necessity of economic development. There is virtually no disputing the beneficent role to be played by credit. But when we raise the question of the terms upon which credit is to be extended we lose unanimity. No one objects to persons or corporations in the rich countries extending credit to developing countries at the going rate of interest or with the object of making a profit. This is viewed as a sound business practice. But, when it is proposed that taxpayers in rich countries subsidize taxpayers in poor countries through the extension of credit on a non-commercial basis--then there is sharp dissent.

No one likes to give money away. And it is psychologically impossible for the rich not to hate the poor. The attitude of the upper class is summed up in the expression "poor and dirty." The prevailing attitude among a large part of the population of the rich countries is that the underdeveloped countries are poor because the people there are lazy--despite the back-breaking toil which is the daily lot of most inhabitants of poor countries. So, one begins to understand that the question "is aid necessary?" is not rhetorical. This is a question which will concern us throughout this study.

But, even if we could agree on the wisdom of extending aid there would still be a question of how to administer it. Should the rich countries set up bureaus to dispense largesse throughout the world? Should such a function be handed over to the United Nations? Or would it be wise to hand over some of these funds to the World Bank? It is this last possibility with which we shall be concerned and particularly with the organization which has come to be called the International Development Association.

OBJECTIVES

One of the objectives of this study is to trace the history of this idea for an International Development Association. It is fascinating to observe the route that this proposal followed, in the United Nations and especially in the United States of America. In fact, it may have set a precedent in foreign policy making in the United States. At least one author has maintained that the Monroney Resolution concerning the International Development Association represented a significant departure from the traditional role of the United States Congress in the foreign policy field.[6]

What was the role of the United States Government in establishing IDA? This study presents the attitude of the American Administration, as it developed, toward this agency. Apparently there were some significant changes of attitude concerning the necessity for a new international financial institution. What caused these changes? We look for proof for the view that the United States endorsed the recommendation for IDA only to offset the drive for SUNFED, that is, the Special United Nations Fund for Economic Development. In IDA, the United States has more than 25 per cent of the votes, whereas in SUNFED it would have had only one vote. It might be reasonable to assume that the United States Government would prefer an IDA-type arrangement to the SUNFED proposal, but was this, in fact, the choice? The argument that the spectre of SUNFED caused United States' policy to favor IDA has been widely circulated.

In addition to determining the view of the United States Government toward IDA, we also want to determine the attitude of the International Bank for Reconstruction and Development toward such an innovation. A certain school of thought holds that the Bank was coming around to the position that something similar to IDA was needed long before the Monroney Resolution saw the light of day. There is the contrary view that the Bank not only failed to recognize the need for IDA but actually opposed the idea. Andrew Shonfield has reported that Eugene Black, then President of the World Bank, said, during the early stages of the discussions on IDA, that "he had never like the idea of 'soft loans,' but if they had to come he was going to make certain that he was the man who handled them."[7] There have been those who have suggested that the Bank captured IDA in order to kill it or at least to dilute its effectiveness. Those persons who were strongly in favor of soft loans can point to the small scale of IDA operations to date and feel reinforced in this view. One goal of the study is to clarify the attitude of World Bank officials to the establishment of a soft loan agency under Bank supervision.

In tracing the history of IDA's birth, we want to examine three issues which arose. First to be considered is the question of soft loans. There was, in 1958, and still is significant opposition to the whole idea of soft loans to underdeveloped countries. And yet the member governments of the World Bank have put up more than a billion dollars for just such soft loans. What were their reasons? What were the arguments that went on concerning this issue? The second significant issue which arose was the proposal to use the local currencies of the less developed countries to finance development. This was a crucial part of Senator Monroney's proposal and yet the International Development Association has not loaned any local currency to anyone. What were the problems of using local currencies and could these problems be overcome? The third issue to be considered is the question of bilateral as opposed to multilateral aid. Some of the support for the Association came out of frustration with bilateral aid programs and out of the feeling that something better was possible.

Another objective of the study is to outline the manner in which the Association is organized; its relationship with the

International Bank; its method of operation; and its major problems. In particular, we are interested in the allocation problem that has arisen in disbursing the money entrusted to this organization. Previously, the World Bank had been able to finance any sound project, presented by a creditworthy country--by selling bonds in the financial markets of the world. However, the funds allocated to the International Development Association have finite limits. Which projects should get loans from the Bank and which from IDA? What should be the basis for deciding--the situation of the country concerned or the type of project involved? What criteria have been established for making these decisions?

LIMITATIONS

This is not a study of the desirability of foreign aid. Neither is this a weighing of the arguments for multilateral as opposed to bilateral aid, although some of these arguments will be given as historical background. The need for soft loans is not treated in an exhaustive fashion although many of the arguments favoring establishment of the International Development Association rest upon the need for funds in addition to hard loans attainable from the International Bank for Reconstruction and Development and conventional loan institutions. But just what is meant by the expression "hard loan?" A hard loan is traditionally defined as one which the lending country can finance out of its own borrowing. Hard loans contain no element of subsidy to the underdeveloped countries. They usually have a duration of less than 30 years. Soft loans are defined as loans which cannot be financed out of borrowing in the market, and are normally made for something over 15 years. Grants are, of course, in a different category altogether. For whatever reasons, grants seem to have been rejected as a foreign aid device by both the donor and recipient countries. Grants will, therefore, not be considered in this study. Much of the case for a Development Association rests on the inadequacy of hard loans alone to meet the development task. Certainly this is the basis of the World Bank's support and they have conducted elaborate and sophisticated studies to show that soft loans are necessary.[8]

It has not been possible to report the arguments that have taken place in the world press concerning the International Development Association. It would have been interesting to have studied the reactions to IDA in the press of the Soviet Union, India, Ghana, West Germany, and all the other countries of the world. Unfortunately, this was not possible. We have had to rely on speeches made by the Governors of the International Bank in order to capture most countries' reactions to the establishment and operation of the International Development Association. The debate that took place in the United States is given fuller coverage because of the accessibility of the data. The reactions of some other countries were obtained through personal interviews.

Just what is an underdeveloped country? Fortunately the problem of definition does not concern us here. We limit our discussion to those countries that are members of the International Development Association and have been allowed to put up 90 per cent of their initial subscription in their own currency (the Part II countries); a total of 76 countries as of June 30, 1964. These 76 countries were located in North, Central, and South America, Western Europe, Asia, and Africa. One Eastern European country (Yugoslavia) is included.

The operations of IDA are studied from September 24, 1960, when the Article of Agreement entered into force, to September 30, 1964. This covers the early formative period and the period in which the basic policy decisions were made, and ends with the September, 1964 meetings of the Board of Governors of the Association.

Perhaps the largest disclaimer to be made for this study concerns a theory of economic development. Although there most certainly is a theory of economic development underlying the operations of the International Development Association, it is not the purpose of this study to delineate that theory. Such a task has perhaps already been undertaken[9] and a further elaboration is a challenging task for another occasion.

SOURCES

The chief source for the study is the International Development Association. Much of the material that was used has been published; however, reliance is placed on unpublished materials and personal interviews and correspondence with staff members. While tracing the history of the proposal for IDA in the United States considerable use is made of public documents of the United States Congress, the National Advisory Council on International Monetary and Financial Problems, and various boards and committees. Interviews with officials in the legislative and executive branches of the United States Government provided helpful information.

In assessing the significance of the International Development Association as a new approach to foreign aid, the opinions of some leading development economists are presented. These opinions were solicited in personal letters which are in the author's possession. In attempting to measure the impact of IDA, representatives of several countries were contacted. In addition, a number of references are made to the works of academic observers of the organization.

METHOD

Chapters 2 through 7 are essentially historical in nature. From the sources previously mentioned, the history of the idea of an International Development Association is traced. These chapters contain a rather complete account of the important forces that shaped the creation of this institution. In Chapters 2 through 7, the author does not attempt to evaluate the arguments, the proposals, and the policies that were put forth, although some of the author's judgments are expressed where deemed appropriate.

Chapters 8 through 14 contain an analysis of the problems that have confronted IDA and of the solutions that have been found. An analysis is made of the criteria being used in making loans. The crucial factors in decision-making are isolated and patterns in the types of projects approved are highlighted. These chapters are concerned with the allocation problem that has arisen. Some of the significant criticisms of IDA are examined. We study some proposals for IDA's future.

Can IDA's success be measured after only 4 years operation? What was hoped for when it was established? Has this been achieved? Does the past 4 years experience suggest any need for expansion of the organization? What are the major criticisms of IDA? These are some of the questions which the author attempts to answer. It is not possible to test IDA in a controlled experiment, by setting up a different type agency, to see if another approach would have been better. So, ultimately, a subjective judgment must be made as to past effectiveness and as to significance for the future.

CHAPTER **2** THE UNITED NATIONS AND THE INTERNATIONAL DEVELOPMENT ASSOCIATION

THE PROPOSED UNITED NATIONS ECONOMIC DEVELOPMENT ADMINISTRATION

The debate concerning the establishment of an International Development Association was very long and wide-ranging.[1] Very early in the life of the United Nations, proposals were made for the establishment of such an institution. The ninth session of the Economic and Social Council, held in 1949, heard a report favoring a United Nations Economic Development Administration or "UNEDA." This proposal was put forth by the Third Session of the Sub-Commission on Economic Development. The idea came from the Chairman of the Sub-Commission, V. K. R. V. Rao of India.

The Sub-Commission pointed out that the economic development of underdeveloped countries involves large-scale investments over a long period of time and that not all of these investments would yield the immediate returns which would be demanded by commercial investors. Yet, some of these projects were more essential to development than commercial investments in mining and manufacturing.

This group noted that the International Bank for Reconstruction and Development had indicated its willingness to expand its activities in financing economic development projects. But,

> on a realistic assessment it cannot be assumed that the Bank could, in the foreseeable future, be able to make a significant contribution to the massive investments required for economic development involved

> over a long period. Moreover, even if the finance available through the Bank could be increased . . . the terms on which it would be available under the policy established by the Bank limit the effectiveness of this financing to underdeveloped countries. There are fields and types of investment required for economic development which can neither satisfy the preconditions required by the Bank, nor carry the interest charges involved, nor be liquidated within the period required.[2]

After having written off the International Bank, the Sub-Commission turned to the proposal by its Chairman, Mr. Rao. This proposal was deemed to be deserving of consideration and it was commended to the attention of the Economic and Social Council.

What was the Rao proposal? After having surveyed the field of international financial agencies, Rao concluded that there was no international agency for: (1) Financing projects which were not bankable; (2) Aiding underdeveloped countries in the preparation and execution of development programs; (3) Co-ordinating technical assistance activities; (4) Promoting projects that extended over more than one national frontier. He, therefore, suggested that such an agency be established.[3]

The functions of the United Nations Economic Development Administration would be: (1) To make technical assistance available; (2) To co-ordinate technical assistance activities of the specialized agencies of the United Nations; (3) To assist underdeveloped countries in the procurement of needed materials; (4) To finance such schemes as could not be financed through normal banking institutions; (5) To promote regional developmental projects.[4]

Rao proposed that UNEDA be financed through the contributions of member governments. These would be in the currencies of the countries concerned and expenditures would be subject to the approval of the country whose currency was used. Rao stated that, for the time being, the bulk of the resources would have to come from the United States of America. No definite figure was indicated for the total budget or for the United States' contribution.

Assistance would be given in the form of loans and not of grants, although the terms of repayment would be liberal and the interest rate would only be nominal. All assistance would be conditional on the receiving country providing a share (as much as 50 per cent) of the costs of the projects financed.

Projects would have to meet an economic test, "in the sense that their completion will result in raising the productivity of the underdeveloped areas and the standard of living of their people."[5] Rao saw UNEDA as a complement to the existing channels of international finance and not as a substitute or alternative to these channels. He was particularly insistent that the agency would be expected to operate in a business-like manner and that no new bureaucracy be set up to administer the program. To accomplish these goals, he urged that most of the projects undertaken be carried out through the specialized agencies of the United Nations, that is, the Food and Agricultural Organization, the World Health Organization, the International Labor Organization, the United Nations Educational Scientific and Cultural Organization, and the World Bank.

The United States member of the Sub-Commission, E. G. Collado, took rather strong exception to Mr. Rao's proposal. The gist of his dissent follows:

> I believe sincerely that the most effective and desirable pattern of organization of the domestic economy from the economic and social points of view is that which gives greatest emphasis to free private enterprise and institutions guided and even regulated and supplemented by government where necessary in the broadest interests of the people and the nation. This is the pattern which has brought great benefits to my own country and, I believe, to many other . . . nations in various stages of economic development . . . . I therefore believe strongly that the United States should co-operate fully in sound economic development of under-developed countries, that it should look primarily to American private enterprise to provide abroad investment of capital and technique, and that it should rely fundamentally on the International Bank for Reconstruction and Development for financing or collaborating in financing closely circumscribed types of project basic to development not readily susceptible

of implementation by purely private financing.[6]

This position of the United States, enunciated clearly in 1949, was to continue throughout the Administration of President Truman and most of the Eisenhower years. This policy, of primary reliance on private enterprise for economic development --aided and abetted when absolutely necessary by the World Bank-- was used in opposition to Rao's proposal for UNEDA and for all the subsequent proposals for a Special United Nations Fund for Economic Development or for a United Nations Capital Development Fund.

The United States, with its Tennessee Valley Authority, Reconstruction Finance Corporation, Federal Housing Administration, and Federal Land Bank, insisted that the developing countries of the world rely on private capital for their own economic development. The United States seemed to have demanded a purer practice in others than deemed necessary for its own economy. Or, as one observer put it, a Democratic Administration acted abroad as though Robert Taft were really President.

Without United States support, Rao's proposal had no chance of acceptance. He had foreseen that United States support was crucial for the success of UNEDA. And when the United States withheld support, the proposal went no further. The report of the Sub-Commission on Economic Development was, however, circulated to the specialized agencies of the United Nations for their comments.

The Food and Agricultural Organization was impressed with the limitations of the International Bank which the report had described.

> It has only recently made its first loans for outright development purposes, and these largely to relatively prosperous countries.
>
> . . . .
>
> It is limited in its loans for agricultural purposes because of the shortage of development projects adequately prepared and planned, and because of the inability of many agricultural projects to earn foreign exchange to repay them.[7]

This same organization revealed an under-consumptionist bias when it called for the United States to contribute heavily to economic development abroad in its own interest.

> Looking further ahead, the recent exceptionally high domestic investment rates in the United States and other developed countries are unlikely to be long sustained. So long as the United States maintains its present general economic institutions, including the structure of taxes, business and government finance, and distribution of income among its population, a large and sustained outflow of funds for foreign investment might well be helpful in assuring sustained high levels of domestic employment and economic activity.[8]

As can be surmised, the Food and Agricultural Organization gave the Sub-Commission report quite sympathetic consideration.

The International Bank for Reconstruction and Development viewed the report with antipathy.

> The Sub-Commission considers it unrealistic to assume "that the Bank could, in the foreseeable future, be able to make a significant contribution to the massive investments required for economic development involved over a long period." The magnitude of the task cannot be denied, but magnitude alone cannot determine the pace at which it is undertaken. The report itself admits the dearth of soundly conceived projects and this agrees with the Bank's experience. Rash expenditure now would prejudice the flow of investment in the future; for in the last resort development relies on the savings of the world, which can hardly be expected to be forthcoming if they are misused. Eventually more sound projects may be presented to the Bank than it can finance, but that time is not yet in sight.[9]

The Bank went on to point out that underdevelopment itself implied an insufficiency of skills with which to make development plans and implement them. And in addition to being short of skills, the underdeveloped countries were pictured as being short of the most rudimentary data necessary for planning purposes. In addition, the Bank pointed out that the necessary political and social foundations for development had to be built gradually. Low productivity and living standards were pictured as being just as much the result of bad government, bad health, unsound finance, and lack of education as of inadequate resources or the lack of productive facilities.

The Bank statement expressed an unwillingness to be deflected from its determination to make loans only for sound and productive projects. And any organization which lowered its standards in that respect would be guilty of waste for the sake of ostensibly humanitarian objectives.

> The proposal for the so-called United Nations Economic Development Administration . . . is based on an alleged need for a new international agency . . . /for/ "financing projects of economically underdeveloped countries which are not financially productive in a banking sense" . . . . The Bank itself was established to finance development projects for which private capital is not available.[10]

The Bank pointed out that its own interest rates were not designed to make any profit, so that loans which were made at lower rates would be simply disguised intergovernmental grants. Four of the functions of the proposed UNEDA were examined and each of them was found to be a present function of the Bank or one of some existing agency.

The Bank argued that its experience suggested that for the immediate future it would be able to acquire sufficient resources to finance all sound development projects in member countries that were ready for execution and that could appropriately be financed by foreign loans which were expected to be paid. This did not mean that the Bank's resources were adequate for all the world's development needs. "There is . . . a vast difference between the amount of money which can usefully be employed and the amount of additional external debt which the underdeveloped countries can properly assume."[11] In many cases, these countries did not have very good prospects of being able to repay foreign debt. And since Bank financing must necessarily take the form of external debt, it could only provide a part of the foreign capital necessary for development.

The Bank agreed that there are capital requirements for health, sanitation, and other social purposes which are indispensable for economic development yet which could not yield a direct return. In some of the poorer countries such basic projects as highway construction, irrigation, and land clearing might also be non-bankable projects because the burden of servicing such debt would be too heavy. However, the Bank did not feel it proper to comment on the various proposals that had been made to extend assistance for such projects on a grant basis. The decision on such proposals was felt to be a matter for the governments of the donor countries to make.

THE COMMITTEE OF EXPERTS

After this discussion of the Rao proposal, nothing significant occurred until 1950, when the Secretary General was asked to appoint a group of experts to study this problem. This request was made by the Economic and Social Council in resolution 290 (XI). Tryge Lie appointed five well-known experts to make recommendations as to what could be done to help the developing countries. The experts were W. Arthur Lewis, Theodore W. Schultz, Alberto Baltra Cortez, D. R. Gadgil, and George Hakim, who served as chairman of the group. The experts' report was presented to the General Assembly in May, 1951.[12]

This group concluded that a minimum 2 per cent increase in the per capita national income of the developing countries was necessary. And in order to achieve this 2 per cent, they figured that an annual capital import of well over $10 billion would be required.

They turned to the existing agencies to see if they might meet the need. The International Bank, at that time, was loaning to the underdeveloped countries at a rate well below $300 million annually. Thus, the experts decided that the Bank was not beginning to meet the challenge presented. And there was a significant obstacle in the way of increasing Bank lending. According to its charter, the Bank had to charge rates of interest which would attract funds in the financial markets.

> The amount that can profitably be invested at a 4 per cent rate of interest depends on the amount which is being spent at the same time on improving social capital; and especially on public health, on education and on roads and communications. There is much to be done in this way in the underdeveloped countries before they will be in a position to absorb large amounts of loan capital.[13]

The underdeveloped countries obviously did not have the money needed for improving their social overhead capital. And they, just as obviously, could not borrow the amount of money necessary for such purposes. Yet, without these basic facilities, economic development was extremely difficult.

To meet this problem, the experts proposed that some mechanism be established for transferring grants-in-aid of about $3 billion a year to the developing countries. This was considerably less than 1 per cent of the national incomes of Western Europe, Australasia, the United States, and Canada.

> The principle that the better off should help to pay for the education, the medical services and other public services received by the poorer classes of the community is now well established within every Member nation of the United Nations. The idea that this principle should also be applied as between rich and poor nations is relatively new. It has, however, been put into practice on several occasions.[14]

The experts cautioned that they were not proposing unconditional aid handed out like alms. What they wanted was grants linked to a specific function with international verification that the funds were used properly. And to oversee such a program, the experts took note of a proposal which had been put forward in the United States by the International Development Advisory Board. This Board had urged the establishment of an International Development Authority under World Bank auspices. The United Nations experts recommended establishment of an International Development Authority under United Nations auspices.

The experts took note of the fact that some countries might prefer to set up bilateral programs for development assistance. However, they felt that international administration had definite advantages over such bilateral approaches. For one thing, international verification of expenditure would be more acceptable to the receiving countries. Secondly, some of the Scandinavian and Australasian countries' traditions were more in keeping with international cooperation and such an organization would save them the expense of setting up separate organizations of their own.

The functions of the Authority would be as follows: (1) To decide upon and administer grants-in-aid for specific purposes and to verify their utilization; (2) To cooperate with developing countries in preparation and coordination of plans for economic development; (3) To help in implementing development plans --by procuring technical personnel and equipment; (4) To make reports on the progress of the underdeveloped countries and recommendations for further action.[15]

The types of projects that would be eligible for grants would be: research and education, public health programs, subsidation of farm credit, and improvement of public works. The Authority would also be authorized to cooperate with the International Bank in undertaking projects. In cases where social overhead projects could not meet the Bank's standards for the full cost of the project, the Bank might loan the part that was bankable while the Development Authority would make a grant for the remainder.

The experts were unimpressed by the arguments of many persons that the underdeveloped countries were unready to absorb large amounts of capital. They were "impressed by the results achieved during the Second World War by programmes of rapid and intensive training of industrial workers and technicians."[16] There were no bottlenecks which could not be overcome, if enough money and effort were devoted to the task.

The President of the Bank, Eugene Black, took note of the proposal of the experts in his speech to the Board of Governors in 1951.

> It is my opinion, which I think the record adequately supports, that unless the international situation deteriorates further, we will be able to meet all the

> capital needs of economic development in our member states, to the extent that those needs ought properly to be met on a long-term loan basis.
>
> In view of the record, it seems strange indeed that suggestions are still heard that new ways must be found to increase many times over the amount of intergovernmental loans for development purposes. Such suggestions, in my experience, are usually based on large but hazy calculations of what is available and what really can be used in the form of loan capital for development. . . .
>
> I would like to record my emphatic disagreement with suggestions of this kind. . . .
>
> That is not to say that there may not be other useful instruments in the field of providing capital, on an international basis, for economic growth. The idea has been advanced, for instance, of an international authority to allocate grants for development. Under present world conditions, it does not appear likely that any significant amount of grant capital will be provided on a truly international basis; but the idea has merits that might well be considered in a later and happier day.[17]

Black was referring to the International Development Authority which had been proposed by Nelson Rockefeller's International Development Advisory Board.

He returned to this theme in his 1952 speech to the Governors. He was, throughout the discussion on new institutions, arguing that the Bank was ready to play a larger role.

> Some of the proposals which recently have been made envisage the creation of a new financing institution. If new arrangements come into existence, the Bank would, of course, cooperate with them. But let me point out that new institutions themselves do not create savings. Fundamentally we must work with what we have. I myself believe very strongly that the Bank itself could operate effectively as an instrument for mobilizing European capital, and I doubt that sufficient consideration has yet been given to the role we might play in this respect.[18]

The statement that "new institutions themselves do not create savings" came back to haunt Black as it was used again and again in opposition to the establishment of the International Development Association almost a decade later.

It was Black's position that the International Bank had been established as an international organization, a specialized agency of the United Nations, for the purpose of reconstructing and developing the war-ravaged world. Why not use it for that purpose? In one of the most eloquent passages from Black's many speeches and writings he argued his case for the Bank.

> Economic development is an important objective for the entire community of nations. It is important to less developed countries in terms of production, of standards of living and of continuing national growth. It is not less important to countries that already have reached a high stage of development. Their own livelihood and their own future depend on the progressive expansion of world production and commerce.
>
> . . . Not long ago, the world emerged from a great war which made it necessary, in many areas, to suspend normal processes of economic growth. The nations have had to engage in tremendous effort and to spend enormous sums of money to repair the loss of those years. Surely we would now court disaster if economic development were again to be treated as a secondary problem and more years were to be lost.
>
> . . . .
>
> Let me conclude by restating what, as I see it, we are all seeking in this process of economic development. Expanding world commerce and higher living standards are phrases that mean something important, but they may obscure the fact that both the source and the object of our efforts is the individual human being. In him is the motive power of what we can do, and for him are the rewards of what we can accomplish.
>
> More clearly today than ever before, we know what happens when men live and are treated as masses, as statistics, as servants of privileged classes or as creatures of the state. All during our lifetimes, we have seen them erupt in riot and bloodshed; we have seen them hypnotized and driven to self-destruction in

> war. The threat that faces us today does not lie in the willfullness of a few men; it lies in their ability to control people in masses, and to appeal to other masses who may be willing to exchange one form of subjugation for another.
>
> In that perspective, economic development can be one of the most significant and constructive activities of our time. Through development, we can help give men a chance to satisfy their aspirations not as a mob but as individuals. For one of the striking characteristics of a developed society is the great variety of choice it can offer to individuals; a choice not merely of one 20th century convenience over another; but a choice of work, of careers, of living places, of ideas and of leadership.
>
> Variety of choice is one of the things we are talking about when we talk about freedom. In far too much of the world today, this element of freedom does not exist. Men are likely to think they have a choice only between extremes; between slow starvation and quick revolution; between complete inertia and regimented obedience to political leaders who themselves may represent extremes.[19]

Black was speaking for a middle road between slow starvation and quick revolution. He had seen the results of revolutionary economic development in Germany, Japan, and Russia. He and those who agreed with him wanted to give countries another alternative--so that they might, with outside aid, develop quickly but peacefully. Black saw economic development as a process that should be carefully planned, soundly financed, and competently guided. People of this persuasion are convinced that outside capital can have a very beneficial effect on the process of economic growth, if such outside capital is soundly administered. They put economic considerations ahead of short-run political advantages because they believe that a prosperous world is "far more stable and peaceful than the one around us today."[20]

Despite the pleas of Black and those who agreed with him, however, there was continuing pressure from the developing nations to bypass the International Bank and set up a new United Nations agency.

THE ORIGIN OF SUNFED

The seventh session of the General Assembly passed resolution 622 A on December 21, 1952 which endorsed a request of the Economic and Social Council for a detailed plan for a special fund for financing economic development. The Secretary General, Trygve Lie, appointed a 9-man committee. The members of the Committee made no recommendation as to whether such a Fund should be established. They were merely interested in drawing a blueprint for a successful agency, should the United Nations decide to establish it. They were addressing the same problem faced by the Sub-Commission on Economic Development; that is, the need for non-commercial capital in the form of grants-in-aid, or long-term, low-interest loans.

The Committee recommended that the Fund should depend for its main budget on voluntary contributions on the part of governments.[21] However, they also recommended that the administrators of the Fund should be authorized to accept non-governmental or private contributions in addition to contributions by governments. They encouraged the Fund to appeal for such contributions and made a plea for nations to declare such contributions tax deductible.[22]

It is unfortunate that such a provision has never been made in the establishment of any international aid agency. There is a possibility of a citizen response that has never been tapped in the drive for economic development. But those persons who are familiar with the enthusiasm generated by War Bond Drives, Bonds for Israel Campaigns, etc. can testify to the public's willingness to subscribe to respected causes. Member governments would want the right to refuse such solicitation--but this would probably not be an obstacle in the case of IDA.

There has been a proposal that the International Development Association should launch such a campaign. An English organization has made a proposal to set up projects for a Peace Investment Trust and to gather nickels and dimes--raised all over the world--which would be invested in bonds issued by the IDA.[23] The Charter allows IDA to borrow funds but the organization could not pay interest on the funds borrowed since it does not collect interest on its loans. And there is no need to raise funds for the World Bank by collecting nickels and dimes because the Bank can raise all the funds it can prudently use, in the capital markets, in much more manageable operations. Thus, this idea proposed by the Committee of Nine a decade ago, has never yet been tried.

The Committee made recommendations about the structure of the Special Fund as follows: The Fund should not be established until at least $250 million had been pledged by at least 30 governments; the fund should make both long-term, low-interest loans, and grants-in-aid; the Executive Board would be made up of an equal number of representatives from the major contributors and the other governments; and no mechanism of weighted voting should operate in the Board. This last recommendation has been a serious stumbling block in all attempts to set up a development fund under United Nations auspices. The rich nations of the world are asked to contribute funds to an agency whose policies they would not be able to determine as they now determine World Bank policy. This plan has been hailed with enthusiasm by all the underdeveloped nations but the United States has looked on it with considerably less fervor.

The Committee recommended that any investment projects which could not otherwise be financed should qualify for consideration by the Fund. They pointed out that although non-self-liquidating projects might well constitute a significant part of the Fund's operations, its scope should not be limited to such operations. The Committee went on to say that the Fund should be able to finance revenue producing projects.[24] This recommendation would seem to put the Special Fund in competition with the International Bank and this is just the way many people saw it at the time.

THE SCHEYVEN REPORTS

The eighth session of the General Assembly, held in 1953, asked the member governments of the United Nations and the specialized agencies to comment on the proposal for SUNFED. Raymond Scheyven, of Belgium, was asked to prepare a report on the attitudes of governments toward establishment of a Special Fund. Mr. Scheyven presented his report in August, 1954.[25]

The report made quite a point of the World Bank's limitations in financing non-self-liquidating projects. By virtue of the fact that the Bank must evaluate a country's ability to repay debt in hard currency, there are many countries which are unable to meet banking standards. And this means that "many projects--even projects of very great importance from the point of view of economic development--cannot be financed by the Bank."[26]

There was general agreement on this point among the members of the United Nations. But there was a sharp split as to how this problem should be solved. One group of countries, those considered to be underdeveloped, urged immediate creation of a Special Fund. A second group of countries--including the Federal Republic of Germany, Canada, the United States of America, New Zealand, the United Kingdom, Sweden, and Switzerland--maintained that progress must be made in disarmament before any contribution could be made to financing a Special Fund. The third group of countries--which included Denmark, Italy, Norway, the Netherlands, Belgium, France, Japan, and Luxembourg--expressed the view that it would be regrettable to make the creation of SUNFED contingent upon a reduction in armament costs, and declared themselves ready to contribute to the Fund.[27]

The General Assembly adopted resolution 822 during its ninth session on December 11, 1954. This resolution requested that Mr. Scheyven prepare a further report on the establishment of SUNFED. This Mr. Scheyven did. His second report, dated May 23, 1955, contained some further recommendations as to the structure of the Fund. This report contained a clear statement that the Special Fund should only make investments which could not be financed by private capital or by the International Bank.[28] The Special Fund would provide grants or loans repayable in local currency, but would have no authority to make so-called "fuzzy" loans. This second report of Mr. Scheyven called for close cooperation between the International Bank and SUNFED. A proposal was made that the two agencies might cooperate on the same projects. The Bank could make a loan on conventional terms and the Special Fund could make a grant for the remainder. This is not unlike the arrangement that has been worked out between the International Bank and the IDA in several countries. All in all, this second Scheyven report was much more cognizant of the contribution of the World Bank than was the report prepared by the Committee of Nine.

THE IMPACT OF SUNFED

Debate on the desirability of establishing SUNFED continues to this day. Critics have charged that if the United Nations established SUNFED it would have the Soviet Union in it and that this would ruin the operation from the beginning. It was felt that the United States Congress would be reluctant or unwilling to appropriate funds for any agency which would dispense aid to communist countries or have communist countries on its board. Officials in the United States were not too enthusiastic about the fact that the United States Government would have had to provide most all the money for SUNFED, because experience has been that the Russians have not contributed significantly to either the Technical Assistance Program of the United Nations or other such programs. There was also a feeling in the United States Government that the United Nations could not administer such a program. As one official in the Treasury Department put it, "If SUNFED had been established, it would have been one more organization created which would have spent money incompetently."[29]

The International Bank opposed the establishment of SUNFED because of its political administration--which it was felt would be poor administration. The United Nations is a political organization. Various aid-giving countries might put pressure on the administrators of SUNFED to favor certain countries in the granting of loans. Economic considerations might become unimportant in such a situation. However, the Bank's main objection to SUNFED was based on the fact that SUNFED was going to give lenient loans. Everybody would have gone to SUNFED for financing. The only way the Bank would agree to having another type of money available was to have it in the same building, with the same men making decisions on World Bank loans and the lenient loans.[30] This is the solution that was finally adopted with the establishment of the International Development Association.

There was considerable criticism of SUNFED on other points, also. One point of criticism was the plan to give each country one vote in the deliberations.

> This is plainly regarded as the ideal solution by the underdeveloped countries themselves. It is not unkind to suggest that they may be partly influenced by the thought that they would generally be able to command a majority of the votes in such an organization. They seem to envisage a complete specialization of functions, the donor nations solely concerned with the giving and the receiving nations with the disposal of the funds.[31]

Although the question of voting strength was important in the United States' position on SUNFED, it is the author's distinct impression that the United States' position was based more on competence than on voting strength. The United States' view is that the World Bank has competent people to do the work and that they overcome many problems by only taking on specific projects. Thus, if there had to be a new international agency, the United States would much prefer it under the Bank than under the United Nations.

Harlan Cleveland objected to SUNFED because the proposal did not contemplate a strong director. Cleveland feels that "the World Bank, which is essentially run, not by its Board, but by President Eugene Black and his staff"[32] was a better pattern to follow. Again, he criticized the proposal that "SUNFED, like an international Community Chest, would be dependent on annual contributions by its members instead of starting life, as an investment organization should, with a nest-egg of contributed capital."[33]

Andrew Shonfield has elaborated a charge made earlier that the United Nations simply could not administer such a scheme.

> No doubt it would be able to dole out money to the poor countries each year on some simple criterion--e.g., equal shares for all or some system of weighting according to size of population, or even according to national income. But the United Nations as it now stands is not an executive organ which is capable of exercising discriminating and purposeful control over a development program of this magnitude. And if it were able to do so, the underdeveloped countries . . . would almost certainly like it no better than they like the World Bank or the International Development Association.[34]

Professor Benham gave a little more positive view of SUNFED. He argued that the most effective way of increasing economic aid would be to set up SUNFED. The underdeveloped countries like the idea "partly because they would have had some voice in its affairs; they have no voice in the affairs of an institution such as the International Development Association. . . . They welcomed it also because its aid would have consisted partly of outright grants,"[35] whereas, IDA's charter specifically prohibits grants.

Although SUNFED was never established, the pressure for such an agency has had significant influence. Eugene Black has stated that "the International Development Association was really an idea to offset the urge for SUNFED."[36] This view has also been expressed to the author by officials of the United States Treasury Department.

Benjamin Higgins believes that "the pressure for SUNFED had two results. First, in October 1958 the United Nations Special Fund was established.

. . . .

A more recent response . . . is the International Development Association."[37]

The establishment of these two new organizations, the United Nations Special Fund, under the leadership of Paul Hoffman, and the IDA, within the World Bank, has reduced but not eliminated the plea of the underdeveloped countries for SUNFED.

In fact, the United Nations Conference on Trade and Development held in Geneva in 1964 was the forum for another proposal to establish an agency patterned after SUNFED. The final act of the Conference recommended that

> the United Nations Capital Development Fund should start its operations at an early date to finance on favorable terms in all developing countries . . . national and regional development plans, programmes and projects, particularly in the field of industrialization.
>
> The resources of the United Nations Capital Development Fund should be derived from voluntary contributions.[38]

The conferees in Geneva wanted to convert the United Nations Special Fund, which is now solely concerned with pre-investment surveys and technical assistance, into a fund for making investments. In particular, they wanted this fund to channel money into "areas not adequately covered by other capital supplying facilities."[39]

Thus, we can see that SUNFED still has great appeal to the developing countries. It has never had much appeal in the United States, however, where the International Development Association idea has been pictured as more realistic. It is to the discussion of IDA, in the United States, that we now turn.

CHAPTER 3 THE UNITED STATES AND THE INTERNATIONAL DEVELOPMENT ASSOCIATION

THE GORDON GRAY REPORT

On March 31, 1950, President Truman asked Gordon Gray to undertake a study of United States foreign economic policies and programs. In his report to the President, Mr. Gray pointed out that the Korean conflict and its drain on United States' resources had made it imperative that United States' aid be "channeled to those areas and for those purposes where reasonable performance in the political and economic fields can be achieved. It is important, from this standpoint as well as from others, to develop as far as possible, a cooperative and multilateral approach to foreign programs."[1] Gray recommended that the United Nations and its associated agencies be used as agents for United States' assistance, where possible.

The underdeveloped countries needed firm guidance in the use of outside aid. But, these countries feared such guidance from the United States because it smacked of intervention in their affairs. An international approach was the only practical way to have the guidance which was so essential and escape charges of imperialistic meddling.

Gray argued that there was a very great need for expansion of private investment in the developing areas. And private investment was considered to be the most desirable method of developing countries because it carries with it the technological and administrative skills necessary for success. However, there were very great obstacles to increasing private investment--the paramount one being the state of international tensions existing at the time. Also, the lack of basic facilities which typifies the underdeveloped country was considered a singularly important deterrent to increased private investment flow. And these basic facilities are not attractive to private enterprise because they do not yield a direct financial return or yield a return only over a long period of time.

Gray felt that, in view of the need for social overhead projects and the reluctance of private capital to undertake these projects, the United States should make public funds available for these crucial facilities. And, in light of the limitations inherent in bilateral assistance programs, Gray made quite a strong case for an international agency to handle such an undertaking. Thus, the groundwork was laid for the International Development Advisory Board which was to follow Gordon Gray's reasoning and recommendations and come up with a specific proposal for an International Development Authority. It is to the deliberations of the International Development Advisory Board that we now turn.

THE INTERNATIONAL DEVELOPMENT ADVISORY BOARD

Harlan Cleveland gives credit to Nelson Rockefeller and his International Development Advisory Board, a committee of citizens appointed by President Truman, for first suggesting an International Development Association. This Board pointed out that we had banks to make hard loans and foreign aid agencies to give funds away, but no machinery for employing the techniques which lay between pure loans and pure grants. And this group maintained that there were a great number of projects which could not demonstrate the pay-out necessary for a World Bank loan and which cost too much to be included in a grant program of technical assistance.[2]

President Truman had appointed this Board in November, 1950, to make recommendations in the field of foreign economic policy. Nelson Rockefeller served as chairman of the group. Other members were Robert P. Daniel, Harvey S. Firestone, Jr., James W. Gerard, John A. Hannah, Margaret Hickey, Lewis G. Hines, Bertha C. Joseph, Thomas Parran, Clarence Poe, Jacob S. Potofsky, John L. Savage, and Charles L. Wheeler. The group reached an unanimous decision that the United States should take the lead in establishing an International

Development Authority.

The Board was led to this decision upon viewing the lack of social overhead facilities in the underdeveloped countries. And they felt that "progress in the production of food, raw materials, and manufactures must move along with the construction of highways, the improvement of rail and port facilities, the expansion of electric power for factories, and irrigation to bring in new farm lands."[3] Unless these types of projects were undertaken there would be no success in commercial ventures and attempts to raise living standards would be frustrated.

These improvements in transportation, power, and irrigation were pictured as being so expensive that they were beyond the financial resources of the developing countries. Even with assistance from the then existing lending institutions, such projects were beyond the reach of many of the poor nations. And these projects were often such that no direct income was produced for many years and even if income was produced there was the problem of converting it into foreign exchange to repay overseas investors. By their very nature, these projects had no appeal for private capital and that presented the problem.

What would be the most efficient way of financing these public works? The Board recommended a stepped up bilateral loan program for some of these projects but warned that many of them could not be financed on a loan basis. "Our considered judgment is that such public works can be most effectively financed and developed through a well-managed international agency."[4]

The reasons given for favoring an international agency were as follows: (1) A United States agency would be subjected to diplomatic pressures to approve public works to serve political purposes. (2) Standards and procedures must be laid down in order to operate efficiently and it is difficult for one country to impose its standards upon other countries. And if the United States attempted to enforce such standards it would run the risk of engendering ill will and misunderstanding. An international agency could establish international standards which could be applied equally to all countries. (3) It was felt that an urgent need existed to devise new financing tools which eliminate the emphasis on large-scale United States "giveaways". (4) It was not the United States' duty to single-handedly finance the economic development of the world. The costs should be borne by many countries in a genuine pooling of effort among the free nations.[5]

The Board recommended that all the free nations be invited to participate in the new International Development Authority. The Authority would have its own board of directors to review projects submitted to it, however, the staff would be furnished by the World Bank through the use of a management contract. Thus, the Bank's staff could be used to evaluate projects and could also supervise grants that had been made.

Members of the Board discussed this proposal with the staff of the International Bank and concluded that the staff would give sympathetic consideration to such a proposal. This management link with the International Bank was considered to be a very important part of the proposal for the Development Authority. This was partly because this closeness would make the joint financing of projects possible. The Board felt that there were many sound projects around the world which could not meet the World Bank's requirements. However, if the Development Authority could make a grant for part of the funds, then the Bank could make a conventional loan for the remainder. In fact, the Board strongly urged that the new Authority not be authorized to make grants for the full cost of any project. This was insisted upon because the Board believed that all projects should be able to support at least a portion of the necessary financing on a loan basis and the borrowing country should match to some degree the outside funds provided. A second reason for tying the new Authority to the World Bank would be to gain the advantages of its several years experience in the field. The Board expressed great reluctance to recommend the establishment of a new agency, even under the Bank's aegis. But, "no existing agency is presently organized or has the authority to perform the functions which would be entrusted to the new Development Authority."[6]

Initial funds for the Authority would be $500 million which would be subscribed by the member nations in proportion to their subscriptions to the International Bank for Reconstruction and Development. Each nation would meet its subscription in its own currency. The United States' share was set at $200 million or 40 per cent of the total. The Board considered that the relatively small sum of $500 million should be used as a starter in order to subject the Authority to a thorough testing.

The Board concluded its discussion of the new Authority with a warning.

> There are limits to which we can entrust our interests to new or partially tried international mechanisms. But it is also true that we must strive constantly to develop new international mechanisms which encourage the free participation of all free nations in mutually advantageous association. We must search for mechanisms which avoid the paternalistic approach, seeking instead those which build up a sense of responsibility and self-reliance among other nations and other peoples.[7]

In order to trace the origin of the idea of an International Development Authority, the author contacted Stacy May. Mr. May had served as Director of Research for the International Development Advisory Board and was known to have played a major role in its considerations. Mr. May reported that

> The Board's Chairman, Nelson A. Rockefeller, was the proponent of this suggestion. He had a very strong conviction that if genuine progress was to be made upon development projects of certain types, it would be necessary to provide long-term financing upon terms that were far easier than those currently being offered by governmental lending agencies. As an example, he felt that on such proposals as multiple purpose water-impounding projects standard loans might be practical on the hydroelectric facilities only if grants or loans upon radically better than market terms could be offered to take care of the irrigation and flood control elements of the proposal.
>
> I am not at all sure that Nelson Rockefeller originated the basic idea of loans upon terms that share at least some of the characteristics of grants, but I am very sure that it was his initiative and conviction upon this matter that persuaded the other members of the International Development Advisory Board to incorporate the recommendation that IDA be established.[8]

CITIZENS OF THE WORLD

Certainly the most grandiose proposal for an International Development Association came from a private citizen in the United States, Stringfellow Barr. His book, Citizens of the World, which was published in 1952, contained a complete plan for such an Association under United Nations auspices.[9] Barr outlined the need for further assistance for the developing nations and reported the heated debates which had taken place in the United Nations over the establishment of a special fund for economic development.

> The poor countries want it set up. The rich countries, led by the United States, do not . . . . The most interesting detail of the fight is that one of the few things on which the United States and the Soviet Union now vote the same way is an International Development Authority; they both refuse it.[10]

Where would the money come from? How could the United States, at that time engaged in the Korean conflict, spare the resources? Barr suggested that the United States might be able to get the money in the same place it had gotten the $90 billion spent on defense since the time the Development Authority had first been proposed.

Barr rejected the World Bank as a satisfactory agency to deal with the world development problem.

> Since the World Bank . . . depends chiefly on the New York money market, it examines . . . projects primarily from the point of view of sound banking principles, not from the point of view of human need. Like most banks, it is most willing to lend money to those who least need it.[11]

Barr described the American president of the World Bank (Eugene Black) as being unimaginative and dismissed that agency from further consideration. What the world needed, he said, was a new Development Authority which would lend money to governments of underdeveloped countries for projects that were socially desirable. Conventional banking standards would not be applied. Outright grants might be made in some cases.

The Development Authority would be authorized by a new People's Assembly of popularly elected delegates from all over the world. One delegate would represent each million inhabitants of the world. The People's Assembly would appoint directors for the IDA.

Money would be raised by issuing bonds to people all over the world. Contributions should be made tax-deductible for individuals and corporations. Countries would be asked to make official donations, also. Every nation would contribute in its own currency; and if any nation was unable to contribute even in its own currency, its shares would go on the cuff until it could contribute. Some countries could give a lien on some of their natural resources. Barr thought it important that all countries of the world contribute either in their own money or in kind.

ATTITUDES OF UNITED STATES GOVERNMENT OFFICIALS

Nothing came of any of these proposals at the time they were made. The United States was involved in the Korean conflict for the first years of the 1950's and was not interested in establishing new international agencies. After 1953, the Secretary of the Treasury, George Humphrey, believed that economic development abroad should be accomplished through private investment. Any public funds made available should be used for development projects that would be put on a self-sustaining basis. He opposed anything which resembled a give-away and argued that everything should pay its own way. Any money extended to the developing countries should be a legitimate debt which the borrower expected to repay and the lender expected to receive. And the loan should be made at the going rate of interest. This type of foreign asssistance meant that there was no burden on the United States taxpayers and the funds would revolve. Humphrey felt that, since the Treasury had to pay 3 or 4 per cent to borrow the money, the underdeveloped countries should pay that rate if the United States loaned them money. There was a distinct feeling that aid programs were international giveaways. And if the United States was going to give money away, it should give it away itself--and not let Gene Black do it. Humphrey was not enthusiastic about United States aid programs--much less about the international programs.[12]

There was a feeling upon the part of some Administration officials that the biggest mistake the United States had made after the Second World War was that it didn't put the Marshall Plan on a hard loan basis. For, it was not until after the Marshall Plan that the developing nations got the idea that they needed low-cost loans for development. The 4 to 5 per cent loans of the International Bank in 1946 were the cheapest international money that had ever been seen. Then the Marshall Plan changed all that and everybody got the idea that it was the United States' responsibility to pay for the economic development of the whole world. Some people in the Administration were doing their best to correct this view, which they considered to be erroneous. Their solution was to handle development assistance on a conventional loan basis through such institutions as the Export-Import Bank.[13]

This view had a considerable following until Robert B. Anderson succeeded Mr. Humphrey as Secretary of the Treasury. "Although Secretary Anderson was a business type, also, he was not as hard boiled as Humphrey. Anderson was favorable to our aid program. Humphrey went along with it grudgingly."[14] By the time the Monroney Resolution was formally presented, Anderson was Secretary and a new attitude pervaded the Eisenhower Administration.

THE MONRONEY RESOLUTION

Senator A. S. Mike Monroney, Democrat of Oklahoma, was the author of the resolution that finally led to the establishment of the International Development Association. Senator Monroney attended the meeting of the Inter-Parliamentary Union in Bangkok less than a month after his re-election to the Senate in 1956. While he was attending this conference, he was given a guided tour of Thailand. What follows is his account of that tour. "The Thais had gotten a loan from the World Bank to build a low water dam 50 miles up the river from Bangkok which increased rice production something like 50 per cent. It was a $20 million project and they were extremely proud of it and took everyone to see it.

"The United States had provided $2 million for a highway to Cambodia--in the name of defense--and they couldn't even get the King or Prime Minister to come out and dedicate it. The Thais are a very proud people. They were proud of the responsibility of doing the dam project themselves."[15]

Monroney understood why the people of Thailand felt easier borrowing from the International Bank than they did about getting bilateral loans from the United States. The Thais are historically neutralists and they didn't like being involved in the Cold War. And yet they needed outside capital for economic development.

It immediately struck the Senator that the Western nations ought to try to provide more funds like those of the World Bank. But, the trouble was that the Bank's terms were too high for many countries. Monroney thought that there ought to be some way to lower the terms by mixing hard currencies and local currencies. Part of a loan could be made in hard currencies at the going rate of interest. Part of the loan could be made in local currencies at much lower rates of interest. This would get the effective rate of interest down quite a bit and the United States would be able to use the local currencies that had been accumulated under the Public Law 480 program.

Title I of Public Law 480 of 1954 had established a program to dispose of surplus agricultural commodities to underdeveloped countries. Countries pay for these imports in inconvertible local currencies and the United States had acquired over $1 billion of these currencies by 1956. About 30 per cent of these currencies were available for United States' use over a period of years--to pay for embassy costs, etc. The remaining 70 per cent were available only for loans back to the country.

In addition to his desire to lower the rate of interest, Senator Monroney also desired to get a longer repayment period than the conventional 10 to 15 year loans made by the International Bank.

The possibility of transferring American-held foreign currencies to a new international association seemed a solution to the need for more outside capital on easier terms and without political strings attached. Monroney felt that the World Bank would be the logical place to locate such a new agency. This would put loaning on a multinational basis and would get some of the other countries of the world to share the responsibility. Also, it would give the borrowing countries a greater feeling of obligation to repay their loans since they came from an international agency of which they were members. The International Bank was known around the world as a soundly administered institution and Gene Black had won the respect of world leaders during his long term as president.

While in Bangkok, Monroney presented his ideas to the meeting of the Inter-Parliamentary Union. He called for "strengthening and enlarging the International Bank and the scope of its work." He suggested that some Marshall Plan counterpart funds were available to the United States which could be pooled with the funds of other nations to increase the capital of the bank. And he mentioned the Public Law 480 funds that were available.

He was of the opinion that the Marshall Plan countries probably had local currencies, also, that could be added to the World Bank and, thus, such nations might be able to re-cycle these original relief funds into doing double duty in reconstruction and development. Besides, the use of Marshall Plan counterpart funds would give a needed boost to Europe's exports.

On his way back from Bangkok the Senator visited Manila. He told the Manila Daily Bulletin that there was a feeling in Congress that the give-away basis of American foreign aid was losing, instead of winning friends for America. "Asian Countries," he said, "would rather have long-term, low-interest loans from rich countries to finance their economic development programs than aid given on a more or less free or counterpart basis. . . . America . . . should siphon her aid to this institution [the World Bank] instead of extending grants . . . [in] the nature of doles or charities."[16]

Senator Monroney and Gene Black are personal friends; so when the Senator got back to Washington he discussed his idea with Black. He also talked to Christian Herter, then Under Secretary of State; Douglas Dillon, then Deputy Under Secretary of State for Economic Affairs; and Senator J. William Fulbright, who was at that time Chairman of the Senate Committee on Banking and Currency. The discussions with Black were encouraging. Monroney's conversations with the State and Treasury Departments were also encouraging. In fact, he felt that he got a very enthusiastic reception at both departments. "Then it was rumored that Dulles came back from one of his trips and killed the whole thing."[17] However, Monroney was not discouraged by a rebuff from the State Department. Senator Fulbright thought the idea was worth further study and appointed Monroney chairman of the Subcommittee on International Finance which would give Monroney a platform from which to launch his proposal.[18]

Senator Monroney had originally thought that an international monetary conference would be an appropriate setting to initiate the International Development Association. He had presented this idea of a "second Bretton Woods Conference" to the Treasury and State Departments and to the President of the World Bank.

> I have suggested such a conference in the many, many conversations I have had with the State Department over the months that have elapsed. For reasons which I think are good and sufficient, on advice of people whose judgments we respect . . . I agreed to this resolution, although I originally thought that the other approach was probably better.[19]

Officials in the Treasury Department were aghast at the idea of a "second Bretton Woods Conference." One Treasury Department official went so far as to say the the Treasury finally came around to support the Monroney Resolution largely to head off the possibility of another monetary conference. This opposition to a conference was based on fear that "a group of people would get together who didn't know what they were talking about." This group of people might seriously weaken or even wreck the existing international financial organizations or re-orient those organizations in a direction that was not satisfactory to the United States.[20]

The World Bank was just as opposed to another international financial conference as was the Treasury Department. And the opposition was based on much the same reason, that is, that the conference would get out of hand. They were afraid that the long years of work in establishing the reputation of the Bank would go down the drain in some wrangle among the Finance Ministers. So, the Senator came around to the view that a resolution expressing the sense of the Senate as favoring an International Development Association was the best plan of attack. Consequently, on March 24, 1958, Senator Monroney introduced the following resolution in the Senate.

> Resolved, That, recognizing the desirability of promoting a greater degree of international development by means of multilateral loans based on sound economic principles, rather than a system of unilateral grants or loans, it is the sense of the Senate that consideration should be given to the establishment of an International Development Association, in cooperation with the International Bank for Reconstruction and Development.
>
> In order to achieve greater international trade, development, and economic well-being, such an agency should promote the following objectives:
>
> 1. Provide long-term loans available at a low rate of interest and repayable in local currencies to supplement World Bank loans and thereby permit the prompt completion of worthwhile development projects which could not otherwise go forward.
> 2. Permit maximum use of foreign currencies available to the United States through the sale of agricultural surpluses and through other programs by devoting a portion of these currencies to such loans.
> 3. Insure that funds necessary for international economic development can be made available by a process which eliminates any possible implications of interference with national sovereignty.
>
> It is further the sense of the Senate that as a part of the United States economic aid program funds be subscribed to the capital stock of the International Development Association in cooperation with investments made by other participating countries.[21]

The resolution was immediately referred to the Committee on Banking and Currency. Hearings were held by the Subcommittee on International Finance on March 18, 19, and 20, 1958.

During these hearings, Monroney made a many-sided appeal for support for his resolution. His summation of the arguments in favor of establishing an International Development

Association follow.

> Senator Monroney . . . . I believe that the proposed International Development Association would work better abroad than our present program because:
>
> (1) It removes the political stigma attached to loans from the United States alone by placing them under international banking facilities;
>
> (2) It insures to receiving nations a continuation of long-range project financing by removing the uncertainty of year-to-year appropriations for the annual aid bill in Congress;
>
> (3) It provides a further mechanism by which new nations can develop an international line of credit;
>
> (4) It places the responsibility of passing on the feasibility of projects and requests for loans in a genuine banking facility;
>
> (5) It encourages other nations whose recovery has been helped to assume their proper share of the common burden of the development of new nations; and
>
> (6) It facilitates the use in international trade of dozens of local currencies not now freely convertible.
>
> I believe it would work better at home because:
>
> (1) It takes the matter of economic development of underdeveloped countries out of the arena of domestic politics;
>
> (2) It reduces the cost of foreign economic development by the better use of soft currencies acquired in our program of surplus agricultural commodity disposal;
>
> (3) It reduces the cost of administration of foreign-aid programs; and
>
> (4) It enables the Congress to enact a long-range banking program and thereby remove this portion of our aid from year-to-year consideration on an emotional basis.[22]

In addition to these reasons, the Senator also pointed out the desirability of increasing foreign aid from our own selfish economic interest.

> Mr. Monroney . . . . As more nations break through the

> development barrier and are able to join that select group of countries with rising living standards ànd ability to carry out capital development from internal savings, the markets for western goods will simultaneously expand.[23]

He insisted that the United States was missing a bet in not getting the underdeveloped countries to help each other.

> In talking informally with representatives of foreign governments they have indicated to me that at various times they have expressed to the State Department a willingness to do more than we are now asking or permitting them to do.
>
> I am afraid that we are following a policy where we want to go it alone too much and not encouraging others to make a contribution to developing underdeveloped countries which they feel in their hearts they should do.[24]

In an appeal to liberals, Monroney recited the problems of bilateral assistance and the advantage of multilateral aid. "Direct aid by the United States is often viewed with suspicion. Some leaders play off Russia against the United States in an effort to milk the maximum from both."[25]

The Senator attempted to interject the Russian aid effort into the debate so as to present a challenge to the United States to do as well. In his speech to the Senate, when he introduced the resolution, he said, "The Russians have started an intense economic offensive by offering loans for development purposes that are a better deal than ours."[26]

However, Senator Homer Capehart, ranking Republican on the Committee on Banking and Currency, didn't accept this argument that the United States had to go into the soft loan business because the Russians had.

> Senator Capehart. May I say--and I say it in the kindest spirit--aren't we losing the cold war and losing this battle, likewise, if we completely wreck the private enterprise system, the capitalistic system, by adopting the same kind of methods they do

> in trying to counteract them? Aren't we going to have to sometimes say this is the better of the two systems and we are going to make it work, and make it work on a practical basis, and we are not going to adopt your methods?[27]

Monroney was not going to let his project be tarred with the brush of communism. He replied to Senator Capehart as follows:

> The Senator was properly worried perhaps that we might be adopting the tools of communism in these low-interest, second-mortgage loans. But would it not be a fact . . . that the Communists have adopted grants and unilateral loans, while we are now moving to a capitalistic approach through international banking. We are abandoning the tools now being principally used by the Communists. . . .
>
> We are going to the capitalistic tools. No one can say that banking is communistic. It is the antithesis of communism.[28]

As to the mechanics of the new Association, the Senator was not too specific. He did have an idea of total funds needed to get the organization going.

> As a starter, it seems to me the International Development Association would need an original capital of $1 billion in dollars or hard currency. The United States would probably put up 30 percent of this amount or $300 million, based on our contribution to the establishment of the World Bank.[29]

After the Association had been established, the Senator had a painless plan for keeping it supplied with funds.

> It is likely that more hard currency capital might be needed for 2 or 3 years. If this should prove true, the Congress could commit the $75 million in annual dollar earnings from interest on foreign loans made under previous aid programs and thus meet additional requirements without new appropriations.[30]

It was on the subject of original financing that Senator Monroney aroused the Administration's opposition. For Secretary of State Dulles had just gotten the Congress to appropriate $300 million for the establishment of a Development Loan Fund which would dispense soft loans to underdeveloped nations. And now Monroney had the temerity to suggest that it might be possible to commit this $300 million to the International Development Association.

Monroney continuously presented the IDA as an attractive alternative to the Development Loan Fund because he felt that "We should not establish a permanent State Department bank which would have the possibility of turning our diplomats into bill collectors around the world. We would be using our public relations branch to say 'No' on development loans, and it will be defeating our diplomatic efforts."[31]

The Senator usually referred to the Development Loan Fund as "Mr. Dulles' bank". He insisted that "One of the most important points of this whole business is moving out of being the sole banker of the world--which Mr. Dulles' bank helps to make us become."[32] Senator Clifford Case cautioned Monroney that he would not succeed in establishing IDA by attacking the present program. "I do have the feeling," Senator Case warned, "that it is unfortunate to attempt to gain these objectives by knocking down the present Development Fund and by attempting to show that it is of no value. With this I thoroughly disagree. I think you will not only fail to accomplish your objective, . . . which I share, by the process, by going at it in that way, but you will also very greatly hurt the whole cause of sound foreign aid."[33]

Senator Case was also concerned that Monroney was making it appear that IDA was somehow going to reduce American outlays for foreign aid. Monroney had cultivated this notion in trying to arouse support for IDA, particularly by his local currency ideas. Senator Case argued, however, that the local currency owned by the United States was already being used as well as it could be. "While this is a good idea it is largely being employed now, to the extent that it has value, and . . . it cannot and must not be allowed to appear in the mind of the American public particularly as any real way by which we can substantially cut down our own effort in the field of mutual aid and of foreign assistance."[34]

Senator Capehart was not at all enthusiastic about the establishment of the International Development Association. He could not understand why Senator Monroney and Eugene Black favored giving loans to countries which were not creditworthy. And Capehart was particularly incensed about the interest rate to be charged. "I don't know why, if I am a good credit risk, I should be charged more to make a loan than if I were a bad credit risk."[35]

Monroney often described IDA as a second mortgage operation. The World Bank would take a first mortgage on a project and IDA would take a second mortgage for the unbankable portion of the loan. But, Senator Capehart insisted, "A second mortgage generally carries a higher rate of interest than a first."[36]

Senator Capehart insisted that the United States should loan money to the developing countries only at the going rate of interest in the respective countries. Monroney pointed out that fifteen per cent was the going rate of interest in most of those countries.[37]

To counteract adverse testimony by Secretary of the Treasury Anderson, Monroney invited Averill Harriman and Paul Hoffman to testify.

Harriman favored the establishment of the IDA and insisted that the Soviet Union should be invited to join and contribute substantially to it "in accordance with the country's obviously great capacity." Harriman expressed the view that one of the things that had made the Marshall Plan such a great success was that the Soviet Union was invited to join and refused. This had established the United States' good faith in undertaking this program and the bad faith of the Russians in opposing it.[38]

Hoffman, formerly head of the Marshall Plan program, introduced the need to counteract SUNFED into the hearings.

> Mr. Hoffman . . . . I don't believe we want to get ourselves in a position of competing with Russia, but Russia has become the principal backer of SUNFED, which is the United Nations Development Fund,

> about which many questions could be raised. However, we can't fight something with nothing."[39]

Mr. Hoffman expressed the view that IDA was the best alternative to SUNFED.

The three main issues that were raised by Monroney's proposal were: (1) the need for soft loans; (2) the possibility of using United States' holdings of local currencies in an international aid agency; and (3) the desirability of using a multilateral approach in economic assistance programs. These issues will be treated in the following three chapters.

CHAPTER **4** SOFT LOANS

DEBT SERVICING CAPACITY OF THE DEVELOPING COUNTRIES

Is there a need for soft loans? What are the facts concerning the ability of the developing countries to service hard loans? As mentioned in Chapter 1, the authoritative studies on debt servicing capacity were made by members of the staff of the International Bank for Reconstruction and Development.[1] These studies rely on information supplied to the Bank by debtor countries. The Development Assistance Committee of the Organization for Economic Co-operation and Development publishes statistics, on debt and debt servicing, which are provided by the creditor countries. There is some cross-checking in an attempt to gain reliable information. So far as could be determined, the International Bank is the only source of statistics on the debt servicing capacity of low-income countries. For this reason, considerable use will be made of these studies.

The first study of debt servicing capacity, published by the Bank, covered the decades 1946-1955 and was, on the whole, an optimistic report. Avramovic pointed out that the size of postwar capital flows had been much above corresponding flows in the 1920's and that grants-in-aid had played a very substantial role in the post World War II period. Such grants had served to reduce the burden of debt that normally follows capital outflows.[2]

Avramovic defined external public debt as the

> Long-term debt owed or guaranteed by public bodies in debtor countries. It includes debts of central and local governments, of public agencies and state-owned enterprises. External debt is taken to mean all debt which is contracted and payable externally. Grants-in-aid as well as loans granted by foreign governments but repayable in local currency are not

treated as external loans. Short-term debts with a maturity of less than one year . . . are excluded.[3]

Avramovic estimated that the size of the return flow of service payments (public as well as private) of 36 low-income countries increased by 80 per cent in constant dollar prices from 1948-1955. Public debt service was reported to have risen considerably faster than the return flow on private account.[4] This 80 per cent increase was not viewed with alarm because of the relatively low base of debt service payments at the close of the Second World War. Avramovic concluded, on the basis of criteria to be discussed later, that there was plenty of room for further increases in indebtedness on the part of the developing nations.

How did he measure capacity to meet debt service payments? Primarily, he argued, debt service capacity depended upon two economic factors. First, the debtor country must be able to do without enough domestic income and savings to make payment on the debt. Secondly, the country must be able to convert such savings into foreign exchange. These two are interdependent. "A high rate of over-all income growth, maintained over a long term, almost automatically implies an adequate rate of increase in the supply of commodities which either actually enter international trade or are capable of being internationally traded."[5] In order, thus, to measure debt-servicing capacity, one must look at the country's performance in the fields of income and savings and in the field of foreign trade. The most relevant ratio is the ratio of public debt service to current account receipts.

During the decade 1946-1955 the income of the developing countries grew at a rapid rate. However, Avramovic's statistical evidence indicated that aggregate service payments (expressed in constant prices) grew even faster.[6] In addition to income growth, the developing countries showed a rapid increase in gross savings during the decade under discussion. In the majority of countries considered the marginal savings rate was greater than the average rate, also.[7]

The crucial ratio, as pointed out earlier, is the relationship between service payments and current account receipts.

In 36 developing countries, covered by the study, exports increased 62 per cent from 1948 to 1955. These same countries' debt service payments on public and private account rose by almost 90 per cent in the same period.[8] "As a consequence, the share of external earnings absorbed by service payments increased from about 6.7% in 1948 to 7.7% in 1955. . . . The increase in the ratio of public debt service to external earnings was greater."[9]

By the time that Senator Monroney's Resolution had borne fruit, and the International Development Association was being considered by the member governments of the World Bank, a second study on debt servicing capacity had been issued. The optimism evident in the study published in 1958 was missing in the 1960 report.

Although it was pointed out that the less developed countries had been receiving an increasing proportion of public funds transferred abroad, it was also noted that an increasing portion of these funds was taking the form of loans.[10] This phenomenon is accounted for by the fact that the United States gave Marshall Plan aid to the relatively rich nations of Western Europe on a grant basis whereas the aid to the poverty stricken countries of Asia, Latin America, and Africa was mostly loans and mostly loans on conventional terms, i.e. Export-Import Bank operations.

In addition to the fact that capital was not extended on as favorable terms as before, it was pointed out that the export earnings of the primary producing countries had taken a nosedive during the period of the second study, 1956-1958. And, while primary product prices fell, the prices of manufactured goods rose throughout the period.[11]

As a result of the deterioration in their terms of trade, the underdeveloped countries had to reduce their rate of capital goods imports. It was estimated that these countries' imports were reduced $2.2 billion from 1957 to 1958 or about 10 per cent of the 1957 level of imports.[12]

A third adverse factor had entered the picture during the 1956-1958 period. There was a sharp rise in interest rates on international loans. And there was a marked shortening of the average effective period of repayment.[13]

This second study illustrated the change in the external public indebtedness of 32 developing countries (accounting for two-thirds of the population of the underdeveloped countries outside the Soviet bloc) from the close of 1955 to the close of 1958. The total public indebtedness of these 32 countries had increased from $6.2 billion to $10.1 billion in a period of 3 years. This is a 63 per cent increase. For some of these countries the original indebtedness was so low that any new debt shows up as a high percentage increase. But, for others, notably Brazil, Argentina, and India, the original indebtedness was considerable.

As large as the public debt service burden is in these countries, we must not forget that service payments on private account are about twice as large. In 1955 public debt service payments of these 32 low-income countries were $653 million while service payments on private account were $1,117 million. In 1958 the ratio was much the same. Private service payments were $1,280 million and public debt service payments were $770 million.[14]

Table 1 presents public debt service as a ratio of export earnings for 30 developing countries (for which such figures were available) in 1955, 1956, 1957 and 1958. A drastic worsening of the ratio is evident in the case of Columbia (from 6.1 in 1955 to 21.4 in 1958), Chile (8.8 to 13.2) and Ecuador (4.0 to 9.8). The weighted average for all these countries rose from 4.9 per cent of current account receipts in 1955 to 5.8 per cent in 1958.[15]

The fact that the study ended in 1958 gives, perhaps, too favorable a picture of the position of some countries. It will be noticed from Table 3 that India's public debt service only required 1.7 per cent of current account receipts in 1958. This is not an alarming ratio. However, 1958 was the beginning of heavy borrowing for the Second Five Year Plan and this ratio changed considerably in a very short period.

Despite the greater than 60 per cent increase in public indebtedness of the 32 low-income countries, Avramovic and Gulhati concluded that "the possibilities for further international lending are far from exhausted. There are a great number of countries which are still in a position to assume new long-run obligations."[16] However, this conclusion is tempered with a

TABLE 1. -- Ratio of public debt service to current account receipts

Country	1955	1956	1957	1958
Colombia	6.1	5.2	10.2	21.4*[a]
Chile	8.8	9.3	10.6	13.2*[a]
Brazil	19.7*	10.1	11.3	13.0[a]
Ecuador	4.0	5.7	6.1	9.8*[a]
Haiti	6.5	14.1*	6.5	9.3[a]
Mexico	7.7	7.0	8.8	9.0*
Peru	4.9	8.3*	6.7	7.6
Uruguay	5.6	5.0	6.9	7.1*
Iran	1.3	1.0	3.1	5.5*
Pakistan	2.3	4.1	4.4	5.3*[a]
Panama	0.7	0.7	0.6	4.9*[a]
Nicaragua	4.9	5.3	7.0*	4.7
Fed. of Rhodesia and Nyasaland	2.7	2.8	3.8	4.2*
Costa Rica	0.9	3.5	3.7	4.2*
Paraguay	4.3*	4.3*	3.9	4.2
Belgian Congo	1.7	2.7	3.5	4.0*
Bolivia	4.8*	3.9	2.3	4.0[a]
Indonesia	3.8*	2.9	2.6	3.5
Thailand	1.1	1.4	2.0	2.3*
Philippines	1.5	1.5	2.4*	2.1
Ethiopia	0.4	1.0	1.8	1.9*
Honduras	0.0	0.0	0.6	1.8*
Burma	0.5	0.6	0.5	1.5*
India	0.7	0.7	0.9	1.7*[a]
El Salvador	1.0	1.1	1.1	1.4*
Malaya[b]	0.3	0.6	0.7	1.0*
Guatemala	0.2	0.2	0.5	0.7*
Cuba	1.0*	0.7	0.6	0.6[a]
Ceylon	0.5	0.5	0.6*	0.5
United Arab Republic	0.2	0.2	0.2	0.2[a]

*Indicates peak ratio. [a]Preliminary.

[b]Ratio of debt service to commodity exports.

Source: Data from IBRD Statistics Division; IMF Balance of Payments Yearbook, various issues. Adapted from Avramovic and Gulhati, Table VIII, p. 53.

warning. "Recent experience suggests that at certain points in the growth process, some countries incur substantial amounts of debt in a very short period of time; and this experience may well be repeated in other cases in the future."[17] In some countries uncertain export prospects and already heavy debt burdens made further borrowing difficult if not impossible.[18]

Thus, this second estimate of debt-servicing capacity presented a mixed picture. Although some countries could still borrow safely, apparently there was a growing number that had passed their limit. It was this latter group of countries that particularly pressed for the establishment of some institution like the International Development Association.

THE PLIGHT OF CERTAIN COUNTRIES

Is there some formula which establishes the limit beyond which a country's ratio of indebtedness to export earnings cannot go with safety? Although the International Bank says there is no such formula, in practice, the Bank regards a country as being in trouble when more than 6 or 7 per cent of their external receipts is absorbed by financial obligations abroad. Beyond this point, a special study is necessary to justify granting of further assistance.[19]

What does it mean for a country to go beyond some such limit? The word goes out that that country is no longer creditworthy. "What this really means is that the bankers judge that such a country might in a crisis find the temptation to default on its foreign debt overwhelming."[20] Most observers agree that the danger point has been reached by several Latin American countries, particularly Brazil, and is just ahead for India and Pakistan.

The case of India deserves special consideration. This country contains approximately 400 million people or one-third of those people living in underdeveloped countries (outside the Soviet bloc) today. What happens in India may have a crucial impact on the hopes of other developing countries.

Shonfield cites India as the most dramatic case for soft loans.

> Consider, for example, the arithmetic of India's Third Five-Year Plan, beginning in 1961. Taking the most conservative estimate of what the Indians will need to carry out a substantial program . . . the foreign-trade deficit during this period will average an amount equal to roughly two thirds of India's export earnings today.[21]

What are the chances of increasing India's export earnings? One observer of the Indian economy has said that "As far as 95% of the exports from India are concerned, there is thus little likelihood of any marked increase even over the next two decades. In the past three decades the volume of exports of these items has fallen, and the trend may continue."[22]

Even assuming that the Indians were able to increase exports to the point that the foreign trade deficit was equal to only half their export earnings, Shonfield points out that, "this would mean that by 1966 the debt accumulated over the Five-Year Plan would amount to two and a half times the value of the country's export trade."[23] And this indebtedness would, of course, be on top of the already large debt burden.

If India borrowed the funds necessary to finance the Third Five-Year Plan at 5 per cent interest for a 20-year period, she "would have to find each year a sum in foreign exchange, for interest and principal repayments together, equal to 10 per cent of the total amount borrowed during the five-year period."[24] This would mean that the annual cost of servicing the Third Plan debt would take 25 per cent of export earnings.

But, this is only the beginning. "More than $1 billion will be required for the repayment of external debt . . . during the period covered by India's Third Five-Year Plan."[25] And this amount equals about 10 per cent of India's foreign exchange earnings each year. So, that by 1966, when the Third Plan is completed, India would be requiring something in the nature of 35 per cent of her export earnings just to service foreign debt!

The problem plaguing India in her attempt to increase export earnings is that of many developing countries today. Even though the people save fiercely and limit consumption to a starvation level, there is great difficulty in turning the goods saved into export items. There has not been any substantial increase in world demand for India's traditional exports of tea and jute. Textiles served as a medium for entering the export field for Japan, and India is trying to emulate Japanese experience. But, here the Indians run up against not only tariffs but "voluntary quotas" on textile exports. Even a program of rampant price-cutting cannot overcome such restrictions.

It is important to remember, in considering the problem confronting the Indians, that they are attempting to raise per capita income by 3 per cent a year, starting from one of the lowest income bases in the world. But, the size of the population is such that just to increase per capita income one dollar each year requires an increase in national income of $400 million. Assuming a capital-output ratio of about 3:1, in order to increase national income $400 million an investment of something over $1 billion is required. We should, indeed, "consider the arithmetic of India's Third Five-Year Plan."

India is not alone in her plight. At the 1961 meeting of the Board of Governors of the International Bank, the Governor from Pakistan presented a very similar picture of his country. What are the alternatives for such countries? The Pakistani Governor said they have two. First, they could cut their development plans and programs back to the amount of soft loans available. Or, they could assume conventional obligations that they know they will not be able to repay, in the hope that someone will bail them out.[26] This is a rather unappealing set of alternatives for any government that is trying to win popular support at home and at the same time maintain international respectability.

The Governor of the Bank for Nepal presented a different case. His country is not overwhelmed with outstanding debt. But, the opportunities for investments of a commercial or quasi-commercial pattern are practically non-existent. This is true because the economy needs so many of the basic requirements which yield no direct return.[27]

Is it wise to saddle countries like Nepal and the newly independent African countries with a lot of conventional debt at this point in their struggle for survival? Maybe the West could learn something from the experience of trying to finance India's and Pakistan's development through the use of conventional loans.

Robert Asher has estimated that because of India's past conventional borrowing, Indian "aid requirements will be nearly 25 per cent greater than the $4.4 billion believed necessary for the import of capital goods during 1961-1965."[28] Is it just making more trouble for the future if hard loans are used as the main source of development capital? For, hard loans must increase enough to allow these countries to repay principal plus interest or these countries are led into a very cynical default.

The countries that have passed the sensible limits of debt servicing capacity--India, Pakistan, Brazil, and some of the African countries--do have one other alternative. They can, of course, adopt the communists' method of forced savings in order to achieve capital formation quickly.

THE WORLD BANK AND SOFT LOANS

V. K. R. V. Rao, in giving the Montague Burton Lecture at the University of Leeds in 1960, conceded that his proposal for a United Nations Economic Development Administration was obviously premature in the world of 1949. He recalled the World Bank's comments on that proposal and noted the irony of the fact that the Bank would be concurring in the establishment of the International Development Association only a decade later.[29]

The Bank's management would not plead guilty to inconsistency in their policy. For, the staff of the Bank has had a long-standing policy of opposition to what they call "fuzzy" loans. From the time when John McCloy was president down to today, the opposition to "fuzzy" loans remains strong. And this is not without some reason.

Just what is a "fuzzy" loan? The Bank defined "fuzzy" loans quite early, as loans repayable in local currency or loans where the obligation to repay was not clear. The Bank felt that if loans were made at low rates of interest or with an uncertain duration (as proposed in SUNFED) that borrowers would not take the obligation to repay seriously and this attitude would carry over to the loans made by the Bank and other creditors. Loans repayable in local currency were considered to be nothing but disguised grants.

The staff continued to oppose "fuzzy" loans, but by 1950-51 there came the realization that something else was needed besides conventional loans. "We had to have some kind of soft money in order to carry out the bare minimum that had to be done."[30] Speaking on behalf of the Bank to the United Nations Economic, Employment and Development Commission on May 17, 1951, Richard H. Demuth said:

> We believe that, in some countries, the rate of development cannot be accelerated substantially if the only external capital they receive is in the form of loans which have a reasonable prospect of repayment. If additional assistance is to be given to these countries we believe strongly that it should be in the form of grants, rather than in the form of quasi-loans, and that the grants should preferably be administered through international channels.[31]

The President of the Bank, in evaluating the requirement for soft loans, said:

> There are some in the creditor countries who advocate putting foreign aid on a grant-in-aid basis in order to escape the eventual necessity of taking repayment in foreign goods. On the other hand, there are some who advocate putting all aid on a 100% hard loan basis, ignoring the virtually insuperable transfer problems which this would create. Even if the creditor country is prepared to continue lending and relending on a large scale indefinitely, so that its actual capital investment need never be repaid, the mounting burden of interest can itself become a formidable problem.
>
> It is with such thoughts in mind that I have often endorsed in principle the idea that a significant part of development aid should be extended on terms providing some relief from the transfer burden. I have repeatedly observed that the justifiable and really minimum needs for development capital in the underdeveloped countries are greater than can be met through conventional loans.[32]

This speech came after the proposal for an International Development Association had been made and represents the tenor of thinking in the Bank during the last half of the 1950's.

In a later address, Black argued that, to be successful, development aid must be accepted as a more or less permanent feature of Western policy with a separate and distinct status of its own.[33] "Conventional loans alone will not do the job. A developing country can reach very rapidly the prudent limit of its capacity to assume fixed foreign exchange obligations, as we are learning in the Bank."[34]

Black also had a warning for the world's bankers and politicians.

> To ignore this prudent limit and simply pile loan upon loan is to destroy the very order in international financial transactions which development diplomacy is in part designed to preserve. . . . We can no longer afford periodic wholesale defaults as a means of cleaning out the international financial system.[35]

In order to get around this business of wholesale defaults such as happened after World War I, Black urged the nations of the world to devise a "whole variety of financial instruments, some quite new and novel, if we are to preserve order in the balance of payments of the new nations and to keep in constructive contact with them."[36]

There has been a considerable degree of disagreement on just what form these new and novel financial institutions should take. The second Scheyven Report to the United Nations had presented a proposal for loans repayable in local currency.[37] The Bank looked with considerably more favor on this idea than on the earlier indeterminate loan proposal. And, if properly administered, the Bank would have favored such local currency loans.[38] In 1957 the establishment of the United States Development Loan Fund made local currency loans legitimate and the Articles of Agreement of the International Development Association are clearly designed to permit loans repayable in local currency. The report of the Executive Directors which accompanied the Articles of Agreement specifically mentioned "loans repayable wholly or partly in local currency."[39] Even though such loans are authorized, to date, none has been made. The finance made available by IDA does have a foreign exchange burden even though repayment is spread over a very long period. But, the staff of the Bank is not willing to call even these loans. They are referred to as "development credits" and Mr. Black feels that they are really disguised grants.[40]

How can a no-interest loan made repayable over a 50 year period be distinguished from a "fuzzy" loan? First, there is a definite repayment date set. Secondly, there is a foreign exchange burden. The staff of the Bank would have much preferred outright grants to such arrangements but both the developed and developing countries preferred the "development credit" approach.[41]

And the financial community much preferred no-interest loans to 3 per cent loans. A 3 per cent loan was a "fuzzy" loan--not really a loan and not really a grant. The financial world is full of biases, cliches, and symbols and they felt that there was something very real about this distinction. And since the Bank must rely upon the financial community to purchase its bonds, the Bank must attempt to conform to their expectations.[42]

As mentioned earlier, from 1950-1951 on, the Bank became increasingly aware of the need for more funds for economic development. There was considerable discussion about what should be done about it. As some countries moved into the category in which they could never borrow from the Bank and as more countries approached the end of their creditworthiness, there was no help to offer these countries at all, unless the Bank changed its nature altogether. And it couldn't do that under the Articles of Agreement drawn up at Bretton Woods. There were various proposals that the Bank simply extend the period of repayment on outstanding loans. Shonfield argued that the Bank's reserves of $500 million should allow the bank to make such a concession.

> Granted, the institution must keep up a tough appearance and give a fair imitation of a hard-faced banker, if it is to keep its relations sweet with Wall Street and other money centers. But lengthening the term of a loan, by offering a country, say, an extra five years before it has to begin repaying the principal in annual installments, surely need not be interpreted as a dangerously soft and unbusinesslike

> act, when interest and other charges amounting to a total of over 6 percent per annum . . . are to be paid by the borrower right through the extra five years. . . . . Some people might regard this as a rather good investment . . . . No doubt some of the brokers and investment bankers would shake their heads a little at first, as they invariably do whenever some object on the fixed horizon of banking conventions shifts its position ever so slightly; but they would soon recognize that the security of this highly profitable investment in World Bank bonds had not been reduced, just because some of the loans were going to be left to earn interest for a few years longer.[43]

Such proposals were dismissed by the Bank as long as Black was president and were considered a violation of the trust placed in the Bank by its investors. McCloy and Black had both spent a great deal of time going around the United States assuring bankers and other investors that nothing would threaten the sanctity of the loans made. And any alteration in the terms was felt to be a dangerous violation of this pledge.

By the time Monroney made his proposal, involving the local currency question as it did, the Bank was ready to consider almost anything that did not involve a fundamental change in principles. The _Thirteenth Annual Report of the International Bank for Reconstruction and Development_, published in September 1958, expressed the opinion that the Monroney proposal, although involving complexities which would have to be resolved, was very interesting and deserving of further study.[44]

In his speech to the Board of Governors in 1958, President Black said:

> It would be a sad setback to the efforts and achievements of the past decade if the flow of international development capital should stagnate just when governments in the underdeveloped world have made significant progress in persuading their people to accept the changes and to make the sacrifices necessary for future growth. I can think of no quicker way to destroy the hopes of hundreds of millions of expectant people than that we, to whom they look, should be

> unprepared and unequipped for new situations as they unfold.[45]

Later in the same speech he commented on the need for new supplies and sources of international development capital and the desirability of channeling it through international agencies.[46] This was about as strong support as Black felt he could give in view of his position as head of an international agency and in view of the fact that the Monroney proposal was, after all, only a resolution before the United States Senate--a purely domestic affair.

VIEWS OF SOME DEVELOPED COUNTRIES TOWARD SOFT LOANS

The official view of the Eisenhower Administration toward soft loans was undergoing a considerable change during the last part of the 1950's. With the change in personnel at the Treasury Department--the replacement of George Humphrey by Robert Anderson--there was a noticeable thaw in the position toward non-conventional loans for developing countries. Deputy Under Secretary of State for Economic Affairs Douglas Dillon reflected the new policy of the Administration in his testimony before the Monroney Committee.

He stated that the State Department had estimated the need for soft loans at about $750 million a year in addition to the sums being made available by Western Europe. This $750 million per year had been the goal of the Administration in setting up the Development Loan Fund. However, Dillon argued that if the United States switched this amount of funds from the Development Loan Fund to the International Development Association,

> It would require at least an equivalent annual contribution from the other developed countries. Otherwise, the International Development Association would lose its multinational character and become a mere instrument or tool of the United States. An annual contribution of any such magnitude by the other developed countries over and above their present effort is clearly out of the question for the foreseeable future.[47]

The Administration apparently felt that since the entire soft loan program could not be put on a multilateral basis, it was better not to put any of it on such a basis. Even though the Administration had been convinced of the necessity for soft loans, there was lingering doubt in the Congress.

Representative John Rhodes, of Arizona, was very greatly concerned about the impact of IDA loans on the moral fibre of the underdeveloped countries.

> Mr. Rhodes. Apparently the governing body of IDA has made a policy decision, for at least the time being, not to charge interest. I question the wisdom of it, not only because I think most people who borrow money expect to pay interest, but because it seems to me there is some virtue to charging interest.[48]

Not only was Mr. Rhodes concerned about the loss of virtue that follows not paying interest, he was also concerned about the morality of the United States in making such funds available.

> Mr. Rhodes. However, at some time in the future it seems to me that in the expectation of a normal borrower, he would, at some time start paying interest. I do not think that we are playing fair with the underdeveloped countries if we let them get into the habit of thinking that the moon is made of green cheese and I am afraid this is exactly what we are doing by making this type loan.[49]

Alan Neale has referred to this type argument as a

> more than usually nauseating line. . . . If the poor countries could increase their import capacity sufficiently by raising money on commercial terms, they would do so. This is just what they cannot do. In a capital-hungry world it is obvious that by and large new investment projects in the faster-growing advanced countries will tend to offer a safer and more attractive return than projects in underdeveloped countries and that in a free world market for capital the latter would be outbid nearly every time. This line is humbug and in reality asserts that underdeveloped countries should not get capital at all.[50]

In Europe, there was considerable opposition to soft loans. Germany and the United Kingdom, in particular,

> have raised objections of principle against soft loans, especially with respect to interest rates. The German Government feels that loans at soft terms may impair the role of private capital, distort competitive positions and weaken the function of interest rates in allocating scarce capital among competing uses. Care must be taken, in the view of the German Government, to ensure that the granting of loans at soft terms does not constitute a substitute for monetary and financial discipline on the part of the recipient countries. The United Kingdom Government generally makes loans at the rate at which it can borrow plus a small management charge. It is concerned, in addition, that lending at soft rates might have repercussions on the terms of treasury lending to domestic borrowers, such as the nationalized industries. The United Kingdom Government tries to reduce the debt service burden by extending the period of repayment, now typically at 25 years, and by granting grace periods.[51]

The need for soft loans was a major issue in the negotiations to replenish IDA and will be considered in that context in Chapter 12.

Commander Sir Robert G. A. Jackson has presented an impressive argument against relying on private capital.

> Many of us in the West feel that large movements of capital should be somehow automatic, with capital seeking the best areas of investment and responding to opportunities for profit. This would be the "natural" method and to those who reason thus governmental activities or action by international agencies are felt to be a disturbing departure from the old, free, liberal tradition. It is therefore relevant to ask how the movements of capital occurred in the past and whether "automatic" methods would still bring the same results. . . . We can see that a number of essential elements in the earlier patterns

> of international investment are now lacking. In the first place, the world is much less secure. . . . Today the one-time prop of "law and order" in large parts of the world--the colonial control exercised by European powers--has vanished, and rightly so. . . . .
>
> Furthermore, much automatic investment has vanished, or is vanishing, with the end of colonialism. . . .
>
> Another vital fact is that the whole outlook for private capital has changed. . . . Today the largest potential investor, America, has a vast prosperous internal market.[52]

Commander Jackson's wife, Barbara Ward, has added her voice to those who would argue for more soft loans.

> I do not believe we are thinking about development on anything like a large enough scale. Our sense of proportion in this whole question of economic assistance is still quite wrong. The most revealing figure is that the world can spend 100 billion dollars each year on defense, yet if we produce five billions in economic assistance, we think we are doing very well.[53]
>
> If morals have any meaning at all, they must entail that the hungry are fed, the naked clothed, the homeless sheltered, and all the sons of men given some little share in the world's great patrimony of knowledge and opportunity, of health and hope.[54]

Barbara Ward has given the Western world a large order and one that hard loans simply cannot fill. Some such vision of the world's need must have been in Senator Monroney's mind when he first conceived of the International Development Association in Bangkok in 1956. And along with this need, the Senator thought he saw a way to meet it--through the use of local currencies.

CHAPTER 5 LOCAL CURRENCY

MONRONEY'S PROPOSAL

In Monroney's speech to the Inter-Parliamentary Union in 1956 there was a three-pronged proposal. One aspect concerned the need for more funds on easier terms. The second aspect concerned an international agency to administer these funds. And the third aspect of his proposal was the possibility of using counterpart funds left over from Marshall Plan days and local currencies acquired under Public Law 480 to finance the new agency. When the Senator returned to Washington, he discovered that there were few Marshall Plan counterpart funds still available. So, this idea was dropped. However, he discovered that the United States had around $1 billion in inconvertible currencies of the underdeveloped countries as a result of sales of surplus agricultural commodities. By the time the International Development Association was launched, in 1960, unutilized balances of foreign credits totalled $4 billion.[1]

Monroney wondered why this money couldn't be put to work. He had seen the obvious surpluses, of tea and jute in India, of rice in some of the Southeast Asian countries, of petroleum in the Middle East, of ores in Latin America. And yet, some of these commodities could be used by other developing countries.

One official in the United States Treasury Department suggested that Senator Monroney simply did not understand the use of local currencies. Secretary Anderson's statement to Monroney's committee was supposed to straighten him out on this matter by pointing out that what the underdeveloped countries needed was foreign exchange. This same official pointed out that, to date, the International Development Association has not loaned a peso of local currency--even that which was paid in on subscription. Why should a country put up a million pesos in capital, borrow it back from IDA and pay a service charge on it, when they could go to the printing press and print up the money and spend it? And most of the underdeveloped countries do just that. It was pointed out, however, that the Inter-American Development Bank has used local currency to make loans to a country in its own currency. And such countries have been willing to pay interest on the currencies which they themselves have subscribed.[2]

One of the executives of the World Bank has said that "Monroney thought that local currencies were 'real money'. Gene Black had breakfast with Monroney and luncheons and dinner parties to try to explain it, but he never did succeed."[3]

MONRONEY'S PUBLICITY CAMPAIGN

Monroney had been a newspaperman before going to Congress and had a considerable respect for the influence of the press in getting an idea accepted by the public. He also had a number of friends in the newspaper business. He kept up a steady stream of ammunition to these people on the International Development Association and particularly on the local currency aspect. Several papers editorialized in favor of his proposal, including the New York Times, the Washington Post, and the St. Louis Post Dispatch.

The Dayton (Ohio) Daily News editorialized on March 1, 1958, in support of Senator Monroney's resolution. The editorial strongly endorsed the local currency aspect of the proposal. "Such a bank could facilitate many three-way trade-and-loan deals such as Russia so easily arranges, with satellites handy for absorptive marketing, whereas free-world tariff barriers render them difficult for this country to make."[4]

The Des Moines Register was not optimistic about the local currency feature but felt that it might have some value.

> It would not do India much good for an international agency to lend back rupees for economic development. These rupees would represent a claim on Indian resources. What India needs is capital from abroad.

> Nevertheless, there is some value in the "local currency" loan feature. In some of the poorer countries, banking facilities are so inadequate, that the "Monroney bank" would serve a valuable function just in providing long-term financing machinery.[5]

A good many economists have pointed out the need to do something about United States holdings of local currencies.

Peter Kenen has made the point that U. S. balances of local currencies are increasing rapidly and that if present trends continue the United States will be the largest holder of some countries' currencies. These U. S. holdings will inhibit countries from making their currencies convertible. This is an anomalous position for the United States since it is such a strong proponent of currency convertibility.[6]

The Senator concluded that the reason the underdeveloped countries were not able to buy each other's surplus goods was a lack of usable currency. And here was the United States holding $1 billion in the currencies of these very countries and not making any use of it! It did seem like a most reasonable solution to transfer United States' holdings of these currencies to an international institution. It would be able to use them to purchase surplus commodities and transfer them to places where they were needed. This would mobilize wasted resources, and it would increase the tempo of economic development without costing the United States taxpayer one cent.

Monroney had another reason for wanting to put these local currencies to work. He could foresee that as this store of local currency mounted each year, there was going to be a powerful movement to cancel them out. "Sooner or later these currencies must be forgiven or written off or they must be used."[7] As a past member of the Banking and Currency Committee of the House and a member of the Senate Committee on Banking and Currency, Monroney had come to believe in sound international financial operations. The idea of writing off all these currencies did not appeal to him as a move designed to engender respect for international obligations and a sense of responsibility for debts. It also would involve disillusionment for the United States taxpayers who supported Public Law 480 because they thought the United States was getting a *quid pro quo* for these surplus commodities.

HEARINGS ON THE MONRONEY RESOLUTION

By the time the hearings on the Resolution had started, Monroney had acquired a considerable amount of ammunition on the local currency question. It was to become the central issue in the hearings.

Secretary Anderson came to the hearings laden with questions concerning the local currency aspect of IDA.

> Secretary Anderson. . . . (1) Is local currency available in countries that might have capital goods available for export to other areas?
>
> (2) If there are such holdings, would the countries permit their use for financing exports?
>
> (3) Would they be willing to have the currencies turned over to an international agency for this purpose?
>
> (4) Would financing through this agency within the country be favored by countries now receiving loans repayable in local currency from United States programs?[8]

In addition to his questions, the Secretary had a good many statements to make about the local currency issue. He pointed out that, "Although the United States holds title to large sums in local currencies, these have been acquired only under specific agreements with foreign countries that their use would be limited in various specific ways, and generally these limitations do not permit their use for financing exports."[9] The Secretary also emphasized that local currencies loaned back to the developing countries would not add to these countries' real resources.

He made much of the fact that Public Law 480 had specifically authorized the financing of goods purchased in one country for the use of another country. This was exactly what Senator Monroney had in mind. And yet, the Secretary maintained that "only very small amounts of currencies generated under the program have to date been agreed upon for this purpose."[10] Mr. Anderson's interpretation of this experience was that such transactions were almost impossible to effect.

Douglas Dillon, Deputy Under Secretary of State for Economic Affairs, echoed the testimony that had been given by Anderson. Dillon argued that our stock of local currency could not be used to remove resources from the country whose local currency is concerned.

> We cannot, for example, use our holdings of Brazilian cruzeiros to buy up Brazilian coffee, cocoa, or cotton--Brazil has no capital goods for export--and ship that coffee, cocoa, or cotton to some other country. And even if we should do so with the consent of the Brazilian Government, we would be reducing by that much Brazil's export earnings in hard currencies and its capacity to pay for the capital resources needed for its economic development.[11]

Senator Monroney answered that he was not concerned with commodities that could be sold in world trade. His interest was in using surplus commodities of the underdeveloped countries and he was convinced then and is still convinced that exchanges of such commodities could be arranged. He used the expression that the developing countries should sell for "money, marbles, or chalk."

> I am talking about a worldwide operation where there are many kinds of surpluses that go unused, that rot on the ground because the neighboring country does not have the foreign exchange to buy the rotting crop except as it converts its local currencies to hard dollars.[12]

Monroney maintained that the United States Government had not really tried to effect transfers of surpluses between underdeveloped countries.

The State Department prepared a memorandum on local currencies for the use of the Committee. In this memorandum, it is pointed out that "unless they receive at least equivalent resources in return the less developed countries cannot provide resources to other countries without a setback to their own economic growth. If the United States were to use a less developed country's local currency to remove resources from it for use by other countries we would cause such a setback."[13]

This statement does no damage to Monroney's proposal because he did not propose taking resources from the less developed countries without putting anything back in. He was proposing an exchange of resources between countries with complementary needs. The State Department insisted that "To the extent that it is feasible, this sort of exchange is already going on through normal commercial channels.

. . . .

There is no present obstacle to trade between the less developed countries which would be removed by United States governmental action in lending these countries each other's local currencies."[14] Senator Monroney would not reconcile himself to a world where people starve in one country while surplus food rots on the ground in an adjoining country. The State Department view, however, was that there was no solution to this problem.

Senator Monroney thought the Administration position on local currencies was contradictory. On the one hand, the Secretary of the Treasury insisted they were practically useless for economic development. They didn't add any real resources to the country to which they were loaned. They could not be used in international trade. And yet, on the other hand, the Administration kept pushing Public Law 480 loans repayable in local currencies and had even established the Development Loan Fund to receive repayment in local currencies. During Deputy Undersecretary of State Dillon's testimony, Senator Monroney said: "You can't have it both ways. If your case is true--that these funds are of no use--then the repayments that the State Department gets back in these same local currencies also have no use and, therefore, we are adding to a stagnant pool of frozen currencies."[15]

DEBATE ON LOCAL CURRENCIES

During the 1959 meeting of the Board of Governors of the Bank, local currencies became the subject of an extended debate. The developed countries, led by the Netherlands and the United Kingdom were particularly opposed to the local currency aspects of IDA.

The Governor from the Netherlands stated that his Government was

> not without concern about the possible monetary and commercial implications of the utilization of so-called local currencies for international investment purposes. We are particularly concerned about the inflationary consequences of the utilization of such currencies accumulated in the past, and about the distortion of international trade that may result from the limited usability of inconvertible local currencies if made available for foreign payments. We, therefore, want to stress that the financial operations of the IDA should in no way aggravate the problems of monetary instability and trade restrictions which in many countries continue to exist, despite the great--and to a certain extent successful--efforts of the International Monetary Fund and the GATT to reduce their significance. We would defeat our own purposes if the IDA were to become an institution creating or even stimulating the very tendencies the Fund and the GATT are opposing.[16]

The Netherlands Governor introduced the International Monetary Fund into the debate on local currencies and surely some mention must be made of the Fund's opposition to anything which smacks of bilateral trading arrangements or of barter. This is in line with the classical liberal tradition of free trade.

However, Andrew Shonfield has argued that it is not in line with the realities of the twentieth century.

> One way in which the underdeveloped countries could surely help to relieve the pressure on their balance of payments is by trading more among themselves. It is not just a matter of taking in each other's washing. Surplus production of a commodity runs to waste in one country, while in another people go short of it, because the mechanism of exchange fails to function efficiently. A lot more food could and would be grown in the great surplus agricultural area of Asia, which runs from Burma across the Southeast-Asian peninsula, if there were an assured market for it. But it only needs one good rice harvest for Burma to be faced with the nightmare of surplus stocks. That is what has happened recently. There are no adequate

> storage facilities, the rice rots, the price falls; and next time, the peasant does not bother to grow so much or to bring it to market.
>
> The reason given for the Burmese failure to sell the rice to the Indians is imply that the Indians cannot afford it. That is true in the sense that the Indian government is not prepared to allocate anything out of its very inadequate reserves of foreign exchange to pay for additional imports of rice. . . . If Burma demands to be paid, like everyone else, in sterling or some other convertible currency, it will be left holding its surplus rice, and everybody will be that much poorer.
>
> Indeed, one would have thought it elementary that these nations should be encouraged to engage in barter trade wherever this helps them to put their actual or potential surpluses of production to some useful purpose. It came as a shock, therefore, when I was in India at the end of 1959, to run into a mission from the International Monetary Fund engaged in a vigorous effort to break up an Indo-Burmese barter agreement. The IMF started by hurling anathemas. What the Indians were doing was a sin against the principle of untrammeled multilateral trade, with equal freedom for all exporters to enter a market.[17]

Some persons have argued that Monroney's proposal to use local currencies to facilitate such barter arrangements merely put a mask on them. It was still essentially barter and was condemned as such by some of the member governments of the International Bank.

The United Kingdom joined in attacking the local currency proposal. "We have considerable doubts about the use of local currencies by IDA. . . . We shall want to be clear how such use could be arranged without resulting in distortions of normal trade."[18] The Governor from Canada participated in the debate, also. He echoed the speeches of the Governors from the Netherlands and the United Kingdom, in that he was concerned about contributing to inflation, aggravating the exchange problems of borrowing countries, and contributing to uneconomic trade diversion.[19]

The Governors from India and Pakistan also expressed opposition to the local currency aspects of IDA. The Governor from Pakistan said that

> It would be unrealistic to expect the less developed countries to . . . agree to the use of their local currencies, whether in the shape of counterpart funds or otherwise, in the form of unrequited exports . . . I am sure that the option to determine the time when a less developed country will be in a position to spare some of its production for helping other developing countries must rest with the countries concerned and not with the institution.[20]

The Governor from India was in agreement with the Pakistani Governor on this issue. He presented a closely reasoned argument in opposition to widespread use of local currencies by IDA.

> The proposal before us has raised the question of the utilization of the accumulations by one country in the local currency of another. These accumulations cannot, obviously, be used in a manner that amounts to making that much exports available without corresponding payment. Nor can they be used as a source of additional internal finance without creating inflationary pressures in the process. These funds are a resource only notionally, the impact of the initial loan in real terms being represented by the imports financed from it. The subsequent transactions are only an accounting device. It is true that with the accretion of an external resource, a measure of domestic credit creation might be appropriate, but the measure and timing of this credit creation have to be judged in relation to the over-all economic situation rather than in terms of the apparent accumulations as such.[21]

Thus, it can be seen that not only the developed countries (especially the large trading nations), objected to the local currency aspects of IDA, but the countries that had received large quantities of agricultural surpluses under Public Law 480 objected, also. Both groups of countries were afraid of a reduction in their exports brought about by three-cornered trade arrangements. It was a little strange, however, to attack Monroney's proposal as inimical to free multilateral trade, while supporting Public Law 480. The whole agricultural surplus disposal program, no matter what its merits, is an exception to the principles of free multilateral trade.

When the International Development Association was established, the Articles of Agreement had a provision dealing with local currencies. Article III, Section 2 (a) states that

> The Association may enter into arrangements, on such terms and conditions consistent with the provisions of this Agreement as may be agreed upon, to receive from any member, in addition to the amounts payable by such member on account of its initial or any additional subscription, supplementary resources in the currency of another member, provided that the Association shall not enter into any such arrangement unless the Association is satisfied that the member whose currency is involved agrees to the use of such currency.[22]

J. Burke Knapp, Vice President of the International Bank, in discussing this provision with the author emphasized the phrase "as may be agreed upon." Knapp pointed out that the International Bank had been most reluctant to assume the responsibility for administering these local currencies. Thus, this provision in the Articles is extremely important. No government, including the government of the United States, could even donate local currencies to the International Development Association without the agreement of the Association.[23]

The local currency debate came back into the limelight in the discussions concerning augmentation of the Development Association's funds. Some members of the staff of IDA feel that local currencies could be loaned to the underdeveloped countries. They argue that there is a great deal of sense to loaning these currencies so long as they represent real savings. If the money has not been obtained from savings, then it is purely inflationary--that is just the same as printing it. But, if the country has taxed savings to contribute to the Association, why shouldn't they be loaned?

There is a question of workability in connection with IDA use of local currencies. Could the Association keep track of the currency as it worked its way through the country's financial system? Could IDA insure that the money really did represent savings?

> At first sight it might seem obvious that the release of monies obtained from savings would not be inflationary. There is, however, a very important question of timing. What could happen--and in fact often happens--is that funds are accumulated from genuine savings, but that during the period while this accumulation is exercising a deflationary effect, the local government is expanding the money supply through other channels. The immediate result is neutral, but if then in a subsequent period the impounded savings are released, the result can be a serious inflationary impetus despite the original source of the released funds.[24]

IDA has decided to require countries to pay local currency costs of projects out of their own currency rather than using IDA holdings of such currencies. This ensures participation by the Part II countries and is apparently easier for IDA from an administrative point of view.

The United States has not transmitted any of its holdings of local currencies to the Association. The Treasury Department felt that Public Law 480 authorized such transmission but, nevertheless, included specific authority in a bill introduced in 1960. The bill was part of another matter and for an unrelated reason did not pass. The Administration has not proposed legislation since then on this matter.

Thus, it can be seen that one of Senator Monroney's ideas for the International Development Association has been abortive. He is still optimistic that something can be done with these currencies and, meanwhile, his goal of putting more of the United States economic aid program on a multilateral basis has been realized.

CHAPTER 6 MULTILATERAL AID

PROPONENTS OF MULTILATERAL AID

When Senator Monroney proposed the International Development Association, his experience in Thailand was fresh in his memory. He had seen the enthusiasm with which the Thais regarded their dam that had been built with World Bank funds. And he had seen their reluctance to exhibit their new highway that had been paid for with United States' defense support funds. This experience made a lasting impression. It seemed quite obvious to the Senator that an international aid agency was more effective in encouraging economic development than was a bilateral program. In coming to this view, he was joining a number of economists who had been arguing along similar lines for years.

Alec Cairncross has pointed out the historical reasons why the Thais and others have viewed bilateral programs with suspicion.

> The export of capital has always been associated in the outlook of the under-developed countries with imperialistic influence and the improper exercise of power by lending countries in order to secure property rights or advance the commercial interests of investors. The setting up of the Bank was, from their point of view, a blow against imperialism of this kind. They were far more willing to welcome capital from an international institution than to rely either on private investment or on loans from friendly governments.[1]

One does not have to look far to find persons from the developing countries that will agree with Cairncross. The Governor of the International Development Association from Sudan, at the 1961 meeting of the Board of Governors, pointed out that IDA's greatest strength was its international character. He urged the rich countries to look upon aid as a basic aim of foreign policy and not as an expedient for securing immediate diplomatic advantages.[2]

By channeling aid through an international agency, the industrialized countries are telling the developing countries that they put development ahead of diplomatic advantages. There is growing disenchantment with foreign aid as a cementer of alliances. If the goal had been economic development instead of transient alliances -- one wonders if foreign aid programs wouldn't have been more successful.

One of the most significant problems in administering a bilateral aid program is the fact that the underdeveloped world includes over a hundred different countries and territories. Few industrialized countries can claim expert knowledge of all of them. In fact, few countries can claim complete understanding of any developing country, no matter how long or close a relationship between them. International organizations have a unique advantage in this respect. Their relationship with the developing countries is the relationship of a cooperative organization with its members.[3]

Another problem with bilateral programs--although nobody ever talks about it--is the fact that strong firms influence governmental decisions. It is never admitted but it is a fact. Firms are out of orders--they go to the foreign aid dispensing agency and say, "It would be a fine thing if we had some orders. Why don't you grant credit to Somalia?" This is exactly the purpose of such institutions as the Export-Import Bank of Washington but this kind of influence spreads to the other aid dispensing agencies as well. It is hard to argue against industries' pleas when they have unemployed resources available. The problem with this is that the unemployed resources may not be able to produce what Somalia needs most. Or the terms of credit may be inappropriate for the developing country--but who can resist the offer of a loan?

Related to the influence of large firms on the aid program is the opportunity for venality that exists in a bilateral program. In the case of supplier credits a contractor goes into a developing country and says "I will build you a dam and get you the money for it." All his competitors are lining the pockets of the governmental officials, so he has to do it, too. Bilateral aid programs are vulnerable to the ubiquitous problem of corruption in high places. There is more than one case of funds intended to build a dam having gone to line the pockets of the Minister of Interior. Or the money winds up in the Prime Minister's brother's-in-law non-existent construction company. In international organizations there is no problem of supplier credits. The projects are chosen and the contractors must come in and bid on them. The lowest bidder in international competition gets the contract.

The really big value of the international agencies is that they can look at the economy as a whole. They can advise countries on the priorities they should follow. An example is Colombia, where the World Bank has focused the country's attention on railways. These projects are designed to give the best economic returns. Politics are ignored. The World Bank has no politics. A developing country can threaten to vote against the United States position on Red China in the United Nations or it can threaten to revoke treaties covering U. S. bases. Thus, the United States is in a vulnerable position in telling another country what its priorities ought to be. So, it winds up asking, "What would you like us to do?" The Bank and IDA are not vulnerable to such political pressure.

Another source of strength for the multilateral aid agencies is their permanence. IDA and the Bank have charters extending into perpetuity. This quality of permanence allows them to make long-range plans, policies, and procedures. Competent staff members can be selected. Bilateral aid agencies, on the other hand, are considered to be temporary and their continued existence is subject to annual review. The United States Agency for International Development is the successor of the International Cooperation Administration, the Mutual Security Agency, and other short-lived organizations. AID operations are subject to violent changes in policy, staff, and levels of funds. It is difficult to operate effectively in these circumstances.

Recently, the most persuasive argument for bilateral as opposed to multilateral aid has been the impact on the balance of payments. It is argued that bilateral aid can be tied to a country's own exports and thus aid imposes no burden on the balance of payments. The debit item in the capital account is offset by a credit item for the exports. It is upon the basis of this argument that the United States ties virtually all of its military and economic aid to U. S. exports.

But, what are the assumptions underlying the arguments for tied aid? First, it is assumed that the items being exported by virtue of the aid would not be exported without the aid. Is this an altogether valid assumption? If the machinery or equipment that is being exported is for a really vital project, might it not be sold whether the aid were given or not? If the aid-giving country is competitive then it should be able to sell some of its goods to developing countries whether it provides aid or not. Or, what about the case of agricultural exports? If the U. S. did not make wheat available under Public Law 480, would some wheat be sold to developing countries anyway? And if the U. S. makes aid available to a country, doesn't this free foreign exchange holdings to be spent in other countries?

The only case where tying of aid could be clearly demonstrated to be of benefit would be in the case of a country with unemployed resources that could be used to provide the goods and services needed. In that case the provision of the aid would provide domestic employment and increase national income.

The case of Public Law 480 is of interest here. The United States Government collected taxes from the taxpayers as a whole, the Government transferred these taxes to farmers as payment for their surplus crops, the Government saved on storage costs of surplus commodities, the merchant marine received employment in transporting the commodities, and the multiplier effect on government spending tended to increase the national income. The United States shipped very valuable commodities to the underdeveloped countries. But, in no sense did it cost the American people anything.

Thus, insofar as there are unemployed resources in any sector of the economy, and if the goods shipped by virtue of bilateral aid would not be shipped anyway, then it could be argued that tied bilateral aid imposes no burden on a country's economy. We have seen how the agricultural interests in the United States have seized upon this truth and have used it to their own great advantage. The industrialists and industrial unions have apparently not perceived this point or else lack the power to get a P. L. 480 program enacted for surplus industrial goods.

In any case it can be seen that the arguments in favor of tied aid are not applicable in all cases. To make a sweeping policy of tying aid is not an effective act. It makes no sense to tie aid for those items that are produced by fully employed sectors of the economy and that are produced by industries that are competitive. Such aid could be handled by a multilateral institution with no adverse impact on the balance of payments. And it would be as well to admit that such aid was a burden on the economy. If fully employed resources are diverted from producing for domestic use to producing for international use, this is a burden. Then the decision must be taken as to whether the burden is worth bearing. The proponents of assisting developing countries would have a stronger case if they would admit that such assistance did sometimes impose a burden but that the burden was worth while. It is not possible to demonstrate that aid never imposes a burden on the economy. The case for aid would be further strengthened if it could be demonstrated that aid went for the most essential projects and that such projects were efficiently planned, built, and operated. This type of assurance cannot be given for many projects financed with bilateral aid. Such assurance can be given for the projects financed by the World Bank, or IDA.

The main problem with tied aid is that it raises the cost of development. Geoffrey Wilson, Vice-President of the World Bank, pointed out in 1963 that the Bank had found wide variations in tender prices from different countries. In one case, suppliers from six countries quoted prices for equipment for a cement plant that ranged from $176,000 to $450,000. Although the high and low bidders were both Western European countries there was 150 per cent difference in their prices. The Bank has found that a range in prices of 20 to 40 per cent is to be expected. Thus, when a tied loan is extended it may mean that the borrowing country is paying a premium of 20 to 40 per cent. Wilson reports that on occasion suppliers even raise their prices when they know that they will not have to contend with international competition. When a borrower has a World Bank loan, however, he is required to purchase his equipment at the lowest possible price.[4]

A very practical reason for turning development efforts over to an international agency was given, by the Maxwell Graduate School, to the United States Senate Committee on Foreign Relations. "Programs which induce change raise touchy political problems. There is consequently a strong case for multilateral management of such programs in the whole field of technical aid and investment loans for economic development."[5] This group pointed out that certain local special interests are bound to be adversely affected by the changes which come about as the result of development efforts. Why should the United States Government be blamed for such changes? An international agency is less bothered by such pressures.[6]

Another reason for extending aid on a multilateral basis is the fact that saying "no" loses friends. If a developed country refuses aid to a developing one, it will be accused of trying to protect a foreign interest or it will be taken as a mark of opposition to the government in power. A rejection by a multilateral institution would not be so construed.[7]

The plight of the underdeveloped countries in dealing with so many different aid programs has been demonstrated by the story of one country that applied for technical assistance from the United Nations. The technical assistance needed was learning how to apply for loans and grants from all the different aid-dispensing agencies.

In addition to the arguments given by economists and developing countries there is an argument put forward by an American businessman in favor of international channels for aid.

> I question, however, whether from a standpoint of either the lender or the borrower it is wise for one national government to borrow from another. Among the reasons in support of this view are, first, it is difficult for a lending national government to put such a transaction on a thoroughly businesslike basis and, second, the collection of loans given by one country to another presents great difficulties. For these reasons I think that as rapidly as possible lending and borrowing among nations should be on an international basis.[8]

Raymond Mikesell has been able to detect a noticeable shift in United States public opinion in favor of multilateral aid. He gives three reasons for this shift. First, the relative deterioration of the United States' balance of payments has led to a desire to share the burden of economic assistance. Secondly, there is a changed attitude toward development assistance.

Formerly it was tied to short-term objectives as part of the United States military program whereas it is now seen as a long-run process designed to assure national independence and democratic progress in the developing countries. Finally, Mikesell believes that a major factor in the change has been the influence of the World Bank and its long-time President, Eugene Black. Confidence in Black and the Bank are credited with winning Congressional and Presidential support for the International Development Association. The change that has come about originated as much in the Congress as in the Administration, as evidenced by the Monroney Resolution.[9]

RESERVATIONS CONCERNING MULTILATERAL AID

Despite all the problems inherent in bilateral aid, despite the oratory and shifting of opinions, most aid is still on a bilateral basis. During the period 1956-1962 approximately $50 billion was made available on an official and private basis to the underdeveloped countries by the developed countries. More than 90 per cent of this was on a bilateral basis. The high water mark for multilateral aid was 1962 when approximately 10 per cent of all long-term aid was made through multilateral agencies.[10] This percentage may go up or down over the next few years but is unlikely to change drastically in either direction.

Developed countries prefer bilateral aid for many reasons. Aid is a way of keeping control and influence where a country has economic interests. If developing countries act in a way which the aid-giver does not like, then the aid is stopped. French refusal of further aid to Tunisia in 1964 is a perfect example of this use of bilateral aid.

Apparently a good many people subscribe to the view of one United States Government official who argued that "the under-developed countries don't care where they get the money. Sure, State Department money is political. But let's not get around politics. Our aid money should be for political gain. Not for securing the election of someone we like in Ruritania--not that type. That doesn't get us anywhere. But, development loans should go where they will help us. Our political objectives are important."[11]

There is fear in some quarters that multinational agencies might be governed by political forces in making loan decisions. And it is pointed out that in some countries, notably in South America, the World Bank is rather unpopular with large sections of the public.[12] These two caveats should be given along with the obvious advantages which multinational agencies have, although it certainly seems unlikely that the International Development Association, with its weighted voting system, is in any immediate likelihood of being governed by political forces inimical to the West. And the Bank's unpopularity may be caused by its insistence on responsible governmental policy which is unpopular with many.

The Brookings Institution has enumerated two reasons why the United States might not wish to turn more economic aid over to the World Bank. First, it is argued that not all nations which the United States wishes to assist are members of the Bank. Secondly, some countries may not wish to submit their loan requirements to the scrutiny of the Bank, especially when its membership includes governments which are not on friendly terms with the applicant.[13]

There is a feeling in some countries that the World Bank is dominated by the United States Government and reflects its policies. C. Wright Mills has pointed out the connection between the IBRD and the Chase Manhattan Bank. John J. McCloy, who became Chairman of the Board at Chase in 1953 was a former president of the World Bank. He was succeeded at the World Bank by Eugene Black who was a former senior vice-president of Chase.[14]

The first President of the World Bank, Eugene Meyer, is reported to have resigned because of United States' interference in running the Bank.[15] The United States does have more than a fourth of the total votes in the Bank. The United States, United Kingdom, France, Germany, and Canada command a voting majority over the ninety-seven other member countries. Thus, it is difficult to envision policies, to which the United States was violently opposed, continuing for any great length of time. There are times, however, when the management of the Bank does follow its own good sense rather than U. S. policy.

One of the reasons which some members of the staff of IDA give for not wanting to accept any greater portion of the United States aid effort is the fear of United States domination. Of course, if the United States and Western Europe increased their contributions pari passu this objection would disappear.

One final reason rich countries prefer bilateral aid concerns the drive for autonomy among bureaucracies. A man in the U. S. Agency for International Development can refuse aid. If aid were channeled through IDA, this would eliminate this decision making authority. It will be seen that this factor was of some significance in determining the U. S. contribution to the replenishment of IDA's resources (see Chapter 12).

IMPORTANCE OF THE FRAMEWORK FOR ADMINISTERING AID

Roscoe Drummond has summarized the arguments for multilateralizing aid in his report on the 1961 Conference on Tensions in Development. It is widely recognized that countries must keep account of their taxpayers' money. Thus, most economic aid is bilateral. But, it is also widely recognized that developed countries cannot stipulate conditions to developing countries in the same manner that multilateral agencies can. It is easiest to lay down conditions when the recipient country itself is a member of the organization disbursing aid. It would, thus, be highly beneficial if the developing countries themselves could become donors of economic aid. They could devote something of their admittedly inadequate resources to helping other underdeveloped countries. They could, perhaps, come to understand the problems of donor countries.[16]

This point was made time and time again by Senator Monroney in his drive to get the International Development Association established. The Senator felt the West was missing a real bet in not getting the underdeveloped countries to help each other. It would not only help them to see the problem from the donor's position. It would also give them a feeling of responsibility that the resources entrusted to them not be squandered. There is, for various reasons, a limited amount of resources that can be raised for economic assistance. When any nation wastes its portion it penalizes other nations in the growth process. IDA was an attempt to instill this idea into all the developing countries.

This will not be achieved by simply getting the nations of the West together to give their aid through consortia. Dag Hammarskjold pointed this out in a press conference after his return from Africa in 1960.

> I will not in this context repeat what is common knowledge. For those countries, it is infinitely easier to receive financial assistance and technical assistance by experts and so on through an international body than on a bilateral basis, and it is infinitely easier for them to receive it through an international body of which they are themselves members than through any other international body of which they are not members. That is to say, internationalization of aid is not achieved by switching from the system of one country giving another country aid to a system where one group of countries gives a country aid. The bilateral character is then maintained. It is not until and unless the receiving country feels that this is an act of solidarity within an organization where they have equal rights with the donors that you really reach the optimum point not only psychologically but politically and economically.[17]

Hammarskjold's argument is reinforced by Barbara Ward. She points out that the framework in which aid is given is almost as important as the aid itself.

> On the side of the developing nations, friction and resentment spring inevitably from the fact that while political independence is now (save in parts of Africa) a fact, economic independence is not. The "Southern" areas of our planet have not yet the capital or the skills needed for the forced-draught development that is demanded by their relative backwardness and growth of population. They must still look to the North, and there is still an element of dependence inherent in their situation. It follows that the frame within which assistance is given is of immense political importance. If the Western powers give aid for practical purposes--to

> stop Communism, to make clients, or to back nations agreeing with their views--then the assisted countries feel they are being used as means, not ends. This is, after all, one definition of subordination or dependence. . . . . The context of aid giving is of vital importance. If we see the transfer of capital and skills from the developed North to the underdeveloped South as part of a joint, world-wide effort to create a modernized world economy, the idea of interdependence is written in to what we do. But if we aim only at Cold War maneuvers, the subordination of the developing lands to our Western policies is inescapable.[18]

SENATE PASSAGE OF THE MONRONEY RESOLUTION

Despite the urgings of economists, businessmen, and international civil servants, the Eisenhower Administration was not at all enthusiastic about the idea of rushing down to the International Bank and handing over the foreign aid funds. Deputy Under Secretary of State Dillon, in his testimony before Monroney's subcommittee, argued that the State Department had "found generally, with the exception of the Middle East where tensions are very high, that the countries concerned indicate at least to us that they would just as soon, if not prefer, deal with us directly rather than with a multilateral institution."[19] And Senator Capehart was not too impressed with the arguments in favor of multilateral aid, either. He said that the "only thing I have heard about so far from you, Mr. Chairman, in favor of it is that people would like us better if we loaned our money in conjunction with some other country rather than loaning it to them directly, which to me is a silly argument. I do not think there is any truth to that statement at all."[20]

Despite the objections of Senators Capehart and Bricker, the Senate Committee on Banking and Currency accepted the arguments in favor of multilateral aid. In the report on Senate Resolution 264, the Committee gave three reasons for putting aid on a multilateral basis.

> First, because the advantages of development accrue to all members of the international political community, it seems only fair to share the costs of the development program among all who can participate. Second,

> a lending institution including both debtors and creditors gives a greater measure of assurance that the loans will be repaid. Third, governments may sometimes prefer international loans because they remove any possible implication of political interference in internal affairs.[21]

Senators Bricker and Capehart did not concur in this report. They condemned the "use of a Senate resolution to usurp the usual diplomatic procedure employed in negotiating the formation of a new international institution."[22] Furthermore, they argued that "The resolution does not urge any course of action that the State Department could not initiate itself through ordinary channels."[23] Thus, the only possible explanation was that "the purpose is to force the administration to adopt a policy that it has not deemed wise heretofore."[24] And the Senators were in hearty agreement with the State Department's lack of action in this sphere, because they were convinced that "there is no need for the proposed IDA."[25]

In addition to a majority of the Senate Committee on Banking and Currency, the Senator from Oklahoma was finally able to convince the Eisenhower Administration to support his resolution. There were several changes in the resolution, at the request of the State and Treasury Departments, but on May 20,1958, the official position of the Administration became one favoring enactment.

The revised resolution reads as follows:

> Resolved, That recognizing the desirability of promoting a greater degree of international development by means of multilateral loans based on sound economic principles, it is the sense of the Senate that prompt study should be given by the National Advisory Council on International Monetary and Financial Problems with respect to the establishment of an International Development Association, as an affiliate of the International Bank for Reconstruction and Development.
>
> In order to achieve greater international trade, development, and economic well-being, such study should include consideration of the following objectives:

> (1) Providing a source of long-term loans available at a reasonable rate of interest and repayable in local currencies (or partly in local currencies) to supplement International Bank lending activities and thereby permit the prompt completion of worthwhile development projects which could not otherwise go forward.
>
> (2) Facilitating, in connection with such loans, the use of local and other foreign currencies, including those available to the United States through the sale of agricultural surpluses and through other programs.
>
> (3) Insuring that funds for international economic development can be made available by a process which would encourage multilateral contributions for this purpose.[26]

What brought about the change of policy on the part of the Administration? One official in the Treasury Department has attributed the change in policy to all the favorable publicity Senator Monroney got for his resolution. "The Treasury would have held back on IDA until today unless Monroney had gotten all the publicity, the Senate Resolution, etc."[27] Monroney attributes the change, in large part, to the publicity and favorable editorial support. However, he points out the role of Eugene Black in getting the Resolution endorsed. "Black gave a dinner for a bunch of Republicans and told them it was alright and they decided to support it."[28]

The pressure for SUNFED was important, also. As Paul Hoffman had pointed out, "You can't fight something with nothing." IDA appeared as a good, cheap alternative to the contribution the United States would have had to make to SUNFED. All these reasons and more contributed to changing the Administration's view of the matter. On July 23, 1958, with Administration support, the Resolution sailed through the Senate by a vote of 62-25. And, thus, the International Development Association was on its way.

CHAPTER 7 THE INTERNATIONAL DEVELOPMENT ASSOCIATION IS ESTABLISHED

THE UNITED STATES GOVERNMENT LAUNCHES THE INTERNATIONAL DEVELOPMENT ASSOCIATION

The Monroney Resolution, as it had been passed by the Senate, requested the National Advisory Council on International Monetary and Financial Problems to study the possibility of establishing an International Development Association. The Council was established by the Bretton Woods Agreement legislation and consisted of the Secretary of the Treasury, the Secretary of State, the Secretary of Commerce, the Chairman of the Board of Governors of the Federal Reserve System, and the President of the Export-Import Bank. When other agencies are vitally concerned with the subject matter under discussion they are invited to the meetings. At times the Mutual Security Administration, the Agency for International Development, and the other aid agencies have been regular members.

Before this Council made any reports and prior to the meeting of the Board of Governors of the International Bank in September, 1958, Secretary of the Treasury Anderson wrote President Eisenhower and proposed that informal discussions be undertaken during these meetings concerning the establishment of an International Development Association. The President agreed to this proposal. Thereafter, Secretary Anderson and his party went on a trip around the world--on the way to and from the New Delhi meetings of the Board of Governors. They talked to the Chancellor of the Exchequer in the United Kingdom and the Finance Ministers of Germany, Italy, and Japan. "Only Japan was enthusiastic. Germany and the United Kingdom definitely did not want it. They wound up supporting it as a result of a horse trading operation. They agreed to support IDA in exchange for some things they wanted. The United Kingdom and Germany still don't like it very much. We talked about using local currencies to the Finance Ministers--using Brazilian lumber to build a project in Greece because we have lots of Brazilian cruzeiros. All the underdeveloped countries actively supported the idea for IDA."[1]

The German representative with whom Anderson talked was Economic Minister Ludwig Erhard. He saw Erhard during the meetings in New Delhi. Erhard felt that the Monroney Resolution was a wooly-headed idea which would undermine the World Bank. His fear was that the debtor countries would have a choice between the IBRD and the IDA and that soft loans would sweep the whole interest structure away. The Central Bank of Germany was strongly opposed to IDA based on the non-revolving character of the IDA fund--it would require continuous replenishment by member governments. This raised Germany's budget problem. The Germans have a passionate fear of budgetary imbalance as they are still painfully aware of previous inflations. They think their current prosperity won't last and the government will have to borrow to cover obligations it has made and this borrowing will start the whole inflationary psychology over again.

Germany was also afraid that IDA appended to the World Bank would be dangerous to the Bank. There was a fear that IDA would destroy the trust which the Bank enjoyed in the capital markets. And it was feared that IDA would increase the desires of the underdeveloped countries. They would come to expect more than the rich countries chose to give them. And once established, IDA might have a life of its own--as international agencies tend to do. Thus, Germany would have favored aid on an ad hoc basis.

After the meetings in New Delhi, Anderson had a second conversation with Erhard concerning IDA--this time in Tokyo. Anderson's main points in all these meetings concerned the spectre of SUNFED if IDA were not established. He argued that the World Bank was a much more logical place to put aid than the United Nations and that there was need for more aid on soft terms. By the time of the Tokyo meetings Erhard was considerably more sympathetic toward IDA and had cautious support from the German Central Bank. Both Germany and the United Kingdom expressed serious reservations concerning soft loans. Their feeling was that if soft loans were to be made available they should be made on a bilateral basis. They were anxious that soft loans not interfere with the international credit structure.

The French were not opposed to IDA but considered themselves as already doing more than their share in the field of soft loans. Most of France's aid has gone to her former colonies in the form of budget support. Much of this has been on concessionary terms. Thus, France was not enthusiastic about further contributions on soft terms but was willing to go along.

During Secretary Anderson's speech to the Governors in New Delhi he dwelt on IDA at some length. He pointed out that although the U. S. had no blueprint to offer at that time that the Government was giving serious thought to the proposal for IDA. The main facet he emphasized was IDA's ability to make loans repayable in local currency.[2] This is interesting in view of the fact that Monroney had planned for loans to be made in local currencies--not repayable in them.

The Secretary of the Treasury serves as Chairman of the National Advisory Council on International Monetary and Financial Problems. Thus, Anderson must be given a great deal of credit for pushing the proposal for IDA through the Council. The Council studied the Monroney Resolution from July, 1958, to January, 1959, when it submitted an interim report to the Chairman of the Senate Foreign Relations Committee. This report merely indicated that discussions had been held with foreign governments and that study was continuing.

On August 19, 1959, the Council submitted the report requested by Senate Resolution 264.[3] The language of this report is in marked contrast to the testimony of Administration witnesses on the Monroney Resolution. The report depicts the Council, if not bubbling with enthusiasm, at least reconciled to the idea of an International Development Association. It states that "On the basis of its studies thus far . . . the Council is convinced that the International Development Association would form a valuable adjunct to the International Bank, and would effectively extend the field of operations of the latter."[4]

The reasons given for support of IDA follow those adduced by Senator Monroney. First, the Association would allow the World Bank to loan to countries which could not assume the full foreign exchange obligation of a conventional loan. Secondly, it would allow countries to finance projects without providing all the local currency themselves. Thirdly, it would provide a multilateral agency with great flexibility in lending operations.[5]

The report indicates that there was reluctance on the part of some countries to accept the World Bank shares as appropriate for IDA. One proposal, to overcome this objection, would have those countries whose recent growth warranted it purchase debentures issued by IDA in addition to their prorated share.[6]

The underdeveloped countries had indicated, during the course of the 1958 conversations, a desire for more coordination of lending activities. The hope was held out that the Association might provide this coordination.[7]

The National Advisory Council concluded its report by saying that it considered the International Development Association as both feasible and desirable and that it would be in the best interest of the United States and the free world to proceed with efforts to establish such an organization.[8]

The Council decided that the best approach to establish IDA would be to have the Executive Directors of the Bank draw up a draft of the articles of agreement for submission to member governments. Consequently, Secretary Anderson proposed such a step to Eugene Black in a letter dated July 31, 1959. This letter is appended to the report of the National Advisory Council. In it, Secretary Anderson stated that he was convinced that a sufficiently broad base of support existed for IDA among member governments so that a carefully worked out plan would meet with widespread acceptance. President Black forwarded the Secretary's letter to all the member governments of the Bank. In his forwarding letter Mr. Black stated, "I am fully in accord with the suggestion of the Governor for the United States that our meeting in September should be the occasion for taking action looking toward its consideration and, as I would hope, toward the establishment of an International Development Association."[9]

Along with the letter, Secretary Anderson sent some guidelines for use by the International Bank's Executive Directors in drawing up articles of agreement for the International Development Association. These guidelines contained the following provisions: (1) The purpose of IDA would be to promote economic development of less developed members whose needs could not be met by the International Bank. To this end, IDA should finance sound projects of high priority. (2) Membership in IDA should be available to any member of the Bank. IDA should be a separate financial entity, but should be manned by the staff of the International Bank. (3) Voting should be on a weighted basis, according to capital subscribed. (4) IDA should have an authorized capital of $1 billion. Members would pay half of their subscription immediately and the rest over a 5-year period. (5) The United States would contribute about $320 million. (6) IDA's resources should be reconsidered every 5 years. (7) Members would make their subscription partly in gold or convertible currency and partly in their own national currencies. (8) Twenty per cent of each country's quota would be freely disposable by IDA. IDA would have authority to suspend the obligation of the less developed countries to pay in convertible currency. (9) IDA would have authority to borrow from member governments and other sources. (10) Arrangements should be made for IDA to receive the currencies of one member from another member.[10] The staff of the International Bank had worked with officials of the Treasury Department in drawing up these guidelines.

THE BOARD OF GOVERNORS' DEBATE ON THE INTERNATIONAL DEVELOPMENT ASSOCIATION

The Views of the Developed Countries

President Eisenhower, in welcoming the Board of Governors of the International Bank to Washington in 1959, stated the United States' view that the new Development Association must be closely integrated with the Bank. "Thus, there will be assured the wise expenditure of its funds and the effective coordination of its activities with other institutions. In our view, no other mechanism can perform this task for the free world as well as would the proposed IDA."[11] Treasury Secretary Anderson, following President Eisenhower, made a very strong case for establishing IDA.

The Governor from the Netherlands, J. Zijlstra, posed several interesting problems for the Governors. He stated the Netherlands' view that although they had accepted the decision to double their initial subscription in the capital of the Bank--this did not mean that they accepted this formula for apportioning shares in the future. Shares in IDA should be based on the members' capacity to contribute. He proposed a charter allowing non-members of the Bank to be associated with IDA. The question of voting rights should be open to discussion. The forms of financial assistance to be made available by IDA should not be specified in advance--grants should not be excluded in the charter. The link with the International Bank should not be so close as to preclude close cooperation between IDA and the Special Fund and other United Nations activities. He attached great importance to the observance of certain rules with respect to fair behavior in debtor-creditor relationships and with respect to foreign interests Without assurance that IDA would operate on the basis of such sour principles, the Netherlands would not be prepared to participate.[12]

Ludwig Erhard, the Governor of the Bank from Germany, expressed approval of the plan to allow IDA to provide funds on flexible terms. However, he warned that

> The very allowance for such flexibility would, however, commit the International Development Association and the recipient countries to observe a particularly high degree of discipline in their economic and monetary policies. Only such discipline will avoid the danger that unrealistic aspirations which will later be found to have been harmful are assisted by the new credit facilities.[13]

The theme of this speech of Erhard's was repeated by the German representative at meetings of the Board of Governors following the establishment of IDA.

The Governor from the United Kingdom attached "great importance to the proviso that the subscription of industrialized countries should be convertible, untied, and additional to the existing level of aid."[14] He echoed the argument made by the Governor from Germany that, although IDA funds should be made available on less stringent terms than is possible with the International Bank, nevertheless, the basis of sound international lending should not be undermined. "We do not ourselves much like the idea of concessionary rates of interest."[15]

The Governor from Canada, Donald Fleming, warned that, although there was need for funds on less onerous terms than those of the Bank, there was also need to maintain lending standards. "In our opinion, the distinction between grants and loans should not be blurred, and provisions regarding repayment, while properly less onerous than those which are available in commercial loans or through the International Bank, nevertheless should not be such as to store up trouble for the future."[16]

The Governor from South Africa expressed the view that debtor countries should be assessed for contributions to IDA on the basis of per capita gross national product rather than on the basis of the International Bank's subscription formula. South Africa injected a note of caution into the discussion of IDA.

> At the present time the demand for capital far exceeds the supply. The establishment of the IDA will not create new capital. At most it will mean the redistribution, within limits, of the available capital. Such diversion can and will make an important contribution to the economic advancement of the less developed countries but we must face the fact that there will still not be enough capital to satisfy _all_ the wants of _all_ these countries. . . .
>
> If we were to think that the IDA will provide the answer to all capital prayers of the less developed countries, that it will be the panacea for all economic ills and that it will solve all financial problems, we are bound to be disappointed.[17]

The Governor from Sweden interjected SUNFED into the debate.

> We hold the view that there would have been considerable merits in a solution permitting also other member countries of the United Nations, besides those represented here, to assist in the task of creating a new financial institution of this kind. As you know, projects of a nature similar to IDA, among them the Special

> United Nations Fund for Economic Development, have been considered by the UN for several years, and the matter will come up again before this year's session of the General Assembly. I will make it clear, however, that we--since so many of the prospective recipient countries in the course of this meeting have spoken in favor of the IDA--shall not object to the proposed mandate to the Bank Directors. . . . An attempt should be made to coordinate the work being done in this field here and in New York.[18]

We shall see how Sweden's view changed from cautious support to enthusiastic approval of IDA.

The Views of the Underdeveloped Countries

The Governor from Viet Nam proposed that

> Instead of a single multilateral loan fund, several such development funds might be created within the framework of, or closely tied to, the International Development Association, with each loan fund adapted to conditions and needs of a particular region. Moreover, it could represent a vital step forward, so far as the countries of a specific region are concerned, toward greater regional cooperation in coordinating or harmonizing production plans, trade and payments--much the same as the Marshall Plan and subsequent institutions did in Europe.[19]

This proposal was made right after the Inter-American Development Bank had been proposed to meet the needs of Central and South America and the Arab and African Development Banks had been proposed for those areas. Some of the Asian countries felt as though they were being neglected and saw a possibility of remedying this through IDA. Nothing came of this proposal, however.

The Governor of the Bank from Libya, A. N. Aneizi, spoke quite frankly to the Governors. He pointed out that it might be desirable to modify the practices of the International Bank rather than to set up an entirely new institution. He was concerned with the undue proliferation of bodies with more or less the same aims and objectives. He urged that, if IDA be set up, it finance local currency expenditures so as to avoid undue emphasis on the balance of payments aspects of development programs. He also urged the Governors to modify the voting rights of members so as to enable the underdeveloped countries to have a more effective say in the affairs of IDA than in the affairs of the International Bank. And he pointed out that the underdeveloped countries have to incur substantial outlays for essential projects whose benefits transcend the narrow financial and economic criteria of either the World Bank or the proposed IDA.[20]

The Governor from Pakistan warned that it would be unrealistic to expect the underdeveloped countries to put up money in convertible currencies except in token amounts.[21]

The Governor from India had several points for the Governors to consider. He pointed out that

> A developing country finds inevitably that all its investment needs cannot be encompassed within what has come to be called a projects approach; its needs have to be viewed in their totality in terms of the entire program which it is implementing. I should suggest, therefore, that this wider approach should be stressed while framing the provisions of the IDA, and in this approach, I should add, an element of grants cannot be entirely ruled out.
>
> Secondly, while it is recognized that an international institution should be a cooperative endeavor . . . there is no getting away, on a plane of practical reality, from the fact that the less developed countries are not in a position to assume any large responsibilities by way of subscription or repayment in terms of convertible currencies or of unrequited exports.[22]

The Governor from Ghana made a straightforward address to the Governors.

> I should like to conclude my contribution to this debate by stating what I am sure is the voice of the millions in Africa and the other areas with conditions of life similar to ours in Africa, and who like

> ourselves, are either only recently free or on the verge of nationhood. We have not had the chance to improve our lot as we would wish. In the world of today where the "haves" tend to have more and the "have-nots" to have less, unless we receive aid from the older and stronger nations, some of whom until a while ago were our rulers and ordered our lives for us, the future for us can be but bleak and desolate. May I say that these older and more developed nations, in helping the younger and weaker ones, will only be helping themselves. For us in Ghana, and I believe for all the others, too, whatever help we are given, we should like to feel, is intended primarily to help us stand on our feet and to make us strong economically. Anything less than this may not be welcome.[23]

Apparently the Ghanaian Governor was correct in his assessment that he spoke for other underdeveloped countries, because several spokesmen for other countries spoke approvingly of his address.

David Horowitz, the Governor from Israel, introduced the writings of one of the founders of the Bank, John Maynard Keynes, into the debate.

> "Assuming no important wars and no important increases of population, the economic problem may be solved--or at least within sight of solution--within a hundred years. This means that the economic problem is not--if we look into the future--the permanent problem of the human race."
>
> Keynes was vindicated by subsequent events in industrialized countries. What is needed now is a massive transfer of capital to underdeveloped areas, to vindicate his prediction in the underdeveloped areas of the world.[24]

Horowitz was trying to counter the arguments presented by the West German and United Kingdom spokesmen in favor of "natural" capital movements as a device for allocating scarce capital.

DRAFTING THE ARTICLES OF AGREEMENT

After the debate, the Governors came to unanimous agreement on the resolution introduced by the United States Government and, on October 1, 1959, instructed the Executive Directors, "having regard to the views expressed by the Governors and considering the broad principles on which such an Association should be established and all other aspects of the matter, are requested to formulate articles of agreement of such an Association for submission to the member Governments of the Bank."[25]

When the Board of Governors instructed the Executive Directors of the International Bank to draw up articles, they were giving them a large order. The Governors of the Bank are usually the finance ministers of each member country. Each member has one Governor on the Board and they meet annually, usually in September. For the day-to-day operations of the Bank there are Executive Directors. Each of the five major members of the Bank (the United States, United Kingdom, France, Germany, and India) appoints a Director. The other member countries elect 14 directors to represent their interests. Both the Governors and the Executive Directors have a weighted system of voting--with the number of votes corresponding to the number of shares held in the Bank.

After the meeting of the Governors in September, 1959, the Executive Directors began their task of drawing up IDA's Articles of Agreement. There ensued a process of debate based on draft papers prepared by the staff of the International Bank. The shape of IDA was outlined in these staff papers and was worked out in detail in meetings of the Executive Directors.

There weren't many controversies during this process of establishing IDA. The timing is important to remember. It was only proposed at the September, 1959, meetings that Articles be prepared. And by January, 1960, the approved text of the Articles was ready to go to the Governors. So, discussion only took place over a three-month period. The Executive Directors normally have monthly meetings, but they had special meetings to consider IDA. Everyone interviewed agreed that there were no tremendous battles over the Articles and the timing surely seems to corroborate this.

The chief concern during the drafting was to keep the Articles flexible. Everyone wanted as little to tie the Association's hands as possible. And they were very successful in this. As Eugene Black said, "The result is that we can do what we want. The charter of IDA gives the management and staff the right to do almost anything."[26]

The attitude of the Bank's staff toward IDA is difficult to define. One official of the U. S. Treasury insists that Richard Demuth planted the idea of IDA with a member of Senator Monroney's staff. This staff member was supposed to have put this idea in Monroney's head. A member of the Bank's staff insists that "nobody put anything in Monroney's head"--that the IDA proposal was his own brainchild.

As mentioned in Chapter 1, Mr. Andrew Shonfield stated that Mr. Black said, during the early discussions on IDA, "that he had never liked the idea of 'soft loans,' but if they had to come he was going to make certain that he was the man who handled them."[27] Michael Hoffman, formerly of the Bank staff, hotly disputed this statement. Hoffman argued that the idea for IDA really originated with Eugene Black and Richard Demuth. Black, in particular, is credited with inventing IDA--with taking the local currency idea of Monroney's and changing it into a plan for good project loans on extraordinary terms. Hoffman insisted that Black was very much behind IDA.[28] And, as mentioned earlier, Senator Monroney gave Black a great deal of the credit for getting the idea accepted.

However, some members of the Bank staff have indicated that they thought Shonfield was probably right--that Black didn't want soft loans--but if anybody was going to make them, he wanted to make sure that it was the Bank. This is not inconsistent with Black's own statements. He preferred giving outright grants to the underdeveloped countries. He never liked the idea of soft loans. But, he did realize that if you had soft loans being dispensed by another agency while the Bank was handing out conventional loans, that everyone would go to the other agency.[29] So, it may be that Shonfield and Hoffman are both right. Black recognized the need for money in addition to conventional loans, but he opposed soft loans. However, he recognized that soft loans were the only feasible way to get more money--grants were unacceptable to both the developing and developed countries--and he worked hard to get the soft loan agency tied in with the Bank.

Black discussed his views on this matter at the 1959 meeting of the Board of Governors. This was before the vote to prepare Articles of Agreement. "Should the underdeveloped countries simply want money and not development capital--that is, capital administered to achieve its development purpose--then I suggest this would be the wrong place to come."[30] He might have been intending his remarks for those nations that had been pushing for SUNFED.

At the 1960 meeting, Vice President W. A. B. Iliff stated that the staff realized that the Bank's administration of IDA would be watched carefully. "We have to demonstrate that a bank can handle monies soundly and effectively where an orthodox financial return is not a first consideration."[31] Some of the poorer countries have not yet been convinced that the staff has succeeded, as will be discussed later.

Some of the underdeveloped countries feel that the Bank captured IDA in order to kill it or dilute its effectiveness. There is a current of hostility toward the Bank in some of these countries. They see the rich nations as having given IDA to the Bank in order to offset SUNFED. And they don't expect the Bank to be enthusiastic in trying to expand the Association.

During the negotiations, the views of the Bank staff prevailed on most questions. One of the things that did get changed was the nature of the new fund of easy money. The Bank did not want a new institution created. The United States insisted on a new institution. The staff only wanted a fund that could be administered by the Bank and there was some reason for this. The staff was afraid that if there was a separate institution it would get confused with the Bank in the eyes of the financial community. The Bank has a very good standing with the bankers of the world. If these bankers thought the Bank was putting out funds at no interest--they might be reluctant to buy any more Bank bonds. The United States felt that these bankers and investment dealers were sophisticated people and would be able to distinguish between the operations. The Monroney Resolution had called for a new institution. There was a good bit of popular support for a new institution. And so, on this particular point, the staff was apparently overruled. However, the distinction between the International Bank and the International Development Association is in some ways an imaginary one. Although the funds are kept separate and distinct, the management and staff are identical. Section 4 of Article VI specifies that the Executive Directors of the Association shall be composed ex officio of each Executive Director of the Bank who was appointed by a member of the Bank who is also a member of the Association, or elected by the votes of at least one country who was a member of the Association.

The President of the Bank is ex officio President of the Association and Chairman of the Executive Directors. The President of the Bank is the chief of the operating staff of the Association. He is responsible for the organization, appointment, and dismissal of the officers and staff. The closeness of the relationship between the Bank and IDA has caused Robert Asher to say that although "legally an institution, the IDA appears in reality to be a fund administered by the World Bank."[32] As far as the practical effects are concerned, the Bank staff may not have been over-ruled even on this point.

On such broad questions as the membership and objectives of the Association, there was little dissent. Membership is open to all members of the Bank who desire it. The objectives of the Association are "to promote economic development, increase productivity and thus raise standards of living in the less-developed areas of the world included within the Association's membership, in particular by providing finance to meet their important developmental requirements on terms which are more flexible and bear less heavily on the balance of payments than those of conventional loans."[33]

As has been indicated earlier, there was some disagreement on whether the Association should make loans or grants. The staff of the Bank preferred grants, in line with their views on this subject dating back to 1951. However, both the poor and rich members, especially the United States, preferred loans. So, Article V, Section 2 reads as follows: "Financing by the Association shall take the form of loans."[34] There is a provision for other financing either out of funds subscribed after the initial subscription or, in special circumstances, out of supplementary resources furnished to the Association if these resources carry an authorization for such financing.

"The Association may provide financing in such forms and on such terms as it may deem appropriate, having regard to the economic position and prospects of the area . . . concerned and to the nature and requirements of the project."[35] In the report which the Executive Directors prepared to accompany the Articles for country consideration, they elucidate on this section. This section is intended, they explain, to permit the Association to make finance available in a number of ways. The Association could provide for lenient terms of repayment through the use of loans repayable in local currencies, it could make loans repayable in foreign exchange but having long grace periods, it could lend at no interest, or it could lend at a low rate of interest.

Loans are, as with the International Bank, tied to specific projects and shall be for purposes of high developmental priority. The expression "specific projects" is given a broad interpretation, however, and can include such proposals as a railway program, an agricultural credit program, or a group of related projects. There is also provision for finance other than for specific projects in special circumstances.

Loans may be made to a member, a member's territory, a political subdivision of a member country, a public or private entity in the territory of a member, and to international or regional organizations. In the case of loans which are not made to member governments, the Association has discretion as to whether or not it will require a governmental guarantee, whereas the Bank's charter requires it to secure a governmental guarantee on such loans.

The Association cannot provide financing when such financing is available from private sources on terms which are reasonable or when a loan could be provided by the International Bank. The Association is barred from tying funds to purchases in any one of its member countries and is directed to give attention to considerations of economy, efficiency, and competitive international trade in using proceeds of its loans.

The Association has the authority to: borrow funds with the approval of the member in whose currency the loan is denominated; guarantee loans from other sources; and provide technical assistance and advisory services at the request of a member.

The Association is authorized to enter into a formal arrangement with the United Nations and may enter arrangements with other public international organizations having specialized responsibilities in related fields.

On the question of voting rights in the Association there were differences of opinion. The underdeveloped countries wished to have more weight than they have in the International Bank and to some extent they succeeded. When the quotas of the World Bank were doubled in 1958 the voting strength of the smaller countries was diluted somewhat. In the Articles of IDA, the old formula is brought back. Each original member gets 500 votes plus one additional vote for each $5,000 of its initial subscription. Countries joining after original membership get voting rights as decided by the Board of Governors. All additional funds given to IDA above the original subscription carry no voting rights.

The voting pattern works out as follows: as of June 30, 1964, the United States had put up 32 per cent of the money and had 26 per cent of the votes; the United Kingdom had put up 13 per cent of the money and had 11 per cent of the votes; France and Germany had the same quota which was 5 per cent of the money and 4.5 per cent of the votes; and no other country had as much as 4 per cent of the votes. As new countries come into the Association, these percentages change slightly.

The underdeveloped countries were not at all reconciled to the weighted voting arrangement. The Governor of the Bank from Burma, Thakin Tin, put the case rather bluntly at the 1961 meetings.

> The principle of voting and representation in the management on the basis of the size of stock held by members, though customary for profit-making associations, is hardly comforting to small stockholders in an institution like the Bank which has the avowed object of assisting underdeveloped countries. The latter cannot help

> feeling that they are excluded from deliberations vital to their future and what they get in the way of development loans is largess through the beneficence of large stockholders who dominate the institution by virtue of their voting strength.[36]

On the question of local currencies there was some disagreement, also. As mentioned earlier, the staff of the Bank was not enthusiastic about receiving local currencies from the United States. However, the Articles contain provisions whereby countries may provide supplementary resources in the currency of another member, but IDA must agree before any local currencies can be contributed.

On the question of amendment of the Articles, the IDA procedure is a little simpler than in the Bank. Amendment of IDA Articles can be done by the Board of Governors, whereas in the Bank, the amendment must go to the member governments.

The Articles direct that political considerations not be taken into account when deciding upon a loan. "Only economic considerations shall be relevant . . . and these considerations shall be weighed impartially in order to achieve the purposes stated in this Agreement."[37] Even though this Article is clear in its intent, it is difficult to think that Egypt would be impartial about approving loans for Israel or vice versa.

The two main issues which arose in the discussions were the shares to be contributed by the members and the form in which the member's contributions would be made. First, it was agreed that the total funds of the Association would be $1 billion. There was some argument against fixing such a total in view of the fact that new countries would be coming in and that some of the members of the Bank might not choose to join IDA. But, a total was set. Then the apportioning of shares took place.

One possibility which was considered was contributions based on national income or gross national product. The gross national products of the industrial nations, which would have to subscribe the usable currency, were converted to United States currency on an exchange rate basis and totaled. On this basis, the United States had 57 per cent of the West's gross product, the United Kingdom had 8 per cent, the European Economic

Community countries had 20 per cent, and the other industrial countries had a combined total of 8 per cent. On the basis of United States prices (using the formula devised by Milton Gilbert and Irving Kravis) the proportions were United States--47 per cent, United Kingdom--9 per cent, European Economic Community--25 per cent, and other countries--19 per cent.

Another possibility was the formula drawn up by Paul N. Rosenstein-Rodan. He used both exchange rate and United States price formulae for his computations. On a straight gross national product basis, he concluded that the United States should contribute 60 per cent of the aid burden. By using United States prices to establish a figure for "real" gross national product, he computed the United States' share at 54 per cent. Applying the progressive income tax principle to the real gross national product he concluded that the United States share would be 65 per cent as shown in Table 4.[38]

The idea of progressivity of contributions was welcomed by some of the poorer countries. However, the richer countries saw little to commend such a proposition. No agreement on any formula based on gross national product could be reached. The other alternative was to use the quotas that had been established at Bretton Woods for contributions to the International Monetary Fund and the International Bank. The exact formula for these quotas is not available, but it is known that it took account of the size of gross national product, the ratio of exports to gross national product, the fluctuations in export earnings, etc. All these considerations are more relevant for the International Monetary Fund than they are for the International Bank or the International Development Association.

The United Kingdom, Belgium, the Netherlands and other ex-colonial powers have been strikingly hit by this formula. At the time the Bretton Woods Agreement was drawn up the United Kingdom held great reserves for sterling area trade and had a large share of world exports and imports. By using exchange rates on gross national products, the United Kingdom would contribute 8 per cent and all the European Economic Community countries would contribute 20 per cent. However, by use of the Bretton Woods formula, the United Kingdom's share is 17 per cent and the European Community countries' share is 23 per cent. On a straight gros national product basis, the following countries are obviously contrib ing more than their share to the Bank; United Kingdom, Netherlands

TABLE 2. --Sharing the burden of aid.[a]

	Nominal GNP				"Real" GNP			
	GNP Per Family (dollars)	Number of Families (thous.)	Tax Per Family (dollars)	Contri-bution by Each (%)	Weights for "Real" GNP	"Real" GNP Per Family (dollars)	Tax Per Family (dollars)	Contri-bution by Each (%)
Belgium	5392	2303.2	495	1.1	1.23	6632	729	1.4
Canada	7954	4578.2	1002	4.3	1.00	7954	1002	3.7
Denmark	4774	1152.7	380	0.4	1.33	6349	676	0.6
Finland	3573	1128.5	164	0.2	1.44	5145	449	0.4
France	4815	11,478.0	389	4.2	1.20	5778	568	5.3
W. Germany	4452	14,072.0	326	4.3	1.43	6366	679	7.7
Italy	2491	12,385.7	0	0	1.44	3587	164	1.6
Luxembourg	6084	83.0	626	0.04	1.23	7483	900	0.06
Netherlands	3815	2910.5	209	0.6	1.55	5913	594	1.4
Norway	4895	906.7	398	0.3	1.29	6315	670	0.5
Oceania	4419	4023.7	317	1.2	1.33	5877	585	1.9
Sweden	6228	1889.7	653	1.2	1.30	8096	1033	1.6
Switzerland	6222	1343.5	652	0.8	1.25	7778	944	1.0
United Kingdom	5383	13,075.0	493	6.1	1.30	6998	799	8.4
U. S. A.	11,161	46,141.5	1728	75.2	1.00	11,161	1728	64.4

[a]On basis of progressive income tax schedule of U.S.A. Assumes a family consists of 4 members.

Source: Adapted from P.N. Rosenstein-Rodan, "International Aid for Underdeveloped Countries," The Review of Economics and Statistics, XLIII (May, 1961) p. 138.

Belgium, Norway, South Africa, and Denmark. And the following countries are contributing less than their share; Italy, Sweden, Canada, Germany, France, and the United States. However, the Bretton Woods formula was the only basis on which any agreement could be reached and this was finally adopted.

The United Kingdom, Belgium, and the Netherlands have been unhappy with this decision. They feel that the world situation has changed since Bretton Woods. The United Kingdom subscribed to the Association almost immediately, despite its objections. The Netherlands held off for a while and Belgium and Luxembourg did not decide to join until 1963.

The second major issue involved the arrangements to be made for payment of subscriptions. Were all member nations going to have to subscribe in gold or convertible currencies? Or were the poor nations to be allowed to subscribe in their own currencies? Finally a very ingenious scheme was devised. The members of the Bank were divided into two parts. Part I countries are the industrial nations of the world and would be expected to make their contribution in convertible currency. Part II countries were underdeveloped countries who might expect to be eligible for assistance from IDA and would expect to make most of their contribution in their own currencies.

The decision on which countries would fall into Part I and which into Part II

> presented the Bank with an interesting and rather difficult question. A large number of economic criteria were made available by the Bank, the amount of capital exported by the country, the gross national product of the country, and various other things of that sort. These were reviewed by the Board of Directors. But in the ultimate analysis, the management of the Bank was invited to present a list of those countries which, in their opinion, and based on the background of the World Bank, should be in category I and those which should be in category II. The management presented this list, and the various executive directors who were negotiating the charter discussed it and agreed that this was an adequate list.[39]

The Bank staff relied primarily on per capita income figures for their decision. But there were some negotiations. Most cases were fairly obvious but there were two cases that the staff could not decide--so they asked the countries concerned. Spain said they were flattered to be asked but they did not feel that they were Part I calibre. Finland accepted Part I membership.

Some countries (such as Iceland) came in as Part II countries feeling that they probably wouldn't be able to borrow from IDA because their per capita incomes were too high to justify IDA loans. Japan is an anomaly from a per capita income standpoint. Japan, however, does export capital so it was put in Part I. The decision was based partly on how a country sees itself. Israel, for instance, has a high per capita income but is a massive capital importer. Ireland came in as a Part II country but has a relatively high per capita income. One of the considerations which the Bank staff considered was the fact that Part I countries are required to put up all their subscription in gold or convertible currency, while the Part II countries only put up 10 per cent of their subscription in gold or convertible currency and 90 per cent in their own currency. So, some relatively well-off countries (Iceland again) wouldn't want to put up all their subscriptions in convertible currency due to their own needs. Table 3 shows the countries of Part I and Part II and their proposed initial subscriptions.

There has been little published criticism of the IDA for its policy of requiring the underdeveloped countries to contribute 10 per cent of their subscription in gold or convertible currencies. Ceylon expressed opposition to any further drain on the poorer countries in the event of a future expansion of IDA.[40]

Each country is given five years in which to pay in its original contribution. Currency of Part II countries may be used by the Association for administrative expenses incurred by the Association in the territories of such members; and insofar as it is consistent with sound monetary practices this currency may be used to pay for goods and services to be used for projects financed by the Association in such territories; and when the Association and the country agree on it the Association can use these currencies for projects outside the territories of the member. All members must take steps to maintain the value of

TABLE 3. --Proposed initial subscriptions in the International Development Association (millions of U. S. dollars)

		Part I		
Australia	$20.18	Japan	33.59	
Austria	5.04	Luxembourg	1.01	
Belgium	22.70	Netherlands	27.74	
Canada	37.83	Norway	6.72	
Denmark	8.74	Sweden	10.09	
Finland	3.83	Union of South Africa	10.09	
France	52.96	United Kingdom	131.14	
Germany	52.96	United States	320.29	
Italy	18.16			763.
		Part II		
Afghanistan	1.01	Israel	1.68	
Argentina	18.83	Jordan	0.30	
Bolivia	1.06	Korea	1.26	
Brazil	18.83	Lebanon	0.45	
Burma	2.02	Libya	1.01	
Ceylon	3.03	Malya	2.52	
Chile	3.53	Mexico	8.74	
China	30.26	Morocco	3.53	
Colombia	3.53	Nicaragua	0.30	
Costa Rica	0.20	Pakistan	10.09	
Cuba	4.71	Panama	0.02	
Dominican Republic	0.40	Paraguay	0.30	
Ecuador	0.65	Peru	1.77	
El Salvador	0.30	Philippines	5.04	
Ethiopia	0.50	Saudi Arabia	3.70	
Ghana	2.36	Spain	10.09	
Greece	2.52	Sudan	1.01	
Guatemala	0.40	Thailand	3.03	
Haiti	0.76	Tunisia	1.51	
Honduras	0.30	Turkey	5.80	
Iceland	0.10	United Arab Republic	6.03	
India	40.35	Uruguay	1.06	
Indonesia	11.10	Venezuela	7.06	
Iran	4.54	Viet-Nam	1.51	
Iraq	0.76	Yugoslavia	4.04	
Ireland	3.03			236.
				$1000.

Source: Adapted from Articles of Agreement of the International Development Association (Washington: International Development Association, 1960), p. 29.

their subscriptions. In the event of depreciation, countries must add enough currency to restore the original value and in case of appreciation, the Association will return currency to the member country.

The Articles charge the Association with reviewing the adequacy of its resources at such time as it deems appropriate and at five-year intervals thereafter. If it seems desirable, the Association shall authorize a general increase in subscriptions. When additional subscriptions are authorized, each member shall be given the opportunity to subscribe an amount which will enable it to maintain its relative voting power, but no member shall be obligated to subscribe. Any country may add to its subscription at any time.

The Executive Directors gave the member nations until December 31, 1960 to decide whether they desired membership. And the Articles were to enter into effect upon their acceptance by governments whose subscriptions totaled 65 per cent of the total or $650 million. The completed Articles of Agreement and an accompanying report of the Executive Directors went out to the Governors of the Bank, by mail, on January 26, 1960.

CONGRESSIONAL APPROVAL OF THE INTERNATIONAL DEVELOPMENT ASSOCIATION

On February 18, 1960, the National Advisory Council submitted a special report on the International Development Association.[41] This report contained the Articles of Agreement for the Association and a statement of the Administration's reasons for favoring United States' participation. The arguments which were used in the debate on the Monroney Resolution were repeated but with some changes in emphasis. This report emphasized that the less developed countries themselves would be contributors to this new institution.[42] Much was made of the fact that the other countries would provide a larger share of the total resources than would the United States.[43] The possibility of using local currency was still receiving emphasis, although the Council did point out that the magnitudes that would be involved could not be predicted.[44]

President Eisenhower wrote a letter of transmittal for the report in which he stated that "I am convinced that participation by the United States is necessary."[45] Thus, since 1958, the Administration's reaction had run the gamut from determined opposition to IDA, through indifference, to lukewarm approval, until by February 18, 1960, membership had become necessary.

President Eisenhower's recommendation that the United States participate in the International Development Association went to the Congress in February and both houses of the Congress called early hearings on the proposal. There was the feeling that early United States action was necessary in view of the role of the United States in proposing IDA. And it was also thought that early United States approval would encourage the other nations to act speedily. Secretary of the Treasury Anderson and Under Secretary of State Dillon presented the Administration's case.

Secretary Anderson's testimony before Subcommittee No. 1 of the House Committee on Banking and Currency left no doubt concerning his stand on United States membership in IDA. He introduced his statement with this sentence. "I wholeheartedly support enactment of this bill."[46] He went on from there to reiterate arguments that had been made earlier in favor of the Association. However, he did introduce some new points of emphasis.

One of these concerned the fact that the underdeveloped countries themselves were putting in 10 per cent of their subscriptions in gold or convertible currencies.

> This, it seems to me, will give a sense of fiscal discipline, because all of them will be looking at the fund thinking in terms that, when these hard resources have been exhausted, the borrowers as well as the lenders have to be putting back some hard currencies in order to maintain the activities of the International Development Association.[47]

This particular item became one of the crucial points upon which the United States was insistent. Anderson pressed for agreement on the principle that, not only must all countries make some contribution in gold or dollars on the first round, but, that any replenishment of capital would also involve a gold or dollar contribution by the debtor as well as the creditor countries.[48]

Some of the Representatives indicated concern that the establishment of the International Development Association might be detrimental to the United States' balance of payments. Secretary Anderson was reassuring on this point.

> We are contributing about 32 percent of the funds to this institution, and the normal practices of the World Bank indicate that about 29 percent of the identifiable purchases under World Bank loans on an international competition basis are made in the United States.[49]

He conceded that these figures would indicate that the establishment of IDA might lead to some temporary addition to the United States' balance of payments problem. However, he argued that IDA was a long run attempt to solve this problem "on the basis of establishing a world in which we can become larger exporters, and other people better customers."[50]

The strongest implied criticism came from a member of the committee who was not even at the hearings. Representative Wright Patman, of Texas, had sent a list of questions which he wanted Secretary Anderson to answer. The questions concerned the interest rates that had been charged by the Export-Import Bank and the International Bank from 1946 to 1958. Patman called attention to the rise in interest rates on Export-Import Bank loans from 2.77 per cent in 1948 to 5.20 per cent in 1959 and on International Bank loans from 4.25 per cent in 1947 to 5.64 per cent in 1958. The Congressman was implying that it was the United States Government that was responsible for raising these rates and that this action was the reason that some such measure as the International Development Association was necessary.

Another line of criticism which came from the House Committee was based on the action of the International Bank in extending a loan to the United Arab Republic for the purpose of dredging the Suez Canal. This loan had come right at the time that the United Arab Republic had denied Israeli ships, or ships bound for Israel, access to the Canal. Some 25 per cent of the membership of the House of Representatives had objected to the Bank over this loan. The Bank had, nevertheless, granted the loan. This had considerably angered some Representatives and several of them expressed their unwillingness to establish IDA under World

Bank management.

There was very little criticism or opposition in the Senate hearings. Most of the Committee on Foreign Relations were obviously quite favorable to the establishment of IDA. There were some questions concerning coordination between IDA and United States' aid activities so that borrowers could not play off one against the other and so that duplication of effort could be avoided. The Administration spokesman assured the committee that the United States Executive Director of IDA would sit as a member of the Board of the Development Loan Fund so that such problems ought not arise.

A surprising degree of unanimity existed among the business and labor groups of the United States on the advisability of joining the International Development Association. Only three groups, the Farm Bureau, the National Foreign Trade Council, and the Merchant Marine Institute, expressed reservations concerning IDA.

As far back as 1956, the Research and Policy Committee of the Committee for Economic Development had called for an expanded program of public investment in underdeveloped countries under World Bank leadership where an international approach was advantageous. This group favored giving the World Bank additional capital contributions and authority to make grants and development loans repayable in local currencies.[51]

The Chamber of Commerce of the United States supported IDA from the start. The Chamber was anxious to have assurances that loan funds would not supplant private capital. The National Association of Manufacturers had no particular policy position with reference to IDA. The U. S. Council of the International Chamber of Commerce sent a representative to testify in favor of United States membership in the Association.

The National Farmers Union made a strong statement before the House Committee on Banking and Currency favoring United States participation in IDA. The National Grange sent a letter of support as did the National Council of Farmer Cooperatives. The Farm Bureau actually did not oppose the establishment of IDA; they merely wanted to insure that if the United States joined IDA it be with the firm understanding that the United States Development Loan Fund's appropriation be reduced by the amount of the appropriation to IDA. Their letter pointed out that "there is a limit to the amount of capital funds the U. S. Government can provide to other countries."[52]

The bankers of the United States sent three spokesmen to welcome the establishment of IDA. John J. McCloy, Chairman of the Chase Manhattan Bank, James S. Saxon of the First National Bank of Chicago, and Tom B. Coughran, Executive Vice President of the Bank of America, served to represent the bankers as strongly in support of United States participation in IDA.

The American Federation of Labor-Congress of Industrial Organizations made a very strong case for United States participation in the International Development Association. The spokesman did have two reservations about the new Association. One was that, in turning IDA over to the World Bank, the influence of individuals with the traditional bankers' point of view might outweigh the views of those who recognize the need for flexible, nonbankable loans for economic development.[53]

The labor spokesman also questioned the size of the appropriation for IDA. The September, 1959, convention of the AFL-CIO had adopted a resolution which called upon Congress to authorize effective United States financial support for IDA. It did not appear to the AFL-CIO representative that a contribution of $320 million constituted effective support. He expressed the hope that Congress would expand the resources of IDA so that it would be assured of at least $1 billion a year.

> We must recognize that, unless the more fortunate, industrially advanced nations of the free world, and especially the United States, which is still by far the richest, are prepared to make available to the less developed countries economic assistance on a scale commensurate with their minimum needs, they will reluctantly, but inevitably, turn to the Soviet Union.
>
> This is an important reason for increasing the capitalization of the International Development Association substantially above the presently contemplated level, but it is by no means the only one.[54]

The Congress turned a deaf ear to this plea.

Other groups which endorsed United States entry into the Association were the National Council of the Churches of Christ in the U. S. A., the United Christian Missionary Society, and the Women's International League for Peace and Freedom.

The Merchant Marine Institute questioned the advisability of multilateral foreign aid because the United States would not be able to require that goods be shipped in American vessels. The National Foreign Trade Council passed resolutions at both its 1958 and 1959 meetings which questioned the need for another inter-governmental financial institution. The Council felt that any necessary aid should be given on a bilateral basis and that such aid should not be repayable in non-convertible funds. However, by the time the bill to establish IDA came before the Congress, the Council was reconciled to IDA and did not testify against United States membership. They did publish a statement which questioned the local currency aspects of IDA and which regretted that no reference was made in the articles of agreement to the need to prevent any financing which would be inimical or injurious to private enterprise.[55]

Why was there so little opposition to United States participation in IDA? Such participation cost more than $300 million. At the same time that legislation establishing IDA was sailing through the Congress there was very bitter and determined opposition to the bilateral aid program. Some persons have suggested that the Congress is usually enthusiastic about any new aid program. All proposals for re-orienting the foreign aid program are seen as panaceas at their first introduction. Thus, the IDA merely slipped through on its newness as did the Inter-American Development Bank and the Development Loan Fund a few years earlier. Some people were, thus, expecting the hard fight on additional funds for IDA that actually took place in 1964.

Another interpretation has attributed IDA's popularity to the intensive publicity campaign which Senator Monroney waged throughout 1958-1960. Editorials favoring IDA appeared in 40 newspapers around the country during this period. All the major newspapers in the country carried extensive stories and articles on IDA, many in a friendly vein.

Certainly the fact that IDA was to be managed by the staff of the World Bank had considerable influence. Gene Black's reputation is quite phenomenal among United States lawmakers. They credit him with a wizard's touch when it comes to managing a difficult operation.

Congressional approval for United States participation came on June 30, 1960. An appropriation of $73 million for the first installment of the United States on its initial subscription was approved on July 14, 1960, and on August 9, 1960, the United States deposited its instrument of acceptance with the International Bank. The Articles of Agreement had specified that the Agreement would enter into force when it had been signed on behalf of governments whose subscriptions totaled not less than $650 million. This point was reached on September 24, 1960, and the International Development Association became a reality. Operations of the Association were begun on November 8, 1960, when the Executive Directors held their inaugural meeting.

CHAPTER 8 FUNDAMENTAL POLICY DECISIONS (1960-1962)

BASIC PHILOSOPHY UNDERLYING POLICIES

The first President of the Association, Eugene Black, stamped the Association with his basic views on the development process. His views underlay the basic policy decisions made during the first two years IDA was in operation and these views were expressed on many occasions. He believed that economic development cannot be based on expediency; that although political processes in a democratic society make it difficult for a government to take the long-term view--still development is a long-term process. Development cannot be carried out on a sporadic basis. It cannot be a means of winning votes, nor a means of promoting the interest of certain sectors of the country. And this reminder must be given to the developed countries, also. If their aid is to be really effective, they should look to the fundamental conditions of the country. They cannot base policy on "fever charts of international tension."[1]

For a man whose life long job has been to allocate capital, Eugene Black had a surprising attitude toward the role of capital in economic development. He always argued that too much emphasis was placed on capital, particularly foreign capital, in the process of development. He believed that the social institutions of the country, the distribution of wealth, the opportunities available to the people, the educational system's effectiveness, and the competence of government officials--that all these factors were just as important as foreign capital in economic development.[2]

The quality of foreign capital was of much more concern to Black than the quantity. He argued that outside sources could supply only a small margin of the resources needed. Therefore, the best use of economic aid was to promote "proper" standards in the art of managing the country's resources.[3] The staff was fond of reminding the underdeveloped countries that many nations developed without huge inflows of external capital. In particular, Western Europe was cited as the prime example of an area that developed without outside aid. The same was true of Japan before World War I. And, of course, the Soviet Union developed recently without outside aid.[4]

Mr. Black eschewed as far as "efficiency" permitted the ideological aspects of development. He thought that the World Bank should concentrate on economic development as though its only aim were higher consumption and greater comfort. He endeavored to remove ideology from economics and to strive to achieve higher material living standards as an end in itself.[5]

The simple explanations for underdevelopment were never very popular with Black. He argued that it was not just the lack of capital per se, of savings per se, or of entrepreneurship per se which stood in the way of growth. He argued that there was no single cure for underdevelopment. One simply could not improve education and expect that to bring about development, nor could one import a lot of foreign capital and expect that to work. The solution to the problem of underdevelopment lay in illuminating the opportunities for growth and development. He referred to this as the primary task of economic diplomacy. And once the opportunities were visualized then many of the traditional obstacles to development would appear much less formidable.[6]

None of Black's critics have ever attacked him because IDA did too much. A number of people have claimed that it did much too little. Black's answer to this charge would run somewhat like this: IDA should not substitute sympathy for understanding of problems in allocating resources. The surest way of defeating the ultimate objective of economic development would be to use carelessly or ineffectively the scarce resources which had been entrusted to IDA. And that is the reason that IDA insisted on the same standards of investment for IDA projects as for Bank projects.[7] Black did not deny the consideration which should be given to human suffering. He was well aware of the political pressures on the governments of the developing countries. But he urged that economic aid be dispensed "sensibly", while taking these considerations into account. He admitted that this is extremely difficult to do because the political problems facing the governments of these countries are excruciatingly difficult. The governments themselves are acting as the primary agents of change in societies which are undergoing a wholesale transformation. In the West, of course, this role was taken by the entrepreneurs; governments could confine themselves to governing. Today governments are taking the initiative in development themselves, either because there are no entrepreneurs or because only the government can raise the necessary capital. To help these governments perform their functions without generating extravagant forms of political injustice and cruelty was the major objective in offering economic aid.[8]

SOME EARLY POLICIES

With Black's philosophy forming the foundation for decisions, what fundamental policies did the Association choose? As to the terms of financing, it was decided that IDA would not make loans repayable in local currency. On this point there was general consensus among the Executive Directors, and the staff was opposed to local currency loans.

The terms that have been adopted for all "development credits" extended to date have been identical. The credits must be repaid in foreign exchange. They have a duration of 50 years, amortization is to begin after a 10 year grace period; thereafter, 1 per cent of the principal is repayable annually for 10 years and 3 per cent is repayable annually for the next 30 years. A service charge of 3/4 of 1 per cent per annum on the amounts withdrawn and outstanding is charged to pay IDA's administrative costs.

The second Annual Report of the Association dilated these conditions. The staff did not intend that these concessionary terms should result in the extension of financial subsidies to the actual projects on which IDA funds were employed. So, in the case of revenue-producing projects, IDA requires that the credit be invested on a normal business-like basis and that the price of the goods or services produced by the project be fixed at levels which will make the project remunerative.[9]

If IDA should lend soft money for a project with a high rate of return inside the country--then IDA would be subsidizing the borrower vis-a-vis his competitors, which was no part of IDA's purpose. So, the policy has been that IDA credits for commercial projects are passed on to the government and from the government to the ultimate borrower at rates of interest comparable to the rates prevailing within the country. An attempt is made not to distort the interest rate structure of the country. An example of this policy is the $5 million credit to the China Development Corporation which was passed through the hands of the Republic of China. The Corporation is paying 12 per cent interest to the Chinese Government and the duration is 30 years. There are no restrictions imposed on the counterpart funds that are generated when an internal organization repays its loan to the borrowing government. There are two reasons why there are no such restrictions. First of all, it is economically meaningless. The local currency generated by repayment of loans does not represent real resources to the country concerned. The use of such resources depends on the current monetary situation in the country. If IDA required a country to hold the counterpart funds--the country could hold them and simply create bank credit in the same amount. So nothing would be accomplished. The second reason for imposing no restrictions is that no objective is to be gained by imposing new restrictions on the countries concerned. These restrictions would require further consultations and negotiations. IDA tries to limit the interference imposed on a country's management of its affairs.

The reason IDA insists that credits which are on-loaned to a domestic organization bear the going rate of interest is clear. Subsidizing revenue-producing activities would be inequitable as between borrowers. And it could lead to a poor allocation of resources. Of course, one result of the policy is that the government concerned makes a profit from its on-lending of IDA resources. This technique is an innovation in international lending. Previously the terms of aid had been related to the project concerned rather than to the circumstances of the recipient country. IDA is paying attention to both.

The First Annual Report carried the announcement that IDA had no policy of allocating its funds in advance. However, it was pointed out that an effort was being made to assure wide geographic distribution, taking account of the priority which should be given to the poorer countries. It was pointed out that it would be necessary to impose limits on credits to some countries which could absorb all the money very quickly.[10] Quite obviously the report was referring to India and Pakistan.

Very early a significant policy question had to be decided along this line. What would be the criterion of eligibility for IDA credits? Would it be based on the type of project or the condition of the borrowing country? It was decided to base decisions on IDA countries rather than IDA projects. Mr. Black's speech to the 1961 meeting of the Board of Governors made it clear that the same standards would be applied to projects financed by the Bank and IDA, although IDA would finance some projects of a more social nature than the Bank, e.g., schools, housing.

There was one early proposal that soft loans be made for some projects where returns were slower in accruing, even though they were located in countries that were creditworthy. In addition, credits could be extended for quick-return projects in non-creditworthy countries. In practice, this would mean two types of operations. IDA would finance education, urban water supply systems, housing projects, etc., in countries that could borrow from the Bank. And, IDA would make credits available for roads, hydroelectric plants, and irrigation projects in countries that had difficulty obtaining international credit. This proposal was rejected. Instead, it was decided to allocate IDA funds to IDA countries.

This led to a certain anomaly. IDA, with a billion dollars (because it catered to the really poor countries), had a much larger clientele than the Bank which had over $7 billion. In addition, IDA could finance a broader range of projects than could the Bank. So IDA had less money, no possibility to borrow, more customers, and a broader range of projects than did the Bank. In an effort to bridge the difference between these two institutions, the Bank decided to finance a broader range of projects itself, including projects of a social nature. The Bank is now willing to finance educational projects and other such activities when they are capable of making an important contribution to economic development.

Thus the Association only lends to countries that are not creditworthy or are exhausting their remaining margin of creditworthiness. The staff is the arbiter of what countries get what terms. The staff decides whether the loan should be made from the Bank, from IDA, or not at all. Three criteria have been established for determining if a country is eligible for credits from the International Development Association.

THE CREDITWORTHINESS CRITERION

First, a country must be near the end of its rope so far as creditworthiness is concerned. Within this category there are two types of countries. The first group are those countries whose foreign exchange situation is such that the staff thinks that further hard loans involve a substantial risk of default. The second group consists of those whose burden of foreign debt service is so high that, while they can borrow on conventional terms some of the external capital which they require to carry out their priority programs, they cannot prudently borrow the whole of it. In these circumstances the World Bank and IDA may combine forces and this is, in fact, what has happened in India, Chile, Sudan, and Colombia.[11] Decisions on creditworthiness or the blend of loans and credits are based essentially on judgment. Ratios of debt service to exports, or of debt service to local budgetary receipts or gross national product cannot be used as rigid criteria.[12]

Since the Association's funds are for countries with a balance of payments difficulty, it becomes necessary to draw up a balance of payments estimate for future years. If minus items cannot be offset by plus items, then the country must either default or reduce imports to a level which would seriously affect the continuity of the development process. Although the Association must have a view of the future balance of payments of its customers, the balance of payments really depends upon two items under the control of other lenders. First, how much are other lenders likely to lend in the years ahead? And, secondly, what debt service liability has accrued because of loans these institutions have already made? There are great dangers in projecting balance of payments situations 10 years ahead for this depends upon what assumptions are made about debt service liabilities the country will have acquired during the period and on what terms such liabilities are incurred. It is necessary to try to predict what other soft loan money is going to be made available and whether the industrial nations will keep their present bilateral programs going.[13]

There is an assumption underlying the need for IDA that the underdeveloped countries are going to continue to get capital mainly on conventional terms. It is, therefore, relevant for IDA policy to consider what everyone else is going to be doing. There is the prospect of the underdeveloped countries receiving all sorts of resources from all sorts of sources. What it boils down to is that IDA policy-makers must guess the other chap's intention.[14]

Despite these complexities, it has been decided that exhaustion or near-exhaustion of creditworthiness is a necessary condition before IDA money can be obtained. But, this ought not be enough. Exhaustion of creditworthiness could be due to improvident policies and IDA was not established to reward the improvident.

THE PERFORMANCE CRITERION

So, a second criterion was established--that some element of good performance in the country should be postulated. Some evidence is required that the country is making a real effort to mobilize its own resources and to gear its financial policy to development. This means that IDA will only assist countries who are mobilizing domestic resources and avoiding inflationary policies.[15]

Good performance is a very appealing criterion but it is also an ambiguous term which is difficult to quantify. It has been suggested that good performance could be measured in terms of the rate of growth of a country considered in relationship to the proportion of investment which has been financed domestically. This would reflect the country's ability to use savings effectively to promote growth and to channel part of the increased income into domestic investment. However, the growth rate is not purely a product of a country's efforts. The rate of growth also depends on a country's resources, on the amount of previous investment that had taken place, and other factors.

Some people stress the country's marginal savings rate in evaluating performance. It is argued that, if a serious effort at development is being made, the country will achieve a relatively high marginal savings rate. It has been hard to establish any standards here, though. There seems to be no correlation between average or marginal savings rates and per capita income levels, and there is no norm for any income level. This may be because it has not been approached in a sufficiently sophisticated way as yet.[16]

Some of the other factors that could be taken into account in considering quality of a country's performance would be the wisdom of public expenditure decisions. Are they based on a systematic evaluation of cost and benefits? How much of a country's investment goes into prestige projects or unnecessary military spending? Are tariff and price policies the result of sectional pressures? Does the institutional framework in agriculture thwart incentive to experiment with new crops and new production techniques? Are industrialization and import substitution plans influenced by non-economic considerations? Is the government capable of making decisions? These types of questions can be useful when supplemented by statistical indications of growth in output and indications of structural change in the economy.[17]

Another possible quantitative measure of performance has been the taxation performance of the underdeveloped countries. How much of the national income has the government been able to collect in the form of taxes for investment purposes? However, there is a low correlation between gross national products and tax levels, also. When exports and imports as a percentage of gross national product are added to a multiple correlation analysis, the fit is much better. The implication is that countries with a high level of exports and imports can tax them easily.[18]

> Pre-investment studies of countries are, except in rare cases, based on investigation on the spot, because experience shows that the inadequate published data can only be supplemented by observations made on the scene. Some judgment of the imponderables must be made based on personal knowledge of the government, of business, and of the farming classes.[19]

These studies of countries seek to analyze the existing structure of the economy, the structural changes that are taking place and the factors that are inhibiting or accelerating growth. Analysis is made of the magnitude of investment, savings, exports and imports, and external sources of capital. The staff tries to arrive at some judgment as to the rationality of policy and the efficiency and speed with which capital investment takes place. In all these assessments, limitations of data are serious. National accounts data may be wholly lacking. Information on savings are likely to be very unreliable.[20]

Many of the things which the Bank has emphasized would be referred to as human resources. Attention is given to institutional bottlenecks; to initiative of the private and public sector; to the quality of the civil service; and to the degree to which a sense of purpose or an air of bouyancy pervades the country.[21] Given the difficulty of quantifying good performance, the staff is driven to all kinds of non-quantifiable aspects. It is difficult to set uniform standards. Different countries require different norms. The newly independent nations cannot be expected to meet the same performance standards required for an older country. This calls for judgment as to which standards to apply.

In evaluating performance, a question arose. To what extent should this reflect good performance up to the present and to what extent should it rest on opinion or hope that performance is going to be good in the future? In some cases, performance has been poor in the past, but IDA money might be used to encourage better performance in the future.

The Bank has used its funds to exert pressure on countries to follow orthodox financial policies. There has, however, been a notable lack of success throughout South America. As Mr. Black observed in 1961, the most discouraging fact about South American governments is their inability to manage their economies without inflation. He pointed out that Brazil and Chile had both had price level changes of more than 80 per cent in a given year. This was not just a matter of one misguided policy. There was something fundamentally wrong. There was something fundamentally wrong too, when tax evasion amounts to 50 per cent of income tax assessments.[22]

What can be done in such circumstances? Mr. Black admitted that "there is little that outsiders can do about these shortcomings other than to withhold support until tolerable conditions exist. I consider that the major reason for the World

Bank's existence is to underline the kind of orderliness in government that is absolutely essential anywhere that economic growth is desired."[23] He was not unduly optimistic about success in bringing this condition about. "No outsider can force orderly government on South America. The problem is one that South America must solve for itself."[24] Some South American countries raise havoc with such conventional ideas. The performance question would be much easier if bad performance was always correlated with stagnation of the economy or if financial rectitude always coincided with buoyant economic growth. But what about the cases where economic growth and high returns to capital have coincided with serious problems in a government's financial accounts? This type of problem is one of the many areas where the performance criterion has had to be weighed along with other objectives.

Andrew Shonfield has warned against an over-emphasis on performance criteria in administering aid. As long as there is a shortage of funds for economic development, it is necessary to choose countries in which the yield on capital is not markedly below the yield in developed countries. The yield should be measured in terms of extra output--not in terms of profit. But, lest we get too obsessed with the problem of economic growth we should remember the ordinary demands of charity. "Poor people have to be helped, even if they refuse to grow."[25]

The countries that have been considered to meet the performance criterion are shown in Table 4.

THE POVERTY CRITERION

The third criterion is poverty. The Articles state that IDA will "provide financing to further development in the less-developed areas of the world included within the Association's membership." Did the drafters intend this to mean loans only to the poorer of the Part II countries--or to any Part II country? The staff interpreted it to mean that loans would only be made to the poorer Part II countries, because it is argued that IDA provides cheap money--tax money from the taxpayers of the rich countries. And, one cannot justify taking money from taxpayers to give subsidies to rich or even relatively rich countries. So, the richer Part II countries--Iceland, Ireland, Israel--have, for all practical purposes, been disqualified from borrowing from

TABLE 4.--International Development Association credits granted through June 30, 1964 (millions of U. S. dollars)

Member in Whose Territories Development Credits Have Been Made	Program or Project	Date of Development Credit Agreement	Original Principal Amount
CHILE	Road Construction	June 28, 1961	$19.0
CHINA	Harbor Dredging	August 30, 1961	2.2
	Ground Water Development	August 30, 1961	3.7
	Municipal Water Supply	September 6, 1961	4.4
	Development of Private Industry	December 1, 1961	5.0
			15.3
COLOMBIA	Road Project	August 28, 1961	19.5
COSTA RICA	Road Construction and Maintenance	October 13, 1961	5.5
ECUADOR	Second Highway Project	May 26, 1964	8.0
EL SALVADOR	Third Highway Project	November 2, 1962	8.0
ETHIOPIA	Road Development	February 27, 1963	13.5
HAITI	Interim Highway Project	November 2, 1962	0.35
HONDURAS	Western Highway Improvement	May 12, 1961	9.0

TABLE 4--Continued

Member in Whose Territories Development Credits Have Been Made	Program or Project	Date of Development Credit Agreement	Original Principal Amount
INDIA	Highway Construction and Improvement	June 21, 1961	$60.0
	Tubewell Irrigation	September 6, 1961	6.0
	Shetrunji Irrigation Project	November 22, 1961	4.5
	Salandi Irrigation Project	November 22, 1961	8.0
	Punjab Flood Protection and Drainage	November 22, 1961	10.0
	Durgapur Power Extension	February 14, 1962	18.5
	Sone Irrigation Project	June 29, 1962	15.0
	Purna Irrigation Project	July 18, 1962	13.0
	Second Koyna Power Project	August 8, 1962	17.5
	Bombay Port Project	September 14, 1962	18.0
	Telecommunications	September 14, 1962	42.0
	Railway Improvement	March 22, 1963	67.5
	Kothagudem Power Project	May 24, 1963	20.0
	Industrial Imports Project	June 9, 1964	90.0
			390.0
JORDAN	Amman Water Supply Project	December 22, 1961	2.0
	Water Supply Project	December 12, 1963	3.5
	Agricultural Credit Project	December 12, 1963	3.0
			8.5
KOREA	Railway Development	August 17, 1962	14.0

TABLE 4--Continued

Member in Whose Territories Development Credits Have Been Made	Program or Project	Date of Development Credit Agreement	Original Principal Amount
NICARAGUA	Managua Water Supply Project	September 7, 1962	$ 3.0
NIGER	Road Project	June 24, 1964	1.5
PAKISTAN	Dacca Irrigation Project	October 19, 1961	1.0
	Inland Ports Project	November 22, 1961	2.0
	Khairpur Irrigation Project	June 29, 1962	18.0
	Industrial Estates Project	November 2, 1962	6.5
	Brahmaputra Flood Project	June 26, 1963	5.0
	Chandpur Irrigation Project	July 26, 1963	9.0
	Dacca Water Supply and Sewerage Project	August 16, 1963	26.0
	Chittagong Water Supply and Sewerage Project	August 16, 1963	24.0
	East Pakistan Education Project	March 25, 1964	4.5
	West Pakistan Education Project	March 25, 1964	8.5
	East Pakistan Highway Project	June 11, 1964	22.5
	West Pakistan Highway Project	June 11, 1964	17.0
	Pakistan Eastern Railway Project	June 24, 1964	10.0
	Pakistan Western Railway Project	June 24, 1964	25.0
			179.0
PARAGUAY	Highway Improvement and Maintenance	October 26, 1961	6.0
	Cattle Project	December 26, 1963	3.6
			9.6

TABLE 4--Continued

Member in Whose Territories Development Credits Have Been Made	Program or Project	Date of Development Credit Agreement	Original Principal Amount
SUDAN	Roseires Irrigation Project	June 14, 1961	$13.0
SYRIA	Highway Improvement	December 24, 1963	8.5
TANGANYIKA	School Construction and Equipment	December 19, 1963	4.6
	Highway Project	February 5, 1964	14.0
			18.6
TUNISIA	Education Project	September 17, 1962	5.0
TURKEY	Development of Private Industry	November 23, 1962	5.0
	Cukurova Power Project	February 1, 1963	1.7
	Seyhan Irrigation Project	May 31, 1963	20.0
			26.7
UNITED KINGDOM			
SWAZILAND	Highway Construction	March 14, 1962	2.8
		TOTAL	$778.35

Source: Economic Staff, International Development Association.

IDA. The estimates of per capita income, used by IDA, for the countries that have received credits are shown in Table 5.

The countries that have received IDA credits have per capita incomes below $300 per year with the exception of Costa Rica and Chile. And some persons would argue that it was a mistake to loan IDA money to Costa Rica and Chile. Underneath this debate, there are two sharply conflicting opinions. One view emphasizes that IDA should help the really poor countries. The other emphasizes the problem of certain countries--higher income countries--which are close to the take-off and which will soon be able to finance their own development. There are several countries in this latter category--Mexico is an example--which have relatively high per capita incomes but which are having difficulties in the intermediate stage of development. A question could be raised about Yugoslavia, also. It might not be eligible based on per capita income, but, based on performance, it is promising. Yugoslavia has had a rapid increase in exports over the past decade. The marginal savings rate has been high. It ought by 1970--if it can keep its momentum--to be able to end its deficit on current account. But, in order to maintain momentum, Yugoslavia will need a very large net capital inflow--on the order of $300 million per annum. The proposals to channel IDA money to countries like these envision charging a nominal rate of interest. For, if capital is provided on conventional terms, these countries will wind up with an enormous external debt. By the same token, they will also have an enormously increased capacity to pay that debt. As of this date, no IDA funds have gone to countries like Yugoslavia and Mexico.

There have been serious objections to IDA's policy of helping only the poorest countries among its members. Spain, Trinidad, and others have pointed out that they have problems in securing capital for public works but yet they are not in the poverty class. As one Governor put it at the 1963 Annual Meetings, they fall between two stools. They are not good enough for the Bank and they are too good for IDA

At the 1962 Meeting of the Board of Governors, the African nations raised questions concerning the allocation of IDA's resources. The Governor from Nigeria pointed out that all of Africa had received only 6 per cent of IDA funds.

TABLE 5. --Per capita gross national product (GNP) at factor cost for countries receiving International Development Association credits through June 30, 1964[a] (expressed in United States currency)

Rank	Country	Per Capita GNP
1	Costa Rica	380
2	Chile	345
3	Colombia	285
4	Turkey	220
5	El Salvador	220
6	Nicaragua	205
7	Tunisia	175
8	Honduras	160
9	Ecuador	130
10	China	125
11	Syria	125
12	Paraguay	105
13	Haiti	95
14	Jordan	90
15	Korea	80
16	Sudan	75
17	Swaziland	70
18	India	70
19	Pakistan	65
20	Tanganyika	65
21	Niger	60
22	Ethiopia	55

[a]Estimates are for the period 1958-1960 and are made on an adjusted exchange rate basis.

Source: Based on estimates made by the Economic Staff, International Development Association.

THE BASIC PROBLEM

Mr. Black expressed the opinion that the major problem that IDA would have to face was the meagerness of its resources. He went on to say that

> There is in sight now a volume of promising applications which, if approved, would absorb a substantial part of the convertible funds initially subscribed for IDA's first five years of operations. India and Pakistan together are already in a position where they could quickly absorb in worthwhile projects all of IDA's capital by themselves.
>
> Some members of IDA cannot yet present concrete proposals for credits because they are not yet able to present adequately prepared and justified projects. But others show every indication of coming forward with very substantial requirements, demonstrating that once a country organizes itself for development it can rapidly build up a burden of debt which may limit, at least temporarily, its ability to borrow abroad on conventional terms. In these circumstances, even on a conservative estimate, IDA's funds are likely to fall far short of the need.[26]

Mr. Black repeated this argument at the 1962 meeting of the Board of Governors and indicated that by mid-1963 most or all of IDA's funds would have been committed.[27] It will be remembered that the Association started its life with total contributions approaching $1 billion. On June 30, 1962, the Association had total subscriptions of $917 million, of which $739 million was in convertible currencies. And, the Articles of Agreement called for review of the adequacy of its resources at such time as it was deemed appropriate and at intervals of approximately five years thereafter. Thus, the impression was created that IDA's first billion dollars was to last for approximately five years. But, was this billion dollars to be committed over five years or disbursed over five years? On this question the Articles are silent.

If it was intended that IDA disburse the whole amount in five years, then commitments would have to take place in the first couple of years, because disbursements follow commitments by a considerable period. There is a necessary lag while projects get underway. However, if the initial amount was intended for commitment over five years--then disbursement would be made over a longer period. The provisions of the Articles for the subscription to be paid in 5 annual installments might lead one to think that this was meant to be committed each year. Some member countries have charged IDA with a breach of faith on this point. They argue that the first $1 billion was for the first five years commitment--not disbursement. The Executive Directors are representatives of bodies politic--although IDA is not political. So, some directors have contributed to this confusion which comes from mixing commitments and disbursements. Some of the wealthy European members have argued along this line, anyway. They are happy to befuddle the issue. At the 1962 annual meeting of the Board of Governors, the Governor from France called for a re-examination of the rate at which loans were being granted.[28]

Whatever the intention of the drafters of the Articles of Agreement and despite the wishes of some member countries, the staff acted on the assumption that the original funds were intended to be disbursed over the first five years operations. They proceeded to commit IDA funds at a rate which would leave the Association virtually penniless sometime in 1963. There is some indication that the staff has acted so as to commit the funds as fast as possible (taking account of the criteria that have been established), in order to get some idea of how much IDA-type money could be absorbed by the underdeveloped countries in a year's time. During fiscal year 1963, IDA committed $260 million and committed $283 million in fiscal year 1964.

In his 1962 appeal to the Governors for replenishment of IDA funds, Mr. Black estimated that IDA would need $500 million a year for the next five years, and therefore, requested replenishment of IDA resources in the amount of $2.5 billion. Of course the Association had no assurance that it would receive this amount. So, it had to make policy based on a budget of only $1 billion.

Most of the problems which IDA faced in establishing policies stem from this inadequacy of resources--from the fact that IDA operations are essentially a sub-optimum operation. IDA resources are such a small percentage of the total of all aid that the staff is not able to pick the optimum solution to the allocation problem. Sometimes it is quite obvious what the ideal solution would be if funds were unlimited. But, they are limited and it is foolish to concentrate too much on the ideal solution--the staff must choose those policies that will work in a realistic situation.

The Development Assistance Committee of the Organization for Economic Co-Operation and Development has estimated that $6 billion of foreign assistance (including surplus commodities and defense support funds) was disbursed in 1962.[29] The Bank (with $600 million) and IDA (with $300 million) together will disburse something on the order of $900 million a year when IDA gets into full operation. Repayments and interest going to the Bank amount to $300 million a year so that the Bank and IDA will be making a net addition of funds of approximately $600 million a year. This is only 10 per cent of all foreign aid extended now and will be something less than 10 per cent in the future if total aid continues to increase.

Assuming that soft loans and grants continue at their present level of $4 billion a year--then IDA will be dispensing approximately 8 per cent of all the soft funds going into the underdeveloped countries. How, with such a small portion of the total resources going into these countries could IDA make a significant contribution? What policies would tend to result in the maximum impact?

One solution to the problem of limited resources would be to concentrate on certain countries. But, could this policy be made effective? If IDA concentrated its assistance on certain countries, would other aid-givers acquiesce in this decision--or would they assist these same countries, also? In the distribution of foreign aid, everyone reacts to everyone else. If IDA chooses t finance certain projects, then other aid-givers will not finance ther But if IDA hadn't financed them, would one of the other aid-givers have done so? How can IDA be sure that its funds are making the maximum contribution to economic development in the underdeveloped countries, considering the role of other aid-givers?

This situation is similar to an oligopolistic model. The IDA and the member governments of the Development Assistance Committee are the protagonists in a situation which involves a certain degree of uncertainty about each other's reactions. Of course, the same countries contribute IDA's convertible funds and their own funds bilaterally, after consultation in the Development Assistance Committee. The parties do, thus, have some information about the others' reactions. IDA does not have information on bilateral aid decisions in advance, so, the analogy still holds. If IDA takes a certain action, it will cause the other aid-givers to react in some way. And, IDA must try to predict that reaction in order to have its limited resources have as much impact on economic development as possible.

The problems of drawing up a consistent policy for the allocation of aid are enormous. It is not difficult to conceptualize a sound aid policy in general terms. That is, IDA can seek to maximize efforts directed toward economic development or can choose to maximize economic product, etc. If IDA had control over enough outside resources, this would be a fairly simple task and with $6 billion of aid, it could allow fairly high margins for error and still come out alright. However, when IDA is allocating one-tenth or one-twentieth that amount, the margin for error cannot be large. And here's the real rub. The technical judgments of the impact of any policy are so extraordinarily crude that they cannot be relied on in specific policy cases. It is not known what impact a steel mill or an educational system will have on an economy. Which would add more to economic output? Which should come first? Since there is so little confidence in technical measurements of the impact of any policy chosen, some other checks on policy must be devised. One attempt to devise a consistent policy for IDA was the decision to establish a performance criterion.

GOALS FOR THE PERFORMANCE CRITERION

Some of the different goals which might be established for the performance criterion are as follows:

1. The International Development Association should not reward unsound economic policies of the underdeveloped countries. Lack of creditworthiness should not be due to improper management of the economy--from unwise debt, from inflationary policies, etc.

2. Another goal also mentioned earlier was the possibility of using IDA credits as an incentive to the underdeveloped

countries in order to promote good performance in the future. Some countries have had really poor administration of their economies in the past. Perhaps an IDA credit could be held out as a lure--to get these countries to improve. This would emphasize future promise rather than past performance. Just how much should future plans be considered? Some countries with poor past performance have well constructed and reasonable plans now in effect. Should IDA help them bring their plans to fruition? This raises an interesting dilemma for IDA. How can one justify ignoring past failures in development? But, if IDA doesn't help with these new plans, this may doom them to failure. Thus, IDA's prediction that the plan was going to fail would become a self-fulfilling prophecy. There are countries that the Bank could not have financed on conventional terms. But, IDA has made it possible for the Bank to have an entre into these countries and thus the Bank staff can work with them and help them improve the performance of their economies.

3. One purpose that might be served by the establishment of a performance criterion would be to impress upon the Part I countries that IDA was making good use of the funds entrusted to the Association. Fundamentally, IDA is administering part of the foreign aid effort of the rich Western nations. A performance criterion might be useful in convincing these countries that this administration is sound and should be continued.

4. One school of thought would use IDA credits to obtain maximum results, in terms of economic development from the limited resources available. Performance tests would be used to insure that such maximization took place. This raises the technical problem of measuring the impact of external assistance of various types, and raises another problem, also. Should IDA be interested in getting the most development for its money or should IDA be interested in channeling its funds to those countries which are trying really hard? Some countries are making Herculean efforts with little result. Other countries are having a relatively easy time of it, for environmental and historical reasons, and achieving quite handsome rates of growth--some of the oil-producing countries of the Middle East and South America immediately come to mind. Some people would argue that IDA should place a premium on improvement relative to a country's present position. This would take little account of a country's lack of resources, etc. IDA has chosen, judging from the countries where it has extended credits, to reward effort rather than rates of growth.

As mentioned earlier, there is no simple method of measuring good performance. Just how good should domestic effort have to be in order for a country to qualify for IDA credits? Certainly growth and growth-creating policies should be favored, but, what facets of the economy should be considered in assessing these policies? How many non-economic factors should be taken into account in measuring performance?

The establishment of IDA has presented the staff of the Bank with a whole host of problems. How can the staff rationalize its decisions to make IDA loans as opposed to Bank loans? There are difficulties in explaining these decisions to the developing countries and to the donor countries. And, in addition to the two types of money available now, there are proposals for adding a third class of loans, between IDA credits and conventional Bank loans.

RELATIONSHIP OF STAFF TO EXECUTIVE DIRECTORS

There is an entirely different interest in IDA loans, on the part of the Executive Directors, than is shown toward regular Bank loans. IDA money is public money and has been raised through taxes. The money which the International Bank loans is money that has been raised through the relatively painless method of floating loans in the capital markets of the world. Bank money has, thus, been saved voluntarily and is being loaned to the Bank with the object of earning interest. The Executive Directors representing the richer nations take a purely perfunctory interest in most Bank loans recommended by the staff. Most observers were aware of the fact that Mr. Black and his staff ran the Bank with only nominal direction from the Directors. And the underdeveloped countries' Directors didn't show extreme interest in loans either, because there was plenty of Bank money available for any project that could meet the Bank's standards. The Bank could raise whatever money could be loaned for such projects, so the developing countries were not vying with each other for a limited resource.

This has been altered in the case of IDA credits. The donor governments are interested in what's being done with their citizens' tax dollars. The staff's responsibilities to the rich nations are much different in the case of IDA money than with Bank money. The Part I countries' Executive Directors study IDA credits more critically than Bank loans. And the developing countries have an interest in where IDA money is going. There isn't enough IDA money to go around to all the projects that meet IDA standards. This means that some projects are going to be left out. Every member country is anxious to get its share.

What this all boils down to is the allocation problem faced by the International Development Association. This is a problem which the Bank had not had to face. The Bank could raise all the money it could prudently use. The staff had no experience in allocating scarce resources between competing and equally attractice projects. This has been a difficult experience for the staff--one which has thoroughly tested the ability of a banking institution to dispense funds where an orthodox financial return was not the primary consideration.

THE CALIBER OF THE STAFF

But the International Bank is no ordinary bank. Andrew Shonfield, who is certainly no blind enthusiast where the World Bank is concerned, has defined the essence of the Bank's character quite well.

> There is a body of influential opinion which believes that the Bank ought to be given the leading role in any enlarged program of economic aid to the underdeveloped countries.
>
> That there should be this feeling is a justified tribute to the shrewdness and energy with which the Bank has conducted its business. . . . The Bank has been able to evoke in many of the underdeveloped countries themselves a feeling that it has genuine sympathy and understanding for their problems. This feeling is more widespread, it is fair to say, in Asia than it is in Latin America. But that the view should exist at all among people who have had requests for loans turned down, as well as accepted, by the Bank is a sufficiently notable circumstance.
>
> This is not just the result of good public relations, though the Bank's characteristically American attention to that side of the business has certainly been a

> help. More important is the high caliber of the Bank's staff and the general mood in which it conducts its affairs.[30]

Shonfield goes on to admit of the distinct impression that many staff members are not only people of very high ability but they are also the very slightest bit odd. The author got the same impression upon coming into contact with the staff for the first time. One person suggested that at an earlier date it had been thought the staff was "faceless", and so could do with a few eccentrics. At any rate, a few eccentrics are there now. The staff is markedly unhurried and easy to interview. It has been suggested that "the 'unhurried' look may be due to a considerable British influence. To an Oxonian, it is not quite proper to show signs of doing any work."[31]

Staff members are not at all the type of people one would expect to find in a bank--even in an international bank. And they have such enthusiasm for economic development! It seems that they have not read any of the theories of economic development which demonstrate that such development is practically impossible in the underdeveloped countries of Africa and Asia. If they have read them, they have been left untouched by this message. Almost all development economists agree that economic development is an enormously complicated business where everything depends upon everything else. The underdeveloped countries have been described as having low-level equilibrium traps and vicious circles of poverty, as needing a big push or a minimum effort, as requiring balanced or unbalanced growth depending upon which economist was read. And yet, the staff keeps going about the business of providing money to the underdeveloped countries to build bridges, and highways, and irrigation projects, and schools. They move in a seemingly unsophisticated and simple-minded way to do these things based on a belief that it is good that bridges and highways and schools should be built. And they go at their tasks with such an optimistic attitude that one has the distinct impression that no one on the staff believes in low-level equilibrium traps or vicious circles of poverty.

James Morris has presented an insightful analysis of the Bank's staff. He calls the World Bank a technocracy. What the management says goes. The Board accepts the staff's judgment and has never rejected a formal proposal by the management in all the history of the institution.[32] This would indicate that the Executive Directors are a mere rubber stamp, which is to some extent true. But it is also true that proposals for loans are usually discussed informally among the Board before they are presented formally. The weighted voting system and the generally high caliber of the Executive Directors has made for a harmonious relationship among the many interests in the Bank. The general attitude of the Bank is that it wants its money back and wants it properly used. It has a paternalistic attitude toward its clients, taking the view that it knows best--and owing to the fact that it has an extraordinarily competent staff, it usually does know best. The Bank generally lends money only to countries which show great promise. Although Bank loans have gone to 40 countries, loans have tended to be concentrated. In South America--Colombia, Mexico, Peru, and Venezuela have gotten more than half of the Bank's loans. In the Far East most Bank lending has gone to Japan, Malaya, the Philippines, and Thailand. In Asia, most of the money has gone to India and Pakistan.

The Bank has never had a loan defaulted. Lest too much be made of this, however, it must be pointed out that the United States government has stood ready to loan countries money at times in order to keep their World Bank loans from going into default. A country's international credit rating can be gauged by its relationship to the Bank and no country wants to default on Bank loans. That would be the end of its international borrowing.

CHAPTER 9 PROJECT APPRAISAL

BASIC POLICIES IN APPRAISING PROJECTS

As Alec Cairncross has pointed out, "There is a tendency in the Bank to erect project appraisal into a mystique."[1] And there is certainly a policy of keeping project appraisals made by the International Development Association a deep secret. I attempted to examine some of the appraisals which the Association has made, however, this was not permitted. As a consequence, this particular aspect of the International Development Association must remain shrouded in mystery. The Association is not without its reasons in keeping such information confidential. Many of the country evaluations contain information submitted by the applying country in confidence. In all the appraisals, an attempt is made to report all relevant information accurately and candidly. There are, consequently, matters in these reports that might be highly embarrassing to member governments if they were published. And, since it is known that these reports will not circulate outside the staff, they are not prepared in complete detail or with ultimate refinement. Professor Albert O. Hirschman, of Columbia University, has been engaged to do a two-year evaluation of World Bank projects. He will have access to all information on project evaluation and will thus be able to outline this process for us. In the meantime we must rely on the very sketchy information that has been published.

There is considerable criticism of the Association's policy of limiting its finance to specific projects, no matter how broadly the term project is defined. "An unkind critic would say that the whole idea of financing economic development project by project smacks of paternalism and a pedagogical outlook."[2] However, this project approach is in large part a reaction from the breakdown of the international capital market after the 1920's.

During that period loans were made at high rates of interest for the most nebulous purposes. Many of these loans later went into default. When the Bank began its operations it was thought that more productive use could be made of funds if specific projects were financed. This would provide for a more accurate appraisal of the amount needed and for better arrangements for management and control of the projects undertaken. Consequently, the Articles of Agreement of the World Bank limit loans to specific projects except in unusual circumstances.[3] The Articles of Agreement of IDA carry the same limitation. "Financing provided by the Association . . . except in special circumstances, shall be for specific projects."[4]

Professor Cairncross, who served for a time as head of the Bank's Economic Development Institute, has outlined the philosophy underlying the project approach. Projects are not treated as isolated transactions, but each loan is examined in relation to the rest of the country's development effort. The Bank insists upon a development program into which the major projects are fitted. The Bank also tries to identify the strategic factors in the economy and encourages governments to promote the areas having the most development potential. The staff emphasizes the importance of good management.[5] The Economic Development Institute was established to bring top level officials from underdeveloped countries to the Bank for training in project evaluation and other aspects of economic development.

Criticism of the Association's policy of providing funds for specific projects has been increasing. Some of the arguments presented in favor of soft loans in Chapter 4 can also be used in favor of non-project assistance, i.e., the problems of debt-servicing may get progressively worse as long as aid is earmarked for specific projects. The provision of such resources does not help finance existing debt and may in fact create demands for more foreign exchange to meet the "local currency" expenditures brought about by the project. In the long run it is hoped that projects will contribute to the country's ability to service debt, but the short-run effect may not be so beneficial. The provision for a 10-year grace period before repayment begins on IDA loans is an attempt to solve this problem.

The President of IDA submitted a report on Bank and IDA policies and practices to the United Nations Conference on Trade and Development in Geneva in April, 1964. He maintained that, "where no adequate framework of priorities has been worked out by the national authorities, the Bank's sector investigations and project identification work may, in effect, provide at least the rudiments of such a framework."[6] Thus, there would be no inconsistency between a "project approach" and a "program approach" to economic development. He called IDA's technique a "program/project approach." In any case, the strict project approach once adhered to by the Bank is being altered.

The particular types of projects which have generally been approved have followed a general pattern. The staff found that the lack of basic services was the major physical obstacle to increasing production and raising living standards in the less developed countries. The lack of dependable and economical transportation restricted the size of the market for both industrial and agricultural production. Deficiencies of electric power handicapped the growth of industry.[7]

The same techniques which were used in appraising projects for the Bank have been found satisfactory for evaluating projects for IDA.[8] In order to evaluate the project from an economic point of view it must be determined if the project is able to earn a reasonable return on the capital which must be invested. If there are similar projects in the economy, then this project should earn not less than the return from comparable enterprises. However, many IDA projects are of a public utility or monopoly character and no comparable enterprises can be found. In cases where no comparisons can be made directly some pricing formulae must be developed to approximate competitive conditions.

In addition to the direct returns, there are many indirect returns from dams, roads, etc. Some of these factors which must be considered are as follows: Would the project put idle men and resources to work? Would the project be a stimulus to other economic activities? What impact would it have on the country's balance of payments--would it produce import substitutes or exportable items? Or might the project cause increased demands for imports of raw materials, replacement parts, etc.?

Another important question is whether the project depends upon protection from competition. If it depends upon high protective tariffs for its success, it needs to be looked at very closely. Or if it is to be protected from competition through public utility type regulation, the regulatory agency must be studied in order to evaluate its attitudes and competence.

Project assessment starts with the availability of natural resources and the capacity of the country to exploit its resources. This includes a judgment of governmental efficiency and of private producers' ability. Any project proposed for financing is considered in relation to the country's overall development program. This consideration may reveal that other projects have a higher priority than the one proposed. Priorities are difficult to establish and the guidelines are vague, however, profitability alone cannot be a sufficient test of a project's contribution to economic development.[9]

Profitability would be the simplest criterion to apply. Investment would be made in those projects which yielded the greatest return over cost. This would be easy to explain to businessmen and governments and it would have great appeal to the rich Western nations, where this criterion was used almost exclusively in their developmental stage. It would be universally applicable and, thus, eliminate the problem of justifying investment decisions to the less developed countries.

However, its simplicity and appeal hide the fact that it is, in fact, a totally wrong criterion to apply. For if pure profitability were the basis for investment decisions, many of the very poorest countries would never get a cent of IDA's funds. It is likely that investments in the industrial nations of the world would yield a higher profit than investment in some parts of Africa and Asia. And surely it was not the purpose of the International Development Association to invest in the United States of America.

What, then, can be used as a basis for allocating funds? Paul N. Rosenstein-Rodan has suggested that aid should be allocated where it will have the maximum catalytic effect in mobilizing additional development efforts. His primary criterion is to maximize additional effort.[10] This criterion seems to be used by IDA.

Two types of foreign exchange expenditures are incurred in the construction of an IDA financed project. One is the direct cost of imported goods and services used on the project. The second is the indirect foreign exchange expenditure resulting from the fact that local expenditure on labor or equipment usually leads to increased demand for imported consumer goods and raw materials. Loans for this second type of expenditure are referred to as loans to meet "local currency" expenditure even though, strictly speaking, they are loans in foreign exchange.[11] IDA did not originally make loans for local currency expenditures. The thinking behind this was that IDA should finance merely the foreign exchange cost of the project itself. However, IDA has seen fit to deviate from this procedure. In one loan it financed the entire cost of a project including local currency cost. In another instance it abandoned the project approach altogether and financed the imports of component parts for factories that had already been constructed.

POLICY TOWARD STATE-OWNED ENTERPRISE

IDA feels that wherever possible, governments should reserve their scarce resources for those projects which private capital would not find attractive. A policy of this sort, it is felt, will be likely to act as an inducement to investment by privately owned companies. Loans for state-owned enterprises may be approved in cases where private capital is not available and if the government's participation is compatible with efficient operation and will not have a deterrent effect upon the expansion of private enterprise. As a matter of historical record, governments seeking to develop their own oil deposits have never obtained a loan from the Bank for this purpose. The Bank has taken a position hostile to public ownership of manufacturing industry, arguing that nationalization is calculated to slow down economic development and is not the most fruitful use of capital borrowed from abroad.[12] The one country that has received Bank funds for governmentally owned industrial enterprise is Yugoslavia. These loans were made in the early 1950's and have not been repeated.

The position of the Bank toward governmentally owned enterprise has won the enthusiastic support of the United States of America. In his speech to the Board of Governors in September, 1961, Under Secretary of State George W. Ball reaffirmed United States support for Bank policy.[13]

The government of Yugoslavia does not, however, support Bank policy in this regard. In 1961, the Governor from Yugoslavia argued that industrial development is of the utmost importance for the economic development of the underdeveloped countries. But the Bank has loaned less than eight per cent of the total loans granted for industry as such. The Yugoslav Governor maintained that there is a lack of international financing for industry and that the Bank should move into this field. And in so doing, the Bank should not discriminate between private and public industry.[14]

IDA has been opposed to loaning funds to state-owned enterprises except in infrastructure type projects. But, the Yugoslavs argue that IDA is speaking in the classical sense of infrastructure--of such projects as highways, ports, and canals--which were state-owned projects in the development of Western Europe and the United States. The Yugoslavs believe that the infrastructure must be much broader in the development of the underdeveloped countries today. They think it should include such things as steel mills, thermal power plants, etc. The state is taking a much more active role in the economic development of the underdeveloped countries than it did in the nineteenth century. The Yugoslavs think it has to. They argue that the underdeveloped countries do not have time to wait for private capital to do the job. The United States and Western Europe had time to wait. But, even in the United States all big power dams have been built by the state. And in Western Europe the railways and communications networks are state-owned.

The Yugoslavs are able to see that the capital of IDA was provided by the countries of Western Europe and North America and that these countries are not anxious to provide funds for industries in the developing countries that might compete with them. But, there are certain industries that have served as the means of securing foreign exchange and of financing economic development (the textile industry, for instance, has moved from the developed countries to the underdeveloped countries) throughout history. Of course, it is understandable that the United States and Western Europe would be reluctant to assist this pattern in its course. Although, in principle, it can be seen to be a beneficent thing; the textile factory owners and workers are not enthusiastic about seeing their companies and jobs eliminated. The Yugoslav Government posits that, for this reason, bilateral aid will not be forthcoming to assist any such process. The argument is made that IDA and the International Bank should, therefore, provide such funds.

IDA's opposition to state-owned industry has been based on grounds of efficiency of operation. But, the Yugoslavs maintain that Yugoslav industries are quite competently run. They have secured loans from the Bank as recently as 1963 for other than industrial-type projects. The Bank knows the industries are efficient--but the Yugoslavs believe that the reason they do not receive Bank loans for industry is the Bank's fear of setting a precedent that would have to be honored on a much broader scale in the other developing countries.

PROJECTS IN THE FIELD OF EDUCATION

The types of projects approved by IDA have been very similar to those approved by the Bank. This was only natural since the Bank was set up to handle these particular aspects of economic development. However, IDA was established partly to finance a broader range of activities than the Bank had done. Such an intention is spelled out in the report of the Executive Directors accompanying the Articles of Agreement.

> The Association is authorized to finance any project which is of high developmental priority, that is, which will make an important contribution to the development of the area or areas concerned, whether or not the project is revenue-producing or directly productive. Thus projects such as water supply, sanitation, pilot housing and the like are eligible for financing, although it is expected that a major part of the Association's financing is likely to be for projects of the type financed by the Bank.[15]

In an effort to carry out this mandate, the Association has moved into the field of education. IDA has concluded that secondary education is the field most in need of assistance. There is great pressure on governments to expand primary education as fast as possible until it becomes universal. And at the other end of the scale, most countries regard the establishment of a university as a sign of their independence and a symbol of great prestige value. Consequently, these two areas have received great emphasis and secondary education has been neglected.

> And this has had unfortunate results, since the secondary schools have to perform three essential tasks; first, to provide teachers for the primary schools; second, to prepare candidates for higher education who can man top level positions; and thirdly, to produce recruits for middle level posts in administration, industry, commerce and agriculture. . . . It is these considerations that have led the staff to conclude that much of the aid to be provided by IDA should properly go to the secondary level.[16]

In the field of education there is a lack of research and a lack of planners. This means that some countries which make requests for IDA funds for education do not have good educational plans and do not have the necessary statistical material on which to base such plans.[17]

The following criteria have been adopted for use in appraising educational projects: (a) Any government wishing to borrow must decide for itself that education has a high priority in its general development plan and be willing to devote its own resources to this purpose. (b) IDA would not normally consider an educational project unless it were an integral part of a plan for the whole educational system which was, in turn, related to the overall economic development program. (c) Projects to be financed should have a high priority within the educational development plan. (d) IDA would prefer to finance the most crucial gaps in the system rather than the normal year-to-year growth in the system. (e) IDA would not normally finance any part of the current costs of an educational system. (f) IDA would have a bias toward projects which would have a speedy effect on national productivity. (g) IDA would require some estimate of cost-benefit ratios. (h) IDA would want to be satisfied that the administration of the system was efficient. These criteria are ideals and the staff fully realizes that all projects are not going to meet all these criteria.[18]

In addition to finance, the staff hopes to provide help to countries in planning their educational investments. It also hopes to help them improve their education statistics. Finally, IDA will help by underlining the importance of sound administration and will help get the best value out of the large amounts of money spent on school construction.[19]

PROBLEMS IN PROJECT APPRAISAL

Mr. John C. de Wilde has presented some of the problems involved in evaluating projects. Although economic analysis of projects has improved as a result of experience, there are still serious difficulties confronting the staff. The most important problem is the divergence between market prices and real costs or benefits to the economy. The staff has attempted to use "shadow" or "accounting" prices to overcome the limitations of market prices. The staff takes cognizance of the fact that the opportunity cost of labor may be considerably below the prevailing wage in many underdeveloped countries. Again, the interest rate is often artificially controlled and in these cases it is recognized that the opportunity cost of capital is considerably higher than this rate. IDA is still baffled by the problem of pricing inputs and outputs. In an attempt to devise a yardstick to be used in evaluating projects, the staff has worked toward measuring the cost of capital. It was hoped that some minimum rate of return could be established by which individual projects could be judged.

The Bank recently had a paper on the cost of capital prepared which considered various methods of determining this cost. It examined the interest rate structure in a number of underdeveloped countries to try to find a rate which approximated a free market rate and which would be devoid of any compensation for risk and entrepreneurial initiative and for future loss in the value of money. It also dealt with formulae for the calculation of shadow rates of interest, particularly the formula developed by R. M. Solow and applied to India by S. Chakravarty. The first approach depends upon the correctness of one's hunch that one interest rate was better than another. The Solow formula was more sophisticated but it required national accounts data which are not available. The Solow formula also assumes static relationships in the economy. Third, the national accounts data used in the formula should themselves be calculated at shadow prices. This illustrates the dilemma faced when the staff tries to replace market prices. They are, in principle, confronted with the need to devise a completely new price structure.[20]

Another important problem in project appraisal is estimating the time path of costs and benefits. It is difficult to determine just how demand for goods is likely to develop. In some cases the rapidity with which capacity becomes utilized and the benefits accrue depends on institutional factors, e.g., how fast will farmers adopt new techniques as a result of irrigation? de Wilde says that, in so far as possible, the staff insists that a revenue-producing project produce revenues considerably in excess of expenditures. In cases of government-owned operations, this sometimes causes upward shifts in pricing. But, this is thought to be necessary in order to increase public savings. "With the progressively larger role played by public enterprise, it is important . . . that 'corporate savings' in the public sector should gradually play the same role in financing public investment as this same type of savings in the private sector already does in financing private investment."[21]

Notwithstanding the fact that project appraisal is a complicated and problem-ridden operation, the Association had approved some 57 projects by June 30, 1964, as presented in Table 4. Twenty three of the projects had been in the field of transportation, including 16 highway construction projects, 3 projects for harbor dredging and improvement of ports, and 4 railway development projects. Irrigation projects accounted for 10 of the development credits. Seven credits were for ground water development and municipal water supply projects. Four credits went to finance projects to increase power supplies. Both India and Pakistan have received one credit each for flood protection and drainage. The Association made $42 million available to India to be used by the Indian Post and Telegraphs Department for expanding and improving telephone and telegraph services. The China Development Corporation received a $5 million credit from the Association to assist in the establishment, modernization, and expansion of private industrial enterprises on Formosa. Additional credits for industrialization under private auspices were made in Turkey and Pakistan. And, in its first such operation, the Association made $5 million available to Tunisia for secondary and technical school construction. Since that time additional credits have been provided for education in Tanganyika and East and West Pakistan. One of the most unique credits IDA has granted was in the sum of $90 million to finance the importation of components and equipment for industrial projects in India. This loan was a clear departure from the "project approach." IDA loaned Jordan $3 million to be used to provide agricultural credit. Paraguay received $3.6 million to modernize its cattle industry. Several of these projects involved funds made available by the Association along with a conventional loan for the same project by the Bank.

CRITICISMS OF PROJECT APPRAISAL TECHNIQUES

There has been criticism of IDA policy on project appraisal. The Governor from Viet-Nam made an impassioned plea for more liberal standards at the 1962 meeting of the Board of Governors. He said, "The Association is determinedly adopting the same policies as the Bank . . . aid given to specific projects, high revenue-producing, unquestionable solvency and absolute security. What can be the use of 'concessionary terms' if the necessary conditions to benefit from the assistance of the Association are absent in most underdeveloped countries?"[22] He went on to describe the particular conditions existing in countries with large communist segments. "Creditworthiness . . . depends to a large extent on the prevailing situation of security. But insecurity . . . is a characteristic of underdeveloped countries. Subversion and instability are rather the consequence of underdevelopment."[23]

The Government of Senegal has been critical of the scale of the projects which IDA has financed. The Governor from that country explained that "rural development . . . calls for widespread or scattered efforts such as the stimulation of activities in the rural sector, small-scale water supply schemes, the reforestation of certain regions and the allocation of agricultural equipment and fertilizer to farmers' cooperatives."[24]

Some of the recently independent countries of Africa have expressed their resentment toward some of the more rigid policies followed by the management. Particularly singled out has been the requirement for detailed statistical data (which is not available in many of these countries). There are countries in Africa which do not have a clear idea of total population and they certainly can't provide figures on marginal savings rates and incremental capital output ratios. Some of these countries have a problem in raising the matching funds for local expenses. A third criticism is that IDA has required that a project should have a certain minimum value before financing is available.[25] There are signs that the management is aware of these complaints and is trying to work out some solution so that the very small countries and very poor countries might be able to benefit from membership.

The Governor from Tanganyika pointed out at the 1962 Meetings that they had had a Bank survey mission in their country. This mission had advised them to concentrate on those projects which would bring a quick return. These projects in nearly every case involved a preponderance of local expenditure. But when Tanganyika seeks aid it is tied to external costs only. The implication he drew was that Tanganyika should abandon their carefully considered priorities in favor of larger, more grandiose, but less valuable schemes which suit the established rules of the game.[26] The management of IDA would not agree that this is the implication in this situation. They, no doubt, would say that the situation calls for a great deal of local effort, savings, and investment; after which, outside aid may be called for.

The Honorable Chief Festus S. Okotie-Eboh, the IDA Governor from Nigeria, joined the critics of IDA policy in 1962. He was especially critical of the slowness of the deliberations. He pointed out that the worsening of the terms of trade of the African nations had posed serious problems for those countries. And, he said, "those of us who have to go cap-in-hand, pleading for more aid, do not enjoy this thankless task for we are not professional beggars. . . . If we could earn more foreign exchange from our legitimate trade we could depend far less on foreign aid."[27] However, he was not optimistic as to the possibilities of increased foreign earnings. Therefore, he said, Africa must have more of the kind of loans IDA is making and these loans should be disbursed with less time-consuming delays. The Governor pointed out that economics "is not an exact science. Economists often disagree among themselves and this is a most potent source of delay and frustration to those who want to get on with the job."[28] To overcome this problem, he suggested that more reliance be placed on the opinions of the man on the spot. This might mean that some mistakes would be made, but, "it is better to attempt 100 projects and see 99 succeed than to attempt only 10 even if all 10 were to succeed."[29] The Bank publicizes the fact that it has never yet had a default on a loan.

CHAPTER 10 INCREASING THE RESOURCES OF THE INTERNATIONAL DEVELOPMENT ASSOCIATION

EUGENE BLACK'S PROPOSAL

At the September, 1962, meeting of the Board of Governors Mr. Black proposed a substantial increase in the funds of the Association. He conveyed as strong a sense of urgency as was possible.

He pointed out that Bank studies had shown that between 1955 and 1961, a group of 34 countries, accounting for some 70 per cent of the population of the underdeveloped world, more than doubled its total external public debt. Yet, over the same period, the export earnings of the same group increased by little more than 15 per cent.[1] He went on to discuss the limitations of private capital for investment in social overhead projects. He enumerated the problems inherent in bilateral aid. "Aid which is at the mercy of the variable winds of diplomacy offers a poor basis for the rational programming of economic development."[2] He argued that more aid was needed on comparatively easy terms of repayment. He had, he said, "Advanced a number of arguments whose relation to one another may not have seemed very clear. But in fact they are all relevant to a single and urgent issue--the future of the International Development Association."[3] He reminded the audience that IDA faced the imminent full commitment of its initial funds and that if no new funds were provided very soon--IDA would not be able to enter into any new lending commitments after mid-1963.

> This is not a situation that can be ignored and allowed to drift. To do nothing would in itself constitute a decision to bring IDA's operations to a halt.
>
> If IDA continues to operate at its normal pace, it seems probable that it will during the current fiscal

> year commit something like $500 million. . . . There is no reason, that I can see, to suppose that the demand for worthwhile credits will be any lower in subsequent years. On the contrary, it is my conviction that the demand will continue to increase, and to increase greatly. Experience has already demonstrated, I believe, that IDA is capable of meeting a very real and important need and, in relation to this need, the original capital of IDA was obviously inadequate. But if it is to meet this need--if it is to become a principal instrument for the development of the poorer countries, and not just a minor gesture of good will toward them--it will clearly require a very substantial addition to its resources.[4]

Mr. Black put the case well. Should IDA become a principal instrument for the development of the poorer countries? Or was it to be only a minor gesture of good will toward them--salve for the conscience of the rich so that they could go on ignoring the desperate poverty all around them?

Mr. Black reminded the Governors that it was to IDA, not to the Bank, that most of the newly independent countries would be looking for help. "The future of IDA is therefore the most important issue that I commend to your sympathetic consideration during this week's Meetings."[5]

In Mr. Black's view, the replenishment of IDA's funds was not only the most important item on the international development agenda for 1962, but he argued that the decision to replenish IDA would be the most important decision the Bank's Governors had ever been called upon to make.[6] The Governors approved the following resolution on September 18, 1962.

> Resolved: That the Executive Directors are requested to consider the prospective financial requirements of the International Development Association, and to prepare and submit a report thereon to the Board of Governors of the Association at the earliest date, if possible before December 31, 1962.[7]

This resolution signified the desire of the Part I members of IDA to continue the organization's existence. It initiated more than 8 months of negotiation among the rich countries of the world. The staff of IDA took a hands-off attitude toward these negotiations and decided to let the countries fight it out by themselves. The discussions took place in Paris on an ad hoc basis among the representatives of the major contributing countries. Later, ratification of the decisions made in Paris took place in Washington with more countries participating. IDA sent a Vice-President, Geoffrey Wilson, to the discussion but did not take a leadership role. The three significant questions which these negotiations raised were: the effectiveness of IDA as an administrator of foreign aid, the shares of the participating countries in the replenishment, and the question of the need for such funds as IDA had been given. It is to the last of these questions that we now turn our attention.

NEED FOR MORE SOFT MONEY

The staff of IDA took a strong stand in favor of increasing the amount of soft money available to the underdeveloped countries. Mr. Black pointed out in 1961 that of the total flow of public funds going to the underdeveloped countries during 1956-59, more than half went in the form of outright grants. But, the signs indicated that the proportion of grants and soft loans was decreasing. More than nine-tenths of the soft money came from the United States and France. Few other countries had extended aid other than on conventional terms.[8]

In 1962, Belgium, Denmark, France, the Netherlands, and Norway made most of their bilateral disbursements in grant form. Nearly three-quarters of the disbursements by the United States were also in grants or grant-like forms. The percentage of such assistance in United States aid is declining due in some part to the feeling that the United States is bearing a disproportionate share of the financing on soft terms. Canadian and United Kingdom disbursements were somewhat above 50 per cent in grant form. On the other hand, Germany, Italy, and Japan provided the bulk of their assistance in loans. The volume of loans has risen rapidly between 1956 and 1962 and loans constitute a rapidly rising proportion of new financial assistance.[9]

The staff of IDA has estimated that external public debt service obligations increased over the period 1955-1961 at an average rate of more than 15 per cent per year. Thirty-two low-income countries increased their external public debt between 1955 and 1961 by a factor of almost 2.1. This increase in the total amount of debt was accompanied by a hardening of the average terms. Thus, while total debt more than doubled from 1955 to 1961, service on this debt increased by a factor of 2.5. The ratio of service on external public debt to exports rose from a little over 3 per cent in 1956 to about 7 per cent in 1962. The total outstanding external public debt of the underdeveloped countries at the end of 1961 was estimated at $20 billion, or $14 per inhabitant. The external public liabilities now appear to be $2.5 billion per year, so that capital inflow has to be more than this amount before any net addition to resources takes place. This annual liability has arisen as a result of an annual capital inflow at the rate of about $4 per inhabitant in the underdeveloped countries.[10]

Mr. Black painted a bleak picture of what might happen as a result of this increasing hard debt.

> I do not have to explain to this audience how the machinery of economic development could be overloaded with foreign debt until it sputtered to a halt amid half built projects and mountains of discarded plans. I expect, indeed, that there are some in this audience who can point to projects in their own countries which are at this very time suspended in mid-air, so to speak, for this very reason. Maybe it is a half-finished highway or a hospital that has been built but not equipped. This kind of disruption kills peoples' hope in orderly economic progress and, if it persists, can lead to serious disillusionment.
>
> . . . .
>
> The safe and sane way to minimize these dangers is to maximize the amount of official capital which is supplied at very long term with only a token interest burden.[11]

Will the external public indebtedness of the underdeveloped countries double again every 5 years? Or will the rate of increase go higher? Even if the rate should decrease, IDA was convinced that more soft loan funds were needed.

During the same period that the negotiations on replenishment were being conducted the Economic Staff of the Bank was preparing new studies on the debt-servicing problems of the developing countries.[12] These studies cast considerable light on the question of the need for more money on soft terms. The question of whether there existed a need for an increase in soft credit to the developing countries depends upon the judgment one makes of how serious the debt-servicing problem is for the underdeveloped countries, and on one's judgment of how serious this problem has to be before soft credit terms are provided. There is no question that the rich countries would prefer to extend assistance on hard terms. Such assistance can be provided through voluntary savings of the citizens of the country concerned--a very painless method. Hard loans exert pressure on the developing country to use the money well, also. However, hard loans mean that debt servicing obligations are going to rise. Such obligations increased two-and-a-half times between 1956 and 1962 and such trend seems likely to continue. What are the implications of this increase? What would happen if new capital stopped flowing into these countries? What would be the result if the value of world trade dropped as it did in the 1930's? Or what would happen if export earnings fail to grow in the future?

The underdeveloped countries must sell their goods in order to service and ultimately to repay their debt. But, in eleven countries earnings from merchandise exports were lower in 1961-1962 than in 1955-1956. For some of these countries the problem was a decline in the volume of exports; for others it was the fact that the price of their exports fell.[13] The coffee exporting countries are a particularly instructive example of this problem. In 1962, the value of world coffee exports amounted to $1.7 billion as compared to $2.5 billion in 1954. The coffee countries exported 50 per cent more coffee in 1962 than in 1954 and yet their exchange earnings in 1962 were one-third smaller than in 1954. The resultant pressure on their balance of payments had a debilitating impact on the rate of capital formation and economic growth.[14]

In 1963 the price of coffee started up again. Will this set off another world-wide boom in the production of coffee? Will the fact that coffee prices have risen lead the developed countries to ignore the problems of the coffee producers? If the answer to these questions is positive, despite the experience gained since World War II, then there would seem to be only one conclusion--

the problem of violent fluctuations of demand, supply, and prices is really insoluble.[15] Added to the problem of fluctuations in demand for primary products is the fact that the international demand for many primary products is increasing at a painfully slow rate. And attempts to expand exports of manufactured goods are met by restrictions on the part of the developed countries.

IDA operations are based on the assumption that violent business fluctuations on the order of the Great Depression will not recur. But, even if this assumption is valid--the problem of short-run fluctuations in earnings poses an enormous obstacle to servicing a large external debt. Much of the debt contracted since World War II is guaranteed by the government concerned and is of a fixed nature--it does not fluctuate with export earnings. So that no matter how little exports bring--the debt service must be paid. And not only must the country pay the service on the debt --it must someday repay the debt itself. Since World War II the developed countries have shown a willingness to extend new loans which offset payments due on past loans. But there is no obligation on their part to continue to do so.

Even if no repayment of debt takes place, the interest on the debt can assume fantastic proportions if all debt is incurred on conventional terms. The Economic Department of IDA has constructed a model to illustrate the dimensions such charges may assume.[16] The model country has the following characteristics: The desired rate of increase in gross domestic product is 5 per cent per annum. The initial gross domestic savings rate is 10 per cent of gross domestic product. The marginal savings rate is 20 per cent. The capital-output ratio is 3 to 1. Since the desired growth rate is 5 per cent and the capital-output ratio is 3 to 1, the required investment rate is 15 per cent of gross domestic product. But, the domestic savings rate is only 10 per cent. Thus, one-third of total investment must be financed by foreign capital inflow. Export earnings are assumed to equal 10 per cent of total income and exports are assumed to grow at 4 per cent per annum. Initial external debt is assumed to be zero. The necessary foreign capital is borrowed at an average interest rate of 6 per cent and with an average maturity of 15 years. With these assumptions, it is found that debt service requires 50 per cent of export earnings at the peak of the debt cycle. But for countries with large populations and low incomes the need for external capital will exceed the figure assumed in the model. If this need is financed on hard terms and if exports do not grow rapidly the rising debt service would put the country in an extremely tenuous financial position which would last decades. Debt incurred at 6 per cent interest doubles every 12 years if interest is capitalized and no retirement takes place. For countries that are starting out with a heavy debt already--such doubling every 12 years means a phenomenal debt burden in a very short period of time.[17]

The model has assumed that the underdeveloped countries can get the necessary capital at 6 per cent interest. But, is it possible that there are countries where the rate of return is lower than 6 per cent? Such countries would not be able to borrow the capital they need at all--or if they did borrow they would be certain to default.[18]

There are three alternatives facing the developed countries. If economic growth in the developing countries is financed on conventional terms, then the creditor nations will have to adjust to very high debt service ratios and balance of payments crises in the developing countries. If this alternative were chosen gross capital exports would have to become very large to yield a net addition to resources in the borrowing country. Such net addition takes place only when gross borrowing is in excess of repayments and interest on prior debt. Since new borrowing carries interest, also, the outstanding debt compounds and this increases the debt service that is due. This solution could not work unless the project basis for loans was abandoned. A second alternative would be to put reliance on hard loans but to put an upper limit on the amount loaned. This would slow down the rate of development in the developing countries and would mean that some profitable projects would not be undertaken for lack of finance. The third alternative is to provide most of the outside funds on soft terms.[19]

Some countries insist that hard loans are necessary because the discipline that the balance of payments exerts is thought to be essential. But, if soft loans are not granted--and if hard loans have to be made in ever-increasing amounts in order to keep a net inflow of capital--isn't this really the reverse of maintaining discipline? IDA tries to maintain discipline by the alternative of tying money to programs or projects. If discipline is maintained by making only hard loans, what is the cost? If the capital exporting countries do not loan the gross amount necessary to keep a certain high level of net investment coming in, they force the underdeveloped countries into a quite cynical default with all the impact that would have on their ability to raise capital, or, the underdeveloped countries are forced to cut back on imports to the point of cutting back development. This latter alternative may have quite a lasting impact. Once momentum for development is reduced, it may be hard to regain. Growth may be slowed down enough that it will cost the rich countries more in the long run than an uninterrupted flow of capital would have amounted to. Or, the chance for achieving development without violence may be lost forever. The prophetic words of the 1949 International Bank Mission to Cuba are recalled in this connection. They (the Cubans) may take advantage of their present opportunity and substitute a growing, dynamic and diversified economy for their present static one, with its single crop dependence. This may be a long and arduous task. It will involve great effort and some sacrifice of tradition and comfort. The Mission believes that failure to choose the dynamic alternatives can bring to Cuba consequences of the utmost seriousness. Control may well pass into subversive but specious hands--as it has done in other countries whose leaders have ignored the trends of the times.[20]

Most of the developed countries accept the pressing need for increased soft loans. The United States Government has argued--against the hard loan advocates--that continuing hard loans is an essentially unworkable policy for lenders because countries will have to go to their legislatures for ever-increasing gross amounts and the legislators won't understand this. Thus, from a psychological standpoint this would be very difficult. The United States Government wants the countries of Western Europe to start making more soft loans so that it can point this out to the Congress and prove that the United States is not alone in this policy and is not carrying a disproportionate share of the cost.

The Germans insist that soft loans are a sloppy way to do things. They propose to loan more and more money on hard terms--to maintain a certain net inflow of capital. But, is it right to make a hard loan to a country even if the project generates foreign exchange enough to service the loan on hard terms? The United States view is that this is selfish and unscrupulous.

A country pre-empts those projects that are self-liquidating--the creditor takes all the improvement in the balance of payments--and this is felt to be unfair to the borrower and unscrupulous to other lenders.

The debate on the need for soft loans has not been settled. The United States, France, Belgium, Denmark, the Netherlands, and Norway are convinced of the necessity for unconventional terms in financing economic development. Canada and the United Kingdom are coming around to this point of view. The Germans and Italians are the hold-outs for fiscal orthodoxy on the international scene. During the negotiations over IDA the soft loan advocates prevailed and it was agreed that additional soft money was needed. The next question that arose was whether the International Development Association had demonstrated its ability to administer a large share of the soft money. A decision on this question hinges on the judgment one makes about the effectiveness of IDA.

CHAPTER 11 EVALUATING THE INTERNATIONAL DEVELOPMENT ASSOCIATION

In order to understand world opinion on the question of replenishing IDA's funds, it was necessary to determine the prevalent attitudes concerning IDA's effectiveness. Each country would decide the question of whether to expand IDA on the basis of its judgment as to how effective IDA had been. In an attempt to measure public opinion on this question during 1962-63 when the negotiations were going on, contacts were made with spokesmen of several underdeveloped countries, with leading development economists, and with spokesmen from the developed members of IDA. Several alternative proposals to a straight increase in IDA's funds were put forward. These will also be presented.

COMMENTS BY ECONOMISTS

Charles P. Kindleberger, of the Massachusetts Institute of Technology, admits to having been quite skeptical of IDA at the time of its origin because Senator Monroney's basic idea was based on a fallacy. Monroney envisioned turning over the local currencies which the United States had acquired to IDA. Kindleberger pointed out that Monroney was attempting to count the same contribution twice. It was a real contribution to the underdeveloped countries to supply them with agricultural commodities. These commodities were paid for in local currencies. To turn around and give these local currencies back would not be a real increase in a country's resources. This is attempting to count the same contribution twice. However, Kindleberger was convinced that IDA as constituted was an effective organization. [1]

Andrew Shonfield, of The Observer, felt that the relative size and importance of IDA and the Bank were all wrong. He argued that the tail was wagging the dog so far as these two organizations were concerned. The decision about the appropriate relative size of IDA and the Bank implied the belief that the main problem of development could be dealt with by means of orthodox Bank loans. Those projects which were not fully bankable were treated as a marginal problem only. In Shonfield's view the unbankable part was the central issue and the most important part of the economic development problem of the day.[2] Shonfield felt that the decision to establish IDA with only a billion dollars as a subsidiary of the World Bank was an example of what was wrong with turning such an operation over to a banking institution. He quotes Black as having argued placidly against the critics of IDA's smallness, that the institution would grow as the need for it and its experience increased. But Shonfield argues that experience was the last thing that was necessary to establish the need for a massive inflow of capital, most of which could not be in the form of ordinary Bank loans. IDA is not well designed to serve the purpose of economic development today. The chief missing element is a sense of urgency. What is required is not the slow accumulation of experience on a series of pilot projects, but a political act of will on the part of the rich countries. Shonfield argues that IDA has become the means of enabling the rich countries to evade the essential problem rather than to solve it.[3]

Shonfield is unfair to Eugene Black in his charge that Black argued against the critics of IDA's smallness. There has been no more forceful critic of IDA's smallness than Eugene Black. He has said again and again that IDA was too small--that her resources were inadequate for the task. However, he is guilty of having the opinion that economic development takes time --that it is not something that can be rushed into with lots of capital and suddenly every country will be producing steel ingots and Nobel Prize winners.

If the Bank's establishment is a typical example, it takes a new institution about 3 or 4 years to get established and functioning effectively. It was hoped that by placing IDA in the Bank, this period of organization could be shortened. It would appear that this hope has been realized. IDA was established in September, 1960, and had granted its first credit by May, 1961. This would appear to be rather prompt action as compared to other international agencies. And these credits have gone to sound projects. Any organization could have given a billion dollars away quickly. But everyone knows that projects that are approved by the staff of the World Bank are good projects.

As far as the size of IDA's original fund is concerned, it is hard to see why Shonfield finds fault with Eugene Black on this matter. When Mr. Black was asked to discuss the major problems in establishing IDA, he replied that there was only one problem and that was getting a billion dollars.[4] What else was he supposed to have done? Why is it IDA's fault that its resources are too small? The author has gotten the impression that the IDA staff, from Mr. Black on down, would have liked to have had more money and certainly they are convinced that IDA needs more money now.

Shonfield is right in calling attention to the fact that a sense of urgency is lacking in this whole sphere of economic development. And it may very well be that IDA was a sop to the underdeveloped countries--a sop that was given in order to salve the conscience of the rich Western nations. If it was this--so be it. IDA has done the best it could with the limited resources made available to it. And the staff of IDA is trying very hard, at this time, to make the developed countries aware of the need for more funds like IDA's.

Max Millikan, Director of the Center for International Studies of the Massachusetts Institute of Technology, had serious reservations about IDA at the time it was established. His fear was that the Congressional support for IDA was based on a desire to eliminate or reduce United States development loans on soft terms. In light of what happened, however, he came to believe that his earlier fears were exaggerated. He had seen little evidence that the existence of IDA led to the reduction of U. S. funds which any more than offset the U. S. contribution to IDA.[5]

It is upon this point raised by Millikan that much depends. Is IDA money in addition to or a substitute for bilateral aid money? Millikan thinks that United States bilateral aid of a soft loan character has been reduced by the amount of the United States' contribution to IDA. If he is right in this, then the main argument in IDA's behalf would be that IDA can administer this amount of money better than the United States Government--an argument to which many people would subscribe. The question would be bilateral as opposed to multilateral aid. If, however, IDA money is in addition to bilateral funds appropriated by the United States Congress and the other parliaments of the Part I countries, then IDA's $1 billion would be a significant increase in total economic assistance.

When Senator Monroney was pushing for IDA, he held out the hope that IDA could be funded out of already appropriated United States aid money--specifically the money of the Development Loan Fund. He also intimated that by using local currency hoards, the United States aid effort could be reduced. This is what Senator Case objected to in Monroney's presentation. However, these two objectives, transferring Development Loan Fund money to IDA and using local currencies to finance IDA, have come to naught.

It is not easy to ascertain how the Congress would have acted had IDA not been established. Would the Congress have appropriated the $320 million which went to IDA to the Development Loan Fund, if there had been no IDA? No one can say. It is my impression, however, that IDA money does represent an increase over what would have been contributed, in the form of soft loans, without IDA. At worst IDA has not represented a more than proportionate reduction in United States assistance.

Millikan advocated that IDA should be expanded as rapidly as possible. However, he would advocate such increase only if Congress could be persuaded to increase the United States contribution to IDA with no more than a compensating reduction in funds made available directly by the U. S. He was of the opinion that a shift of U. S. aid to IDA could be made over time but that a large scale campaign for a radical shift in a short period would be counterproductive.[6]

Barbara Ward, formerly of The Economist, felt that IDA should become a more independent agency while maintaining links with the International Bank. She felt that more United States aid could profitably be channeled through IDA.[7]

Robert E. Asher, of the Brookings Institution, found fault with the terms upon which IDA loaned money. He thought that the use of loans repayable in foreign exchange would limit the total debt burden of the underdeveloped countries to too low a level. He felt that there was a large need for outright grants which, according to its Articles, IDA couldn't make. In view of this limitation, Asher would have preferred that IDA make loans repayable in local currency. "At the same time, it must be recognized that, if the latter is really a loan, it will ultimately have to be repaid in real resources by foregoing goods and services that might otherwise be consumed or invested at home."[8] So far, however, local currency loans have not carried the implication that they would ultimately have to be repaid in real resources and given this history, it would have been hard to get this idea across to the underdeveloped countries. Asher was correct in arguing that local currency loans would have permitted a larger total debt burden than the type of loans IDA made--but IDA would have sacrificed a number of things, if local currency loans had been made. No one would have expected to repay them in real resources. Local currency loans would have postponed the day when currency convertibility could be achieved world-wide. All the objections could be raised against local currency loans from IDA that were important in causing the United States Government's Development Loan Fund to abandon local currency loans in favor of IDA-type credits.

Paul N. Rosenstein-Rodan, of the Massachusetts Institute of Technology, is a believer in multilateral aid. He did, however, have reservations about IDA's relationship with the World Bank. There were advantages to such intimacy in that the World Bank had the best organization and staff on these matters and could therefore provide the service cheaply and efficiently. The dangers were (1) that the World Bank had confined itself to the single project approach. (2) There was fear that IDA would become a waste basket of the IBRD, i.e., that certain marginal projects which would have normally been financed by the World Bank would be passed on to IDA. If that happened, IDA lending would not be truly additional resources.[9]

If IDA financed projects that the Bank would have financed, had there been no IDA, this would, indeed, be a waste of soft loan money. If IDA were wasting soft money, this would be a serious matter. IDA has granted a $2.8 million credit to Swaziland for highway construction. A later announcement of a Bank loan to Swaziland, for the construction of a hydroelectric plant and a thermal plant, presented a picture of Swaziland as a creditworthy country. Two private banks participated in the power loan with the International Bank and the press release announcing the loan carried an account of the rich iron ore resources available.[10] Swaziland's potential exports of wood pulp were touted as being worth $10 million annually. The whole tenor of the report on the Bank loan to Swaziland makes one wonder if an IDA credit to that country were really justified. In defense of IDA, the per capita income in Swaziland was estimated at $70 per year (on an exchange rate basis). It met the poverty criterion of IDA quite handsomely. However, Swaziland is still a British dependency and the Bank loan was guaranteed by the United Kingdom. The fact that this country was still able to secure British guarantees for its Bank loans would increase one's doubt as to the appropriateness of an IDA credit. Perhaps it is this type of borderline case to which Dr. Rosenstein-Rodan referred.

Rosenstein-Rodan believed that IDA, despite the problems, was worthy of additional funds. The case for an increase in funds was especially strong for those very numerous countries which either did not supply enough aid or were particularly deficien in soft loans and grants. These categories included all countries be sides the United States and France. The United Kingdom was doing three-quarters of what should be done. In Rosenstein-Rodan's view, the greatest sinner was Germany.[11] He thus raised a question whic has been raised again and again in discussions of soft loans, and that is the inappropriateness of the West German response.

The Director of the Institute of Economic Growth in Delhi, V. K. R. V. Rao (originator of the proposal for a United Nations Economic Development Administration), argued that the setting up of IDA was a great event in the history of economic development. He felt that IDA was bound to make a significant contribution to the rate of economic growth in the underdeveloped world. He would look to IDA to be the main instrument for the promotion of economic growth, and "the lessening of the differentials in per capita income and levels of living that now make two parts out of this one world of ours." Rao would reform and rejuvenate IDA. His rejuvenation would involve adding a great deal more money. His reform would involve doing away with weighted voting.[12]

Jan Tinbergen, Director of the Netherlands Economic Institute, favored the establishment of IDA as long as a United Nations approach was not possible. It will be remembered that the Netherlands stood ready to contribute to SUNFED as far back as 1954.[13]

Professor Tinbergen preferred the United Nations because he thought that the world as a whole is in vital need of a way of peaceful coexistence. An international order will have to bear on economic and social issues. These issues would be good issues on which to try out peaceful coexistence.[14] Despite his preference for SUNFED, Tinbergen would have urged that considerably more funds be made available to IDA.[15] Tinbergen called attention to Shonfield's comments about handing IDA over lock, stock, and barrel to the head of the World Bank, "to be run by his staff as part of their general business, with no separate offices at all."[16] An independent organ might have been better suited to the task.[17]

Benjamin Higgins, of the University of Texas, would have had the United States "spend as much through the IDA as it possibly can without increasing the American share to a figure higher than has lately become customary for technical assistance--about 40 per cent."[18] Higgins is afraid IDA would lose its international character if much more than 40 percent of its resources came from the United States. Large and regular appropriations for a United Nations grant program could not be expected from the United States Congress. But Higgins felt that it was possible that Congress might increase its contribution to IDA to $800 million, which would permit IDA to have capital funds of $2 billion under his formula. The United States should put pressure on Canada, the United Kingdom, West Germany, and Australia to increase their contributions to IDA; and should urge France to channel a larger share of its capital assistance through IDA rather than through bilateral channels.[19]

How did the people whom IDA was established to help feel about the organization? What were the major problems in their view? To determine their reactions I interviewed spokesmen from some of these countries. These countries could be divided into three groups on the basis of their attitudes toward IDA. One group would be the upper-income underdeveloped countries who have no hope of receiving IDA funds. The second group would be poor countries who have not received IDA funds. And the third group would be poor countries who have received IDA money.

UPPER-INCOME UNDERDEVELOPED COUNTRIES

Venezuela did not join the International Development Association during its first two years of operation. The main reason they didn't join was that they thought it wouldn't be much help to them. They were aware of the intent of IDA to help the poorer of the underdeveloped countries, so they could not see that it was to their advantage to put up their prescribed quota, 10 per cent of which would have had to be in gold or convertible currencies. The fact that they had not joined IDA had not prejudiced their relations with the Bank in any way and they were in the process of negotiating a sizeable loan from the Bank. They did not feel that they had any obligation to help those underdeveloped countries that were poorer than themselves by contributing their resources to IDA.[20]

The second country to be represented in this group was Israel. Israel had joined IDA but felt wronged that IDA policy had been framed in such a way as to exclude them from eligibility for credits. They had numerous quite essential projects involving the education and assimilation of a disparate people. These projects could not be financed through the use of conventional loans. But, since Israel was considered to be creditworthy by the Bank, it was not eligible for IDA credits for these non-revenue producing projects. The spokesman for Israel pointed to the very meagre resource base in his country and the quite phenomenal rate of growth that had been accomplished in spite of this shortage of resources. Why shouldn't IDA help them get over this crucial decade after which they would surely be economically self-sufficient? He felt that because Israel had been so successful in managing its economy, because they had a relatively high per capita income, because their exports were growing at a rapid rate, for all these reasons--they were denied IDA credits. In the eyes of IDA, their worst failure had been the extent of their success.[21]

The third country in this category of upper-income underdeveloped countries was Yugoslavia, which had also had a phenomenally successful development program over the past decade. Their per capita income was close to $400 a year. Their exports had been rising at more than 10 per cent a year. They had been given sizeable loans from the World Bank to spur their development. They were obviously not eligible for IDA credits--

but they joined the Association with enthusiasm, anyway. They recognized the obvious need for increased funds for the under-developed countries. They wanted to participate in making these funds available. Yugoslav support for IDA did not mean that they would have preferred IDA to SUNFED, however. The Yugoslavs would have liked the principle of SUNFED better--there would have been more money available--from countries not included in IDA, i.e., the Soviet bloc countries. This preference for SUNFED was really a matter of principle only, however. Because realistically they saw little hope of establishing a United Nations organization in this field and the Soviet bloc has not contributed much to United Nations agencies anyway.[22]

POOR AND DISSATISFIED COUNTRIES

A second group of three countries expressed varying degrees of displeasure with IDA. These countries would be instantly eligible for IDA credits on a per capita income basis. None of them had, however, received IDA funds. Egypt was not particularly bitter about the fact that they had not gotten any money from IDA. They would have liked to receive IDA money. They felt that most IDA money was going to India. The Egyptian spokesman pointed out the desperate poverty in his country. He could not understand why IDA had not seen fit to make money available to them.[23]

The spokesman for the second country in this group, Nigeria, echoed the comments about IDA money going to India. He had the distinct impression that IDA was not set up with the African countries in mind. It was not established to help Africa--but to help India. The rich countries felt that it would be a great blow if India went to the communists. That is why the rich nations were so anxious to help India and extend them loans. But India was already far overextended insofar as conventional debt was concerned. India couldn't service any more hard loans. And that is the reason IDA was established.[24] This man was not at all optimistic about the size of the replenishment of IDA. Why should the United States give anonymous loans through IDA when she could give bilateral loans and attach strings? And, in his view, all bilateral loans have strings. The United States may not require that other countries come here and worship her, but there are political strings. That is why Nigeria would much prefer international aid. There are no political strings on IDA money. There are stiff requirements, there are delays in negotiations, and the aid must be planned and used efficiently. For these reasons, the finance ministers complain that IDA is too tough and too slow. Because Africans felt that IDA would not be replenished very substantially and also because they felt that IDA was not established with Africa in mind, they put their hope in an African Development Bank. The Nigerian spokesman felt that the Bank could be making soft loans itself. The Bank is very rich now. It should lengthen its terms or lower its interest rate in this man's opinion.[25]

The third country in this poor and dissatisfied group was Viet-Nam. The spokesman for Viet-Nam was very bitter because IDA was applying the same standards as those used by the World Bank. A country must be considered to be absolutely secure and stable before it can get IDA money. This is of no help to Viet-Nam. He was outraged because India was getting all the aid from IDA. He believed this was true for two reasons. First, there are so many Indians on the staff of the International Bank. When Vietnamese apply for jobs they are told they are not qualified. Indians on the present staff decide Vietnamese are not qualified. Secondly, there is the argument that India must be helped so that it can become the show case or model for all Asia to follow. But this man argued that India cannot be such a show case. No one in Southeast Asia wants to follow India's example. He said that they had admired the Japanese very much even though they had resented their occupation at the time. They liked the way the Japanese went about things--the efficiency with which they had developed their country. This is not true in the case of India. And anyway, he argued, Southeast Asia doesn't need any show case. All countries should develop equally. India is no more crucial to the West than any other Southeast Asian nation. India could not stand for a minute if all the other countries of Southeast Asia fell to the communists. All the countries are crucial--none more than others. They should all be treated alike.[26]

IDA's personnel recruiting policies have come in for criticism from other sources. A complaint is heard from many of the underdeveloped countries that the higher staff levels of the organization contain no representatives from the underdeveloped countries. This is a difficult problem. If the poorer countries send their top planners and economists away to work in an international organization, they are going to have fewer trained people left at home to run the country. Most of the underdeveloped countries are short of this type of person. Thus, it would make no sense for them to further deplete their already thin ranks. However, one can see the other side, also. They feel that a Nigerian or an Egyptian would be much more sympathetic with their problems than a German or an American. They feel that a person who is concerned about what type of motor car to buy next year might show little understanding of people who were concerned about where the next meal is coming from.

ENTHUSIASTIC RECIPIENTS OF FUNDS

A spokesman for Tunisia was very enthusiastic about IDA. Here, he argued, we have a very capitalistic institution (the International Bank) coming around to a socialist approach--providing money to countries at very low or zero rates of interest for such projects as education. This is not a capitalist undertaking--to provide money at no interest for things like education. This man argued that it was a socialist endeavor and he welcomed it. He was interested and encouraged by the evolution in the thinking of a man like Eugene Black--from a conventional banker's attitude in the classical economic tradition to a point of view which enthusiastically embraced the International Development Association. And IDA has posed a bothersome problem for the communists. The communist countries had always refused to join the World Bank and the International Monetary Fund because they considered them to be capitalist institutions out to exploit the underdeveloped countries. But IDA is providing money to the underdeveloped countries on better terms than the Russians are doing--for projects like education--and with no political strings attached.[27]

The ever-recurring theme of IDA funds for India was again brought up. The Tunisian spokesman felt that the high percentage of funds going to India was due to the fact that India had the projects ready to present to IDA rather than to the political factors involved. In addition, India is a very well run country. These things were basic to the decision to help India. He believed that the developing countries in Africa were beginning to get projects ready for IDA and would begin to get more money very shortly. He sensed a great deal of enthusiasm for IDA among the African nations. He felt that there was no realistic hope of establishing SUNFED--it would have had the communist bloc countries in it--which ruled out United States acceptance. So that IDA was the only alternative for international aid. The recognized competence of the IDA staff and the lack of political strings on IDA credits makes them very appealing to all the developing countries. Funds coming from the Bank or IDA will be spent on good projects. They will not be wasted. This is one reason why underdeveloped countries prefer IDA money to bilateral money. IDA money goes for solid economic development and thus the government officials concerned are protected from charges of waste or inefficiency, and IDA policies also protect government officials from internal political pressure to build junk projects.[28]

India was the last country contacted concerning its attitude toward IDA. How does the Indian government justify so much of IDA money going to that country? First of all, they point out that India has gotten only 87 cents per capita from IDA as compared to $5 to $10 per capita in some countries. (See Table 6). Of course, they recognize that IDA's funds cannot be distributed on a per capita basis. India cannot receive her per capita share because of her size. But, at least, they argue, she should not be too much penalized for her size. A second point is that India was ready with projects and other countries were not. Now Pakistan is ready. Africa still is not ready with projects. A third point is that IDA funds should not be considered in isolation. We must consider the over-all aid picture. Some countries get significant aid from the United Kingdom. French colonies get French aid. On a total aid basis, India is not receiving a disproportionate share of aid.

On the basis of debt servicing capacity, India was certainly a prime object for IDA credits. India has borrowed extensively to finance its First and Second Five-Year Plans. And India is going to need a lot of outside capital before it reaches a stage of self-sustained growth.

As can be seen from Table 6, India has received $390 million of the $778 million IDA had committed as of June 30, 1964. Thus, India had received approximately one-half of IDA funds. How does IDA justify having given India such a large percentage? IDA argues that India has almost half the people in the underdeveloped world outside the Soviet bloc. India has considerably less

TABLE 6.--International Development Association development credit commitments per capita as of June 30, 1964

Country	Development Credits ($ millions)	Population 1963 (millions)	Development Credit Dollars Per Capita
Swaziland	2.8	0.3	9.33
Paraguay	9.6	1.9	5.05
Jordan	8.5	1.8	4.72
Honduras	9.0	2.0	4.50
Costa Rica	5.5	1.3	4.23
El Salvador	8.0	2.7	2.96
Chile	19.0	8.2	2.32
Nicaragua	3.0	1.5	2.00
Tanganyika	18.6	9.6	1.94
Pakistan	179.0	98.6	1.82
Ecuador	8.0	4.7	1.70
Syria	8.5	5.2	1.63
China	15.3	11.7	1.31
Colombia	19.5	15.0	1.30
Tunisia	5.0	4.3[a]	1.16
Sudan	13.0	12.8	1.02
Turkey	26.7	30.2	.88
India	390.0	449.0[a]	.87
Ethiopia	13.5	21.4	.63
Korea	14.0	27.3	.51
Niger	1.5	3.1	.48
Haiti	.3	4.34[a]	.07
Total	$ 778.3		

[a]1962

Source: Economic Staff, International Development Association.

than half of the gross national product of the underdeveloped world. India, it is argued, has more than half of the ability to use capital. Some Part II countries were ineligible for loans because of high per capita incomes. Some Part II countries were financed relatively lavishly by others (particularly some Southeast Asian countries and some of the dependent territories). Some Part II countries in South America have always looked to the United States and its Export-Import Bank and now to the Inter-American Development Bank rather than to the World Bank and IDA for funds. Some Part II countries were ineligible for loans on the basis of poor performance.

However, India met all the criteria very well. In fact, some people charge that the criteria were framed with India in mind. The charge that IDA had been set up primarily to help India had some element of truth in it. Before IDA was really in operation there was a commitment of $250 million of IDA funds to the India and Pakistan consortia.[29] The International Bank is sponsoring a consortium for India--with the idea that all external sources of capital taken together should meet India's capital requirements. Why should scarce IDA resources be put there if the consortium has agreed to meet the capital requirements? Basically, the same countries supplied the IDA money and the consortium money, so it is really two paths to the same goal. But, doesn't the presence of the consortium have some effect on India's creditworthiness? Some persons would maintain that it is only the presence of the consortium that has allowed India to be considered creditworthy for Bank loans. IDA argues that the members of the India consortium are reluctant to make any continuing commitment for India and so the consortium is not so significant as it might appear. IDA also argues that India gets a low per capita inflow of capital from all sources even though the absolute sums are large.

IDA policy toward India is certainly the most criticized aspect of its operations. This is true not only among the Part II member countries but among some of the Part I countries as well. Some of the Executive Directors from Part I countries have indicated a disagreement with IDA policy toward India. They point out that you can't keep 80 countries in an organization unless they have some hope of getting funds. These Directors are not in favor of dispensing aid geographically. Some Part II countries do favor a geographical division of aid, but this geographic distribution system wouldn't really satisfy countries. They don't throw their hats in the air in Bangkok when IDA grants a credit to the Philippines. IDA can't grant aid like it was a community kitchen. It must direct its limited aid to places where it gets the best returns. IDA aid must be concentrated if it is to be significant. But there is considerable resistance to concentrating as much aid in the future on India.

ALTERNATIVE PROPOSALS

An intriguing proposal came from David Horowitz, Governor of Israel, at the 1962 meeting of the Board of Governors.[30] Horowitz reasoned that the Bank had plenty of money, but a paucity of projects to finance. On the other hand, IDA had many worthy projects but not much money. Why not merge the two operations? Horowitz would have the Bank borrow money at conventional terms and loan it to IDA countries and IDA projects on IDA terms. The difference between the interest paid by the Bank and the interest charged by IDA would then be made up by the developed countries of the world. Thus, IDA could loan $1 billion a year at no interest and the rich countries would only have to contribute $50 million for the interest payment to the Bank.

If some such plan is not adopted, Horowitz warned, the repayment of interest and principal by the poor countries is soon going to be equal to the total financial assistance extended by the rich nations. In 1958, 32 low-income countries of the world were paying $1,280 million in service payments on private account and $770 million in service payments on public debt.[31] These two flows equalled more than $2 billion in 1958. This compares to total official grants in 1958 of $2.4 billion to <u>all</u> the underdeveloped countries of the world.[32]

IDA gave Horowitz' suggestion serious consideration. It was originally concluded that the proposal was unrealistic because it would involve getting governments to agree to pick up the tab for interest for several years in advance. As more and more funds were loaned, interest costs would rise appreciably. It was not felt that the developed countries would be willing to accept this responsibility. A new look is being given this idea as a result of the United Nations Conference on Trade and Development.

Horowitz proposed a second solution to the imbalance he saw between needs and resources. Why shouldn't the funds of IDA be used as a guarantee fund for loans made by the International Bank? Thus the $1 billion of IDA funds would be held intact to make up any defaults on loans made by the Bank. This would allow the Bank to extend its operations into countries and projects where it had not been before.[33] The Association studied this proposal also and again concluded that the proposal was unrealistic. It was felt that the donor countries would not approve of putting the $1 billion into a guarantee fund. Secondly, it was felt that any weakening of the Bank's standards would lead to a loss of confidence in the Bank by the financial community and a lessening of responsibility on the part of the underdeveloped countries.

Horowitz' proposals did stimulate thinking on the alternatives open to IDA. One idea that was put forward as a result of Horowitz' proposals received some lukewarm support from IDA. This proposal would have the developed countries float bonds, in their own countries, at commercial rates of interest and loan these funds to IDA at no interest. This would amount to a subsidy of the amount of the interest. The appeal of this plan lies in the possibility that the parliamentary bodies in the rich countries would be more favorable to borrowing for IDA than to taxing for IDA. Certainly the interest subsidy would be much smaller than an outright appropriation for IDA. And the amount of the subsidy could be controlled by the donor government rather than being a blank check as in the Horowitz plan.

It might be possible to remove the IDA subsidy from annual parliamentary debates if some type of long-run borrowing authority could be given as has been done for the Export-Import Bank in the United States. This relief from the yearly ordeal of the appropriation process is very appealing to some persons who favor increased aid to developing nations. Nothing, however, has come of any of these proposals to date.

Another proposal for IDA's future came from the Government from Pakistan. This plan was presented at the Board of Governors meeting in September, 1961, by M. A. Mozaffar, Governor of Pakistan. He pointed out that Pakistan had suffered from declining terms of trade over the past 10 years. Is it inevitable or equitable that the burden of adjustment should always fall on the weaker economies? Is it in the interest of the industrial countries to have the primary producing countries continually whipsawed by the terms of trade? The Government of Pakistan, the Governor stated, was of the opinion that a solution could be found which would be in the interest of all. The countries which benefited from fluctuations in terms of trade should contribute some part of their gain to the International Development Association. This would apply to both the primary producers and the industrial nations.[34]

Alan Neale has made a proposal that would increase IDA's resources and help solve the problem of fluctuating terms of trade. He suggests that the rich countries, working through the Organization for Economic Co-operation and Development, agree to impose common flat-rate excise duties on their total intake of certain commodities and to devote the proceeds of such taxation to IDA. He estimates that a 5 per cent levy on all coffee, cocoa, and tea sold in the Western countries would produce $100 million a year.[35]

V. K. R. V. Rao made a dramatic case for expanding and re-structuring the International Development Association.

> Time and compound interest are working against the under-developed world and along with it also the built-in progress in science and technology that is accompanying the rake's progress of compound interest in the developed world, parts of which are already wrestling with the problems arising out of affluence, when surrounding them are vast deserts of poverty, and low levels of living and the dismal tyranny of the economic problem. I have no doubt in my mind that the present situation is fraught with instability and constitutes a much graver menace to the peace of the world than anything that the cold war has produced so far. Oases may exist with impunity in a natural world of deserts, but there can be no security for human oases of affluence in a mass-inhabited world of poverty and low levels of living. . . . I believe the answer is the internationalizing of all aid and the entrusting of this international aid to an organization like the International Development Association. Only I do not think it can take such a major job in its present form, certainly not as an

> affiliate of the International Bank, with its peculiar structure of voting rights, and whilst its membership does not include the Soviet Union and Communist China.[36]

Several of the developing countries have suggested that the Bank's reserves be transferred to IDA. The Bank had acquired reserves of over $700 million by the end of 1962. However, this idea received a very cold reception from the Bank's management as long as Black was President. It was felt that this would be a serious violation of trust to the Bank's creditors. At the time the financial community put up the funds for Bank bonds, it was understood that the reserve fund would be available in the case of country default. To use this fund for any other purpose would be a serious breach of faith, it was argued. Some of the staff went so far as to say it would be disastrous for the Bank, if such a transfer were made. Mr. Black told the bond markets that IDA was separate from the Bank and every effort was made to keep it so. To transfer Bank reserves to IDA would destroy the bond market's confidence in the Bank's management, it was felt.

A new type of loan has also been proposed--a low interest loan to countries not really in need of IDA-type credits. Some countries, Mexico, Yugoslavia, etc., are able to pay some interest but are not able to meet much further debt service at conventional rates. It was proposed that the Bank's reserves be used for loans at lower than Bank rates to these particular countries. There were suggestions that regular IDA funds might be used for other type loans than the present 50-year, no-interest rate credits now being extended. Why should all IDA credits be for so long and at no interest? Could some IDA credits be less soft?

This third type loan raised the whole complex issue of justifying 6 per cent loans to some countries, 3 per cent loans to other countries, and zero per cent loans to still other countries. This would really put the staff in an awkward and unjustifiable position. There were already enough problems deciding between Bank and IDA loans. Another type loan would complicate things even further. In addition, there would be a degree of discrimination involved in low-interest loans, that is, the discrimination between those countries getting interest subsidies and those countries paying the going rate. The countries borrowing from the Bank at conventional rates of interest would be paying for the subsidy given to those countries receiving low-interest loans. This would be hard to justify. There was also the possibility that giving low-interest loans might lead to a casual attitude about repayment. This would really be a "fuzzy" loan which, of course, was the target of so much vituperation on the part of the Bank's staff. Because of all the problems cited, there is little prospect for any intermediate interest rate loans by IDA or the Bank.

One other possibility that was discussed was the possibility of lengthening the term of Bank loans. Or, perhaps, the Bank could lengthen the grace period before repayment begins. This would involve some degree of interest risk. Interest rates might rise on the money that would have to be borrowed to complete loans already contracted. In the past, the Bank has loaned on the same terms on which it has borrowed (except for the commission that has been added to go into reserves). If it extended the period of the loan, this would involve borrowing short and loaning long. One possibility would be to put the Bank's reserves to work covering this interest risk. This assumption of interest risk would not involve the outright interest subsidy that would be involved in loans at less than conventional rates of interest. It will be seen that the Bank finally altered its position on several of these proposals.

CHAPTER 12 NEGOTIATING THE REPLENISHMENT

ROLE OF PART II COUNTRIES

Once it had been agreed that there was further need for soft loans it became necessary to apportion the cost of such loans among the member countries. One of the first questions to be decided (and with very little fuss) was that only the Part I members would contribute to the replenishment round.

Treasury Secretary Anderson had insisted that the Part II countries put up part of their contributions in convertible currency when IDA was established. He argued that future replenishments should include contributions from Part II members, also. However, by the time the negotiations for replenishment got under way there was little support for this position. There had been complaints from some of the underdeveloped countries about the possibility of having to give up more of their scarce foreign exchange reserves in order to replenish IDA. Some persons agreed that the Part II members should not have to put up any more convertible currency but felt that they should contribute in their own local currency. But, IDA had not been able to use the local currency that had been contributed when IDA was established. So, it seemed foolish for IDA to keep piling up local currencies that couldn't be used.

The IDA staff argued that they got the Part II members to contribute by having them pay the local currency costs of projects. The view of the staff was that further holdings of local currencies were too much trouble to bother with. The Part I members agreed with this view and agreed to put up all the money for the replenishment, but with no increase in voting rights.

The staff of IDA was on sound economic grounds in opposing an increased contribution in gold or convertible currency from the Part II countries. The staff argued that if the Part II members exported capital they were simply going to need more capital. As one staff member put it, "That's like asking a man standing in the soup line to contribute to the soup kitchen. It makes no sense at all."[1] It would just make the demands on the Part I countries that much greater if the underdeveloped countries had to contribute additional convertible currencies to IDA.

There is nothing wrong with this economic analysis. But, as with some other decisions made by IDA, it ignores the non-economic aspects. In this case, IDA was altogether wrong in not urging a renewed contribution from the Part II members. And such contribution should have been, at least in part, in convertible currencies. It seems to have been considered important when IDA was formed that all members feel that they were making some contribution. All Part II members were asked to make some sacrifice in order to join--they had to put up some of their scarce foreign exchange. This put the underdeveloped countries in the position of being donors of foreign aid and this was one of IDA's greatest advantages over bilateral aid programs. It took the "soup kitchen" tag off of foreign assistance and made it into something that the countries of the world were doing together. It was no longer charity--but a mutual pooling of efforts to improve life for all of us on this planet. Such an arrangement should have been carried into the replenishment of IDA's funds.

SHARES OF THE RICH MEMBERS

Having disposed of the Part II members, the negotiators turned to the question of shares for the rich members. Each Part I member's willingness to contribute further to IDA reflected to some extent that member's evaluation of IDA's effectiveness. So, the question of country shares is related to the question of how well IDA had performed during its first years of operations.

Belgium was originally designated a Part I member of IDA and scheduled to contribute $22.7 million in gold or convertible currency. Belgium did not contribute a cent of their quota to the Association. Why the reluctance to join? Belgium had been the recipient of loans from the International Bank in an earlier period when reconstruction loans were being made. In fact, the Bank had loaned Belgium a total of $76 million during the period 1949-1957. Why, then, was Belgium unwilling to share the costs of helping others, since the Belgian economy is once again prosperous?

The first reason given by the Belgian spokesman was that IDA was established at a time of heavy Belgian expense in the Congo. They were paying the external debt of the Congo that was contracted with Belgian guarantees during the colonial period. They were also paying salary differentials of Belgian nationals serving in the Congo--doctors, engineers, etc.[2]

Secondly, Belgium did not agree with the share assigned to them. The quota used for IDA subscriptions was the quota devised at Bretton Woods for contributions to the International Monetary Fund and the International Bank. This quota took account of such things as exports, imports, currency reserves, etc. These matters are important in apportioning quotas for the International Monetary Fund because the purpose of the Fund is to provide funds in times of temporary crises in a country's balance of payments. However, by the time you come to the International Bank such considerations are already less significant. But, Belgium went along with such quotas in the Bank. It was a once for all thing and only 20 per cent of the $450 million Belgian quota had to be paid in gold or convertible currency. The rest was warranty for possible loans. Anyway that was ancient history, But, by the time IDA came along--this Bretton Woods quota was even less meaningful.[3]

The Belgians argue that a country with a large amount of exports may have little ability to ship capital abroad. Belgium depends on exports for much of its gross national product. But, that does not mean that Belgium is a large capital exporter. The Belgian economy is only one-fifth the size of the French economy, but their Bank quota is more than one-third the French quota. The same would have been true in IDA. Belgium did not want to get a tradition established for using this quota for all questions. They were reluctant to have this quota used for IDA because IDA will require constant replenishment by the Part I countries.[4]

Thirdly, there was some degree of irritation, at the time of the IDA proposal, over the Belgian Congo. The United Nations was <u>persona non grata</u> in Belgium at the time. This followed the United Nations intervention in the Congo. Thus, it would not have been politically wise to go to the Parliament and ask for an appropriation for a United Nations specialized agency. The finance minister must go often enough to the Parliament asking for funds for foreign aid--for the Congo and elsewhere. It would not have helped his case to have asked for funds for IDA membership. "However, this was essentially a question of tactics. If we could have reached agreement on a quota for Belgium--we could have waited a while and submitted it to the Parliament later."[5] Most observers agree that the question of the quota was the primary stumbling block in the case of Belgium. And most observers would concede that Belgium's quota was too high. Belgium was not inflexible on this matter and when a compromise solution was worked out, Belgium came into the Association on the second round of contributions. There was no intimation of criticism of the Association or any lack of conviction that the Association was necessary.

At least one Part I country was very enthusiastic about IDA. On May 28, 1962, it was announced that the Swedish Parliament had approved a special supplementary contribution of $5.8 million to the resources of the Association. The funds were made available in freely convertible Swedish kroner, not tied to Swedish exports nor restricted to use in any specific country. Sweden has made the only such supplemental contributions to IDA. Why did the Swedes do this?

There were several reasons for Sweden's supplementary contributions. First, there was and still is considerable internal pressure to get Sweden into the foreign aid business and to increase Swedish contributions for technical assistance. The labor unions had been especially pushing the government in this direction, although the pressure came from the opposition, also. Although the Social Democratic Party governs Sweden, both parties favor foreign aid.[6]

Originally, Sweden would have very much preferred SUNFED or an expanded United Nations program to IDA. Sweden was ready to contribute to SUNFED. They had already increased their large (for Sweden) contribution to the United Nations activities in the economic development field. They would have liked to channel further economic aid through the United Nations because of the strong support for the United Nations in Sweden.[7]

By 1962, however, Sweden felt differently about IDA. Why? IDA had proven itself capable of administering its funds. It had already assembled a staff which was experienced, capable, and efficient. This was the main point in IDA's favor. Sweden felt that IDA was the best approach to economic aid to the underdeveloped countries. The Swedes had the impression that IDA had been accepted by the underdeveloped countries, too.[8]

A second reason for Sweden's supplementary contributions to IDA was based on uncertainty as to how best to approach foreign economic assistance. Sweden was really just looking around to try and see how to go about increasing foreign aid. No one seems to really know much about how it is best to do this--whether its best to give them a steel mill right away or educate them or just what. No one really seems to know the answer to this--the people who work in this field all have different opinions. Sweden was considering all sorts of approaches. There are considerable drawbacks to bilateral programs. It is difficult for the underdeveloped countries to accept the money from another government--they are sensitive about it and it does raise problems. Sweden does have some bilateral programs--primarily school construction--in India, Pakistan, and Ethiopia. They have built schools and also brought some people to Sweden.

But a bilateral program costs a lot of money. It is expensive to set up and administer and it's hard to find the right people to get it going. It also represents considerable duplication of staff and administrative costs for every country to have its own foreign aid program. So, IDA seemed the better alternative.[9]

The third reason for choosing IDA was that Sweden liked the idea of a multilateral program based on untied loans and a program where purchases would be based on international competition. Sweden must export to live. The Swedish economy is based on exports and imports. They must compete in the international economy and they want the right to compete for all aid funds. They would like for all foreign aid to be on an untied basis and they felt that their own must be. Sweden has traditionally favored free trade and liberal tariff policies and IDA meets this requirement quite well.[10]

The striking thing about these three reasons was the fact that there was domestic pressure in Sweden to increase foreign assistance. I pointed out the contrast between the Swedish and the United States situation in this regard. This was quite understandable in the Swedish view. Foreign aid is a new thing for Sweden. The United States has been at it for 20 years. Sweden may have the same problem in 20 years. The United States Congress and the public is bored with foreign aid. It has been a very long-standing thing. The public wonders when it will end and they are beginning to wonder about the effectiveness of foreign aid--what results have been achieved, The United States, on a realistic basis, has been very generous. People grow tired of being generous.[11] In any event, Sweden liked IDA and supported it with enthusiasm.

South Africa, a Part I member of IDA, expressed itself as unwilling to contribute further, at the 1962 meetings. The Governor, T. E. Donges, explained his country's position as follows:

> We have these large underdeveloped areas, particularly the areas occupied by our Bantu peoples, now evolving towards self-government, which still require considerable amounts of capital for their further development. . . . With our limited resources, it is clear that we cannot afford to incur any very substantial additional obligations in respect of assistance to other less developed countries. While I am in very great sympathy with the objects of IDA and with the proposal before us I feel, therefore, I must make it clear that countries in the special position of South Africa cannot undertake any large new commitments for this cause, however worthy it may be.[12]

At the Vienna meetings in 1961 the Governor of IDA for the United Kingdom, Mr. Selwyn Lloyd, while stressing the importance of IDA, called for a taking into account of the relative capacities of member countries in assessing them for additional contributions.[13] His statement illustrated the British view, held throughout the deliberations concerning IDA, that their share was disproportionately large. Mr. Lloyd's successor, Mr. Reginald Maudling, made the case in more precise terms at the 1962 meeting of the Board of Governors. He made it clear that future subscriptions should be related to the resources and general economic situation of the country concerned. He pointed out that the United Kingdom's contribution was two-and-a-half times as big as that of France and Germany.[14]

Despite the reservation about the British share, there was a considerable amount of enthusiasm for IDA in the United Kingdom by 1962. The British realized that there was a lot to be said for multilateral aid. IDA had justified itself and had done a good job. The British joined the United States in urging a large replenishment for IDA. While urging a large total amount, they wanted to reduce their share from the 1960 quota. The British argued that aid should be on the basis of one's capacity to afford it--not on the basis of a country's exports, imports, reserves, etc., which were important in the Bretton Woods formula. They argued that West Germany and France had caught up with the United Kingdom and should have equal shares with the U. K. There was little balance of payments fear on the part of the British--they expected to get their aid back in the form of purchases in their country. And if they don't get all the aid back--the size of their IDA contribution is not going to break the country. It was hard for the British to understand the furor in the United States Congress over the balance of payments impact of the U. S. contribution to IDA.

The Government of the Netherlands joined the United Kingdom and the United States in arguing for a large replenishment but also arguing for a reduced share for themselves. The Governor from the Netherlands, speaking to the 1962 Board meeting, said that the Netherlands would make a sympathetic response to a call for further assistance to IDA. But, he stated that the Netherlands could not continue to accept for their share the original distribution formula based on the capital subscriptions in the Bank. He argued in favor of national income comparisons as an equitable criterion for apportioning quotas. And he expressed the hope that during the replenishment round the Part I members would not be faced again with the alternative of accepting the "unreasonable" shares assigned them or of abstaining altogether.[15]

The role of West Germany in the replenishment negotiations was somewhat changed from the original German view toward IDA. As has been stated before, Germany opposes soft loans. There has been some relaxation in this opposition but the Germans still prefer to give hard loans than to provide soft loans or grants. West Germany has no ex-colonies to feel tender toward and might have been expected to be a big contributor to IDA. Almost all observers of the aid effort point to Germany as the country that is not doing its share. The Germans just do not like to give money away. They are sensitive on this point, however, and have published a series of full page advertisements in United States newspapers which contain the argument that Germany is, too, doing its share.[16]

What was the German attitude during the negotiations? One participant in the negotiations described the Germans as uninterested in the size of the total replenishment of IDA but interested in some balance between the percentage of their share and the shares of other developed countries. The German Government points to the fact that West Germany increased her percentage share in the replenishment more than any country. They take this as indicative of their new role as staunch supporters of the International Development Association.

The Germans felt that Black's proposal for a replenishment of $2.5 billion was completely unrealistic. They felt that it was nonsense to speak of the demand for this type of money. The demand for IDA credits is unlimited. The real limit is IDA's capacity to ferret out projects that deserve support. Germany did not feel that IDA had demonstrated the ability to dispense $500 million a year. As IDA grows it may be possible, but as of 1962, the West German view was that $500 million a year was an assumption with no proof. West Germany was willing to think in terms of $300 million a year, but there was a negative attitude toward the $500 million idea from the first.

The French felt that IDA came on top of an already large bilateral aid program. France contributes a higher percentage of her gross national product in foreign aid than any other developed country. The bulk of French public assistance (90 per cent) is in the form of grants--thus an even easier burden on the developing countries than are IDA terms. Whereas IDA assistance goes to development projects, French assistance is directed toward technical assistance and budget support. That part of French assistance that does go into investment is aimed more at schools, hospitals, housing, etc., rather than toward economic projects of the IDA type. The bulk of French aid goes to Africa, whereas IDA aid has been concentrated in Asia. French aid is directed toward her former colonies and is a way of keeping control and influence where there are large French economic interests. If the governments of the developing countries do not please the French Government--then France can cut off the aid. IDA doesn't meet these French objectives. Thus, France was not enthusiastic about supporting the replenishment of IDA's funds.

One participant in the negotiations to replenish IDA argued that the small size of the final replenishment agreement ($250 million a year for 3 years as opposed to Black's proposal for $500 million for 5 years) was due to the French. The French held to the figure of $250 million a year for three years and would not budge from it. General deGaulle was in charge of France during the time of the replenishment negotiations and there was no budging him. The French deny this view, however, and as one spokesman said, "The French are not responsible for everything that happens in the world." The French took an attitude toward the replenishment which put them in a unique category during the negotiations. They were not too interested in the size of the total replenishment but put an absolute maximum on the amount (not the share) of their contribution. They felt that in view of their other commitments it would be hard to put in more than $17 million a year. They wound up putting in $20.3 million a year. They did increase both the amount and their percentage in IDA's funds. If the old formula had been applied the French share would have been only $17 million--so that the French view was that their increase to $20.3 million represented compromise on their part. They feel no more to blame for the small total than were the United States or the United Kingdom who argued for a larger total but a smaller share for themselves.

One got the impression that the United States Government was ambivalent toward replenishing IDA's funds. On the one hand, the President of the United States made an unequivocal statement of support for increasing IDA's resources at the 1962 meeting of the Board of Governors. "The work of the International Development Association is particularly important--and this country fully supports the proposal that the Executive Directors develop a program to increase its resources."[17] On the other hand, there was considerable opposition among influential members of the Congress.

One of the limiting factors in the expansion of IDA was the balance of payments problem of the United States.

Representative Passman made this an issue in the 1962 hearings on IDA's appropriation.

> Mr. Passman. But, these countries which earn dollars or other hard currencies from their exports to the amount needed to deal in world commerce, if through the various aid programs we make dollar credits available to the full extent, or even to a partial extent, of the amount needed to pay for what they would import from the United States, then that would make available the money they earn from exports for them to use for whatever purpose they might see fit.[18]

He continued his argument by stating that in the underdeveloped countries

> Some of those dollars are earmarked to buy something that is produced in America.
>
> If we provide for them credits or gifts, or grants, then they can requisition from America what they would normally buy with the dollars which they earn from exports.[19]

John M. Leddy, Assistant Secretary of the Treasury and U. S. Executive Director of the International Development Association at the time, presented information to counter Representative Passman's contention.

> Mr. Leddy. . . . The normal effect of any provision of AID funds or development credits for development purposes in these countries tends in and of itself to increase the total demand for imports into those countries.
>
> Mr. Passman. At least we hoped so.
>
> Mr. Leddy. It has shiftability. It means you have to import more goods to go into the project, it means you have to spend more money internally for labor, et cetera, which then creates a demand for imports. I do not believe that it is correct to say that the effect of lending for development purposes is simply to add to the free dollar resources of these countries.[20]

This is an extremely important point. If it could be demonstrated that untied aid (all IDA loans must be untied in accordance with the charter) leads recipient nations to spend their earned dollars elsewhere, then this would be a potent argument against expansion of this agency. The United States would be patently foolish to give assistance which would tend to drive customers away.

Another fear was expressed in the Congress--where the doctrines of mercantilism are not dead. Some Congressmen were worried that IDA might make loans to countries whose industries might compete with United States firms.

Representative Alexander of North Carolina was very concerned that IDA might loan funds to a textile firm which would compete with domestic industry.

> Mr. Alexander. Do you have any regulations with reference to loans in regard to industrial development in underdeveloped countries which would pertain to the problem of, say, for instance, textiles, which in this country and throughout the world is right much of a competitive business already? Do you have any rules with reference to what these industrial loans would be made for?
>
> Mr. Leddy. There is no prohibition on the making of any particular type loan under the IDA or the Bank. I should repeat, however, that the Bank and IDA have tended to focus pretty heavily on the field of transportation, power, irrigation. There have been some loans to private industry usually through industrial development banks. The industrial development banks, of course, relend the money to a wide variety of domestic industries, which could include a textile industry but there is no general policy laid down in the international institutions as such which would prohibit any particular type of loan or any particular industry.[21]

Although some of IDA's strongest critics were found in the United States Congress, some of IDA's strongest supporters were there also. Senator Monroney succeeded in amending the Act for International Development of 1961 (Section 205 of Public Law 87-195, 87th Congress, September 4, 1961) so that the

President had the power to lend up to 10 per cent of the funds of the Development Loan Fund to the International Development Association. In fiscal year 1962, this would have amounted to $110 million and would be a substantial boost to IDA's resources. However, there was no move to implement such a loan. It would have had to be a peculiar type of loan since IDA does not charge interest and IDA credits will not be repaid for 50 years. If the Congress meant for the President to loan funds to IDA on these same terms, it would have been a most helpful arrangement.

One factor that entered into determining how large the United States contribution should be was fear on the part of the State Department that a large contribution to IDA would hurt the bilateral aid program. Just as IDA fails to meet the political objectives of French foreign aid--it also fails to meet the political objectives of United States foreign aid.

At the beginning of the negotiations in Paris the United States apparently took the position that IDA should get $500 million a year and that the U. S. share should be reduced from 43 per cent to 33 1/3 per cent. On a gross national product basis the United States contribution would have been 60 per cent. If it had been on a progressive basis--the United States share would have been even larger. On what basis, then, did the United States argue that her share should be only 33 1/3 per cent? One argument that was made was that this was approximately the percentage of World Bank expenditures which returned to the United States. Thus, if the United States contributed this share to IDA there would be no adverse balance of payments impact. The whole argument concerning the impact of IDA on the United States balance of payments was exaggerated beyond belief. The IDA contribution was a mere trifle in the United States balance of payments. How anyone could have argued against a United States contribution to IDA on this ground is beyond understanding. A more plausible argument for reducing the United States share in IDA was related to the fact that the United States had higher quotas elsewhere so their quota in IDA should be reduced. Also, United States expenditure for military purposes is for the common interest of all the rich Western nations and this should be taken into account when apportioning shares in IDA.

In any case, the question of its proper share in the replenishment came to be the central feature of the United States position. Instead of taking a position that so much could be contributed and letting the chips fall where they may--there was enormous concern that the share not be disproportionate. It is difficult to believe that the negotiations could have proceeded on this plane but all reports indicate this to be the truth. The United States wound up contributing 41.6 per cent of $250 million a year--which amounts to $104 million a year. At one point apparently the United States would have been willing to contribute 33-1/3 per cent of $500 million a year which would have amounted to $165 million a year. The fact that the United States share did not accord with United States views of propriety caused the absolute amount of the U. S. contribution to be reduced. Surely, in the next replenishment round a more mature position can be taken.

Table 7 indicates the results of the negotiations on replenishment of IDA's funds. The United States, United Kingdom, Norway, Netherlands, Finland, Denmark, and Australia all succeeded in reducing their shares from the original formula. Canada, France, Germany, Italy, Japan, and Sweden all agreed to increase their shares in the new resources. South Africa which had originally declined to participate finally agreed to come in on the replenishment but with a much reduced share. Belgium and Luxembourg had never joined IDA because of their opposition to the original shares assigned them but agreed to become members during the replenishment negotiations. Kuwait had applied for Part I membership after IDA had been established but declined to participate in the replenishment.

Once the total size of the replenishment was agreed to and the shares apportioned it would have appeared that IDA's future was assured. In most countries where a parliamentary system prevails a commitment by the executive is binding upon the legislature. In the case of the United Kingdom, Germany, France, etc., it could be assumed that once the agreement was reached the funds would be forthcoming. However, the United States Congress was under no obligation to ratify the United States agreement to participate in the replenishment. And the legislation to bring United States participation about was defeated in the House of Representatives when it was first presented. It is to this debate on IDA in the United States Congress that we now turn.

TABLE 7. --Proposed participation in increase of International Development Association resources (in millions of U. S. dollars and percentages)

Country	Initial Resources	Proposed Amount of New Resources	Percent Share of Initial Resources	Percent Share of New Resources
Australia	$ 20.18	$ 19.80	2.72	2.64
Austria	5.04	5.04	.67	.67
Belgium	-----	16.50	----	2.20
Canada	37.83	41.70	5.09	5.56
Denmark	8.74	7.50	1.18	1.00
Finland	3.83	2.298	.52	.31
France	52.96	61.872	7.13	8.25
Germany	52.96	72.60	7.13	9.68
Italy	18.16	30.00	2.45	4.00
Japan	33.59	41.25	4.52	5.50
Kuwait	3.36	-----	.45	----
Luxembourg	-----	.75	----	.10
Netherlands	27.74	16.50	3.73	2.20
Norway	6.72	6.60	.90	.88
South Africa	10.09	3.99	1.36	.53
Sweden	10.09	15.00	1.36	2.00
United Kingdom	131.14	96.00	17.66	12.88
United States	320.29	312.00	43.12	41.60
Total	$742.72	$750.00	100.00	100.00

Source: Adapted from Senate Committee on Foreign Relations, Hearings on S. 2214, 1963, p. 9.

CHAPTER 13 CONGRESSIONAL DEBATE ON REPLENISHMENT

The proposal to replenish the resources of IDA came to a Congress that was of two minds concerning the wisdom of such a move. The Senate indicated in October of 1963 that it was enthusiastic about multilateral aid and particularly impressed with the International Development Association, maintaining that, "in the few years of its existence, the International Development Association had compiled a commendable record." The Foreign Relations Committee urged the President to make use of his authority to loan IDA up to 10 per cent of the funds Congress had made available for development lending.[1] During the same year the House had made just the opposite recommendation. This Congressional ambivalence was to be in evidence throughout the discussion of IDA's replenishment.

SENATE APPROVAL OF THE REPLENISHMENT PROPOSAL

The Senate Committee on Foreign Relations held hearings on IDA's replenishment on November 15, 1963, and December 4, 1963. Treasury Secretary Dillon was the Administration spokesman in IDA's behalf. Dillon presented the background information concerning the need for replenishing IDA's funds.[2] He pointed out that Eugene Black had originally proposed $500 million a year. This was resisted by England, France, and Germany, and the United States had not wanted to increase its percentage to provide such a sum. So $250 million a year for 3 years was agreed upon. It was pointed out that this was approximately the rate at which IDA was committing money during 1963.

Dillon pointed out that the negotiations had been arduous and had lasted more than eight months. He was convinced that this was the maximum amount the European countries were willing to contribute and that their shares had been raised as high as possible. The fact that the United States share had only been reduced from 43 per cent to 41.6 per cent was regretted. But he felt that the shares agreed upon during the replenishment round formed a solid base upon which future negotiations could be conducted.

Dillon explained that the President had not used his authority to loan IDA money under the Foreign Assistance Act because such a policy of unilateral lending would undermine the multilateral nature of IDA. He said such a possibility might be foreseen if it could be put on a matching basis. That is, the United States would agree to loan IDA money provided the other Part I countries would loan an equal amount. He felt the other Part I countries would be reluctant to undertake such an operation during the foreseeable future. The Part I countries had made it quite explicit during the negotiations that they would not agree to further increases in IDA funds before 1966.

The Committee indicated two areas of concern in their questioning. The first area of concern had to do with IDA policies toward private enterprise. Senator Hickenlooper indicated concern that IDA might not follow a pro private enterprise line of sufficient hardness. Secretary Dillon was able to assure the Senator that IDA policy toward uncompensated expropriations was identical to or even harder than United States policy.

The second line of questioning was concerned with the United States balance of payments. Senators Morse and Symington indicated that in their view the U. S. should not enter into an agreement to replenish IDA until a comprehensive review of foreign aid and its impact on the United States balance of payments had been undertaken. Secretary Dillon endeavored to demonstrate that the United States would not be irreparably damaged by contributing $104 million a year to IDA for a three year period. He pointed out that the World Bank ordinarily procured around 30 per cent of its goods and services in the United States. Since the U. S. was contributing around 40 per cent of IDA's resources--one could expect that about 3 out of every 4 dollars contributed would return to the United States.

Two citizens groups appeared to oppose, or at least to question the wisdom of, replenishment of IDA's funds. Elgin Groseclose, Economic Consultant, Citizens Foreign Aid Committee, testified that his group was opposed to all foreign aid and as such was opposed to contributing to IDA. N. R. Daniellian, President, International Economic Policy Association, presented evidence to demonstrate that IDA policies were inconsistent with U. S. aid policies. In particular, he pointed out the fact that funds which were loaned to some countries by IDA were reloaned to subsidiary agencies at higher rates of interest. Daniellian also argued that it was inconsistent with U. S. balance of payments conditions to give untied aid. The Chamber of Commerce sent a letter of strong support for replenishing IDA's funds.

The Senate debated IDA on January 20, 1964.[3] Senators Fulbright and Monroney led the effort to pass the replenishment legislation. Senator Fulbright emphasized the leadership role the United States had played in establishing IDA and the role the United States had played in negotiating the replenishment. He argued that this U. S. leadership was based on the conviction that IDA was in the United States interest. It was in the United States interest to have the underdeveloped countries receive aid, assistance, and guidance from the staff of the World Bank. It was in the United States interest to bring the wealthy European countries into the effort to extend soft loans. Fulbright argued that IDA administration of funds was superior to AID administration of funds. IDA had enabled the World Bank staff to assist countries where it would not have been possible on a hard loan basis. He accepted the fact that U. S. participation in IDA would lead to a small drain on the balance of payments. But, he argued, this must be offset against the great importance of IDA to the peaceful development of the world.

The critics of IDA again raised the balance of payments issue. Senator Symington argued that new evidence had come from unnamed bankers which would indicate that IDA would have a very adverse impact on the U. S. balance of payments. Senator Symington also charged that IDA was giving too much money to India, that "IDA is in large part a vehicle for channeling aid to India." Symington was concerned with the fact that the United States exercised only a fourth of the voting power in IDA. He raised the question of whether IDA was the receptacle into which the World Bank dumped its questionable loans.

Senator Javits entered the debate with a strong endorsement of IDA and expressed the opinion that United States aid should be increasingly channeled through multilateral institutions. As for the question of IDA loans to India, the Senator said, "Why not? We are determined to make India the free world's showcase in Asia, and a bulwark of freedom in the face of Red Chinese expansion. I do not wish to be faced again, as a Senator, with what I was faced with in 1948, when I had to face the loss of 400 million people and giving the Communists the balance of power in the world. I would rather vote the money and the resources, within the limits which this country can do it, while there is time.

"I hope that the members of the Senate when they think about how they will vote, will pause to ponder this question: Is India worth saving, or shall we let her go down the drain?"[4]

Senator Clark had gotten figures from the Treasury Department which indicated that over the entire period of their existence, the World Bank and IDA had had a favorable effect upon the United States balance of payments. This computation took account of repayments on loans to the World Bank, interest paid on money borrowed, purchases of equipment, payments for technical services, etc.

At the conclusion of debate the Senate voted by 38-31 to expand the resources of IDA. The closeness of the vote was in marked contrast to the wide support given IDA when it was established. But, in any case, the Senate did vote to authorize increased U. S. participation, and the scene of debate moved to the House of Representatives.

THE HOUSE REFUSES FURTHER FUNDS

The bill to authorize United States participation in the replenishment of IDA was examined by the House Committee on Banking and Currency. The Subcommittee on International Finance held hearings on December 3 and 16, 1963,[5] and the full Committee held hearings on January 8, 1964.[6]

Congressman Henry S. Reuss, of Wisconsin, served as chairman of the Subcommittee on International Finance and conducted the hearings. Reuss' role in the effort to expand IDA's resources was puzzling. On the one hand Reuss seemed to actively support IDA. On the other, his line of questioning depicted a hostile view toward the World Bank and a supra-nationalist concern for United States interests. Reuss has a reputation as a liberal member of the House. But on the IDA question he appeared to be attempting to steal the critics' thunder by anticipating their criticisms and raising them himself. In some cases he handed the critics weapons they may not have had otherwise.

The Executive Director of IDA for the United States during 1962-1964, John C. Bullitt, served as the Administration spokesman before the Subcommittee. Reuss had raised the question of whether part of the World Bank's reserves could not be transferred to IDA. Bullitt indicated that such a proposal had been made during the negotiations concerning replenishment and that the management of the Bank had rather vigorously opposed the idea. The management felt that such a transfer would adversely affect the World Bank's credit rating. After the negotiations had been completed, however, it developed that there was a consensus among the contributors to IDA that it would be a good idea to transfer Bank profits to IDA. Reuss wanted to compel the U. S. Executive Director to move in this direction. He was concerned with the borrowing policy of the World Bank and wished to instruct the U. S Director to insist that World Bank loans not be made in the United States so long as a balance of payments problem existed. Reuss also wished to instruct the U. S. Director of IDA that in any future negotiation concerning IDA funds, every effort be made to further reduce the United States share.

Other Committee members raised questions concerning the possibility of IDA's supplying loans for industries which would compete with U. S. industry, particularly the cattle industry or the food processing industry. This question had been raised at earlier hearings on IDA. Again it was pointed out that IDA took account of the world supply situation for a commodity before loans were approved.

The Committee indicated concern about the fact that the United States share was 41.6 per cent in IDA's replenishment. Mr. Bullitt argued that this was not unreasonable in light of

United States resources. He pointed out that the United States contributed 48 per cent of the United Nations budget, 49 per cent of the World Health Organization's budget, 48 per cent of UNESCO's budget, 41 per cent of the Food and Agriculture Organization's budget, and 40 per cent of the International Labor Organization's budget. So, in relation to other international organizations, the United States share in IDA did not seem out of line. Bullitt did not mention that on a gross national product basis, the U. S. share would have been 60 per cent. Nor did he mention that if the progressive income tax principle had been applied to IDA that the U. S. share would have been close to 70 per cent.

Some of IDA's strongest support in the Committee came from Representative James Harvey, a Republican Representative from Michigan. Representative Harvey had participated in a tour of IDA projects. He had returned from this tour with a very favorable impression of IDA operations. And he made use of the information he had gained on this tour to answer several criticisms which were made. The Committee was not completely satisfied as a result of their session with Mr. Bullitt and requested that they have a session with Joseph W. Barr, at that time Assistant to the Secretary of the Treasury, who had conducted the tour of IDA projects.

The main problem which Mr. Barr dealt with was the question of how to evaluate IDA's effectiveness--and whether additional U. S. participation was warranted. Barr presented several criteria for evaluating IDA, although he acknowledged that all of them were inadequate. One criterion he suggested was growth of gross national product. Another was changes in export earnings. A third was advances being made in educating the people in the countries concerned Barr conceded that statistics on all these indicators were inadequate in the underdeveloped countries. And this seriously limited the usefulness of these criteria. Another possibility Barr suggested was an emergency criterion, that is, IDA had made it possible for India and Pakistan, for example, to pursue their long range development programs without serious setback. So the absence of an emergency or crisis in these countries would be an indication of IDA's value.

IDA projects are long range projects, as Barr emphasized. Railroads, ports, and irrigation projects take many years to build and many more years to have an impact in a country. What IDA was really doing when it financed such projects was to rely on past experience in countries that have already developed. IDA was applying this past experience to the underdeveloped parts of the world. Belief that this same process will work in the underdeveloped countries today is ultimately a matter of faith, in Barr's opinion.

Following the hearings before the Subcommittee, the whole Committee on Banking and Currency called Mr. Bullitt back for questioning on January 8, 1964. Much of the same ground was covered that had been discussed before the Subcommittee, and as a result of the discussions in the Committee it was unanimously voted to refer the replenishment measure to the House for favorable action.

House debate on IDA's replenishment was conducted on two days, February 25 and 26, 1964.[7] At the beginning of debate on February 25 Congressman Reuss moved to substitute an amended bill for the one the Committee on Banking and Currency had originally reported. Thus, the members of the House had a printed bill before them but were asked to vote on a substitute which they had not seen. This blunder was the beginning of a string of tactical errors and procedural maladroitness which played no small part in the defeat of the measure. The protagonists in the House debate were on the one side the anti-aid bloc led by Representatives Passman and Gross and on the other side the members of the International Finance Subcommittee.

Passman led the attack with a viscous, blistering, and utterly misleading presentation. He made the following criticisms of further United States participation in IDA. One, the United States was somehow financing the whole replenishment of IDA's funds because it had in the past contributed aid to the Part I countries that were also contributing to IDA. In Passman's view, these European countries were merely channeling U. S. aid back to IDA and American taxpayers were having to carry the full burden. His second criticism was that communist nations would receive aid from IDA. Passman also feared that IDA would loan money to countries which had expropriated American property or annulled American contracts. He argued that IDA would thwart the decisions of Congress to deny loans to socialized projects where there was unnecessary competition with the free enterprise system. Passman felt that somehow appropriations for

IDA would weaken the movement to bring about sounder business practices in the United States Agency for International Development. (It was never quite clear how this last phenomenon would develop.) Passman also expressed fear that IDA lending would be used to subsidize Latin American governments which had not taken steps to implement internal reforms under the Alliance for Progress.

Representative Gross of Iowa seconded Representative Passman in his attack. "How can . . . the members of the House who vote for this deal go back home and explain this to their taxpayers and voters? How can they explain taking $312 million of their money to hand out to a bunch of foreign leeches?"[8]

Representative Howard Smith of Virginia argued that the IDA appropriation was simply a device to restore part of the funds that had been cut from foreign aid in 1963. And he argued that when you added the interest which the United States Government would have to pay on the $312 million, that in reality the Congress was being asked to contribute one billion dollars to IDA.

Representative Reuss and the other supporters of IDA did a pitiful job of refuting Passman's charges. His charges were not analyzed point by point and answered on the spot as they should have been. This caused some members of the House to think there might be some truth to them. The fact that the House was being asked to vote on a substitute measure added a note of confusion to the proceedings. And the fact that the measure came up on the same day the tax bill had been passed amid pledges of economy in government gave it a very bad psychological climate.

In point after point, members of the House raised issues against IDA that were not valid. Representative Adair asked if it was not possible that IDA could finance the Bokaro steel mill in India in spite of the fact that Congress had expressed its disapproval of this operation. Representative Reuss answered that it was technically possible. That is not the case. All of IDA's replenishment funds together could not have financed Bokaro. In addition, IDA and the Bank have not made a practice of loaning money for government-owned steel mills. Adair also asked if IDA didn't get around many of the safeguards which the Congress had written into the Foreign Aid Bill, and Reuss said that some of the safeguards were not operative in IDA. That again is questionable.

The critics of IDA attempted to infer that there was disagreement among the members of the National Advisory Council on International Financial and Monetary Affairs. The inference was made that William McChesney Martin, Chairman of the Board of Governors of the Federal Reserve System, was opposed to increased funds for IDA. Reuss did answer that he had ascertained that all members of the Council endorsed the replenishment.

Some of the supporters of IDA made a good case for expanding its resources. Representative Moorhead emphasized the fact that through IDA the U. S. got the use of the World Bank staff, the most competent men in the field, at a very nominal cost, to administer foreign aid. Representative Wright Patman argued that not only was the World Bank not loosely administered as had been charged, but he pointed to the fact that they had not had one single default on a loan as evidence that it was more on the reactionary side. Representative Boggs decried the weeping and wailing over United States inability to bear the burden of $312 million for IDA. "Has there ever been a country like the United States of America of today? A gross national product of over $600 billion; corporate and personal income at a record never before achieved by . . . any other nation on the face of this earth." Representative Multer expressed his conviction that the overwhelming majority of the American people were willing to help out and hold out a helping hand not only "to the poor fellow at home but also to the poor fellow abroad to help him get on his feet so he can earn enough to attain a decent standard of living." The proponents of the legislation also pointed out the benefit that would be gained by the United States from the greater incomes of countries helped by IDA. The U. S. would be able to sell more to rich countries than they would to poor countries. It was also pointed out that IDA was the one hopeful sign on the international economic horizon amidst the increasing nationalism that seemed to prevail. But despite these pleas, the House voted 208-188 to recommit the IDA bill to the House Committee on Banking and Currency.

THE MOVE TO RECONSIDER

There was widespread consternation concerning the House vote. The Economist pointed out on March 7, 1964, that the Administration had no choice but to insist on exhuming the bill to replenish IDA, even though a motion to recommit is ordinarily considered the end of a measure. The Economist pointed out that United States failure to ratify this measure would be disastrous for the United States in future international negotiations.[9] Newspapers all across the country editorialized in favor of bringing the bill back before the House. The New York Times pointed out the economic advantages to the U. S. of letting IDA administer a portion of U. S. foreign assistance. A group of 13 international economists wrote a letter to the Times which was printed on March 29, 1964. This group included Professors Machlup, Kindleberger, Halm, Harrod, Scitovsky, Triffin, and others. They pointed out that IDA's defeat was tying the hands of the United States at the United Nations Conference on Trade and Development. They also pointed out the excellence of IDA's past administration. As a result of pressure and the obvious implications for United States prestige if a reversal was not brought about, the Administration succeeded in getting the Committee on Banking and Currency to hold new hearings on March 23 and 24, 1964.[10] This time no Assistant Secretaries were sent. Secretary Dillon and Secretary Rusk made the presentations.

Dillon answered the criticisms of IDA point by point. First, he conceded that the U. S. contribution to IDA was foreign aid and as such was taken account of in the President's budget for foreign aid. He pointed out the really small size of IDA funds as compared to total U. S. aid of $3 billion a year, and he said that the IDA component in United States foreign aid was a particularly valuable segment of that aid, because of the financial policies which had been followed by the World Bank. He pointed out that it was the established policy of the Bank to encourage private enterprise; that these institutions did not make loans to countries which declined compensation for expropriated foreign private property. IDA loans are also for specific projects. So that it would be impossible for IDA money to be used to pay a foreign creditor for his expropriated property. Dillon pointed out that no new commitments of U. S. economic assistance were being made to Part I members of IDA. Thus, the fear that the

U. S. was financing all of IDA's replenishment was unfounded.

Dillon also pointed out that IDA had projects worth $81 million which had been approved and could not be financed because the replenishment had not been authorized. "These are projects which have reached the final stages of planning after many months--and, in some cases, years--of consideration. In many cases, they are key parts of broader development plans, which would have to be reconsidered if the projects do not go forward. This process cannot be turned on and off at random. Lack of continuity means waste and inefficient development."[11]

The question of United States capacity to influence Bank management to follow policies in the U. S. interest was discussed. Dillon argued that the other Part I members had the same interest in sound financial policies as did the United States--they have foreign investments which might be expropriated, also. Thus, the chance of any difference of opinion among the Part I members was considered to be infinitesimal. Dillon pointed out that IDA money would not go to Soviet bloc countries; that no Soviet bloc country was a member of IDA. It would be impossible for a member of IDA to re-lend IDA money to a communist country--because IDA money is tied to specific projects.

As far as Latin America was concerned, Dillon said IDA's policies there were to encourage reform and self-help just as the Alliance for Progress had done. There was no inconsistency with United States policy in this area. He could have added that the World Bank had taken a consistently harder line toward Latin American mal-performance than had the United States. Dillon argued that IDA administration was equal to it not superior to AID administration and pointed out that in many cases World Bank policies had been copied by AID.

He introduced the fact that the World Bank management had reversed its policy on transferring its earnings to IDA and had tentatively agreed to recommend turning over $50 million out of 1963-64 earnings.

Secretary Rusk emphasized that IDA was a complement to U. S. aid activities. He pointed out that the bulk of IDA credits had been to countries where the U. S. had concentrated its efforts, India, Pakistan, Colombia, Chile, China, and Korea. Aid was seen as necessary in order to bridge the gap between the rich and the poor countries. Rusk said that "the need for economic progress in the poorer countries presents the foremost challenge to our existence and to our ability to persevere. Unless we can meet it, our hopes for a decent future on the planet cannot be judged to be bright.

"For political upheavals, arising out of economic despair, inevitably must threaten us all."[12]

The Committee again voted to refer the measure to the House for approval without a dissenting vote. The second House debate on IDA's replenishment took place on May 13, 1964.[13] Several members objected to this second debate and pointed out that normally a motion to recommit a bill is the same as a motion to kill it. There had been an extraordinary amount of maneuvring behind the scenes in order to get the IDA measure before the House a second time. The New York Times reported on March 14, 1964, that a package deal involving several domestic issues had been worked out to ensure passage of the IDA replenishment bill.

The same cast of characters appeared in the second debate that had appeared before, but this time the forces favoring IDA were more capably led. Following the rejection of IDA, former President Eisenhower had written a letter to Republican House members and urged them to vote for IDA's replenishment. In addition, Representative Barry of New York had held a meeting of members who had opposed the bill and had gotten Secretary Dillon to clear up the misconceptions which had existed. All of this work showed up in the debate when earlier charges were answered.

The opponents had not been idle. Representative McClory of Illinois had circulated a letter to members of the House which had raised several questions about IDA. Most of these questions were of the same ilk as had been discussed in the previous debate. The arguments that were brought up against IDA had an implausible ring to them and were refuted on the floor of the House. The vote for passage of the bill was 247-132.

One must comment upon the extreme good fortune that IDA has had in the quality of her enemies. Upon being proposed by Senator Monroney, the main critic was Senator Homer Capehart of Indiana. Having Senator Capehart arguing against IDA was like having two people arguing in favor of IDA. When IDA came back up in the Senate it was Senator Morse who attacked it. In the House debate, the opposition was led by Representatives Passman, Gross and Smith. As long as IDA continues to be opposed by these people, it would seem that its future is assured.

CHAPTER 14 THE FUTURE OF THE INTERNATIONAL DEVELOPMENT ASSOCIATION

What are IDA's prospects? How significant will it be? As has been pointed out, IDA will be contributing no more than 5 per cent of the capital flowing into the underdeveloped countries. Of the more than 100 countries which are considered to be underdeveloped (those countries having per capita incomes of less than $500 per year) IDA had contributed $590 million to 22 countries as of June 30, 1964. These countries contained almost a billion people. Thus, IDA loans amounted to less than $1 per person in the countries that had received loans. How could lending on this scale be significant?

One attempt to make IDA funds have the greatest possible impact was the decision to finance pilot projects in the underdeveloped countries. Such pilot projects are now underway in the fields of education and agriculture. It is hoped that these projects will point the way for similar projects on the part of other institutions and bilateral agencies.

IDA has already had an impact in that it has set the pattern on terms that has been adopted by the United States Agency for International Development and the Inter-American Development Bank's Social Project Trust Fund. The innovation was the combination of low interest rates to countries with balance of payments problems combined with the going rate of interest to the project within the country.

IDA financing has also been a stimulus to additional investment from other sources. Table 8 indicates that IDA funds going into projects as of February 20, 1964, amounted to $591 million. In addition, the borrowing country had put up $1,269

TABLE 8. --Sources of financing in connection with International Development Association credits through February 29, 1964
(in millions of dollars or equivalent)

Country	IDA Credit	Borrower's Own Resources	Other Financing[a]	Total Project Cost
Chile	19.0	37.5	--	56.5
China	15.3	15.0	--	29.9
Colombia	19.5	59.8	19.5	98.8
Costa Rica	5.5	10.9	5.5	21.9
El Salvador	8.0	5.5	--	13.5
Ethiopia	13.5	9.7	--	23.2
Haiti	.4	.6	--	1.0
Honduras	9.0	2.0	2.5	13.5
India	300.0	937.8	105.2	1,343.0
Jordan	8.5	4.3	--	12.8
Korea	14.0	13.2	--	27.2
Nicaragua	3.0	3.0	--	6.0
Pakistan	91.5	79.7	--	171.2
Paraguay	9.6	4.4	--	14.0
Sudan	13.0	36.7	37.9	87.6
Syria	8.5	5.5	--	14.0
Tanganyika	18.6	6.2	--	24.8
Tunisia	5.0	4.2	--	9.2
Turkey	26.7	30.6	--	57.3
Swaziland	2.8	2.4	--	5.2
Total	591.4	1,269.0	170.6	2,031.0
Percent	29	62	9	100

[a] Includes financing from International Bank for Reconstruction a[nd] Development, Inter-American Development Bank, aid from Unite[d] States and other countries, etc.

Source: Adapted from House Subcommittee of the Committee on Appropriations, Hearings on Foreign Operations Appropriations for 1965, March 17, 1964, p. 62.

million of its own resources and had obtained $170.6 million from other sources. Thus, IDA financing had played a crucial role in projects having a total cost of more than $2 billion.

IDA is an ideal answer for those small industrialized nations that want to contribute foreign aid but do not want or cannot afford to set up their own bilateral institutions. Sweden has made several supplemental contributions to IDA since it has been established. The Swedes are convinced that this is a better way than having a small bilateral program of their own. There is some indication that this idea might spread.

Several of the smaller developed nations are expressing increased interest in foreign aid. Norway instituted a special tax in 1963 whose proceeds are earmarked for foreign aid. In Denmark, the Government's contribution to foreign aid has been associated with a public fund-raising campaign initiated by non-governmental organizations.[1] Such countries are likely prospects to increase their contribution to IDA. The Netherlands has decided to restrict its foreign aid activities to those countries for which the Bank and IDA have organized consortia or consultative groups.[2] Although the funds are not channeled through IDA, this decision has the effect of making IDA the arbiter of which countries will receive foreign assistance and which will not.

Two of the Part II countries agreed to make their total subscription available for use in 1964. Ireland and Israel announced such decisions at the Annual Meeting held in Tokyo in September, 1964. Other countries which might take similar steps in the future would be Iceland, Yugoslavia, and Spain. At the 1963 meetings, the IDA Governor for India raised the possibility that India might make her local currency contribution available to finance development in other countries. Steps such as these are a realization of the goal which Senator Monroney had for IDA when he argued in 1958 that the underdeveloped countries could help each other and be better off for having done so.

The management of the Bank agreed to contribute $50 million of its earnings to IDA during 1964. This source of funds will undoubtedly grow in the future. Assuming that $750 million had been committed by June 30, 1964, the staff of IDA projected amortization payments of $23 million per year by 1987. (See Table 9). Now that IDA will have an additional $750 million to

TABLE 9.--International Development Association estimate of development credit amortizations assuming all funds committed by June 30, 1964
(Expressed in millions of U. S. dollars)

Payment Dates	Credit Amortizations	Payment Dates	Credit Amortizations
1972	2.10	1992	23.30
1977	7.78	1997	23.30
1982	11.98	2002	23.32
1987	23.30	2007	23.32

Source: Adapted from House Subcommittee of the Committee on Appropriations, Hearings on Foreign Operations Appropriations for 1965, March 17, 1964, p. 73.

commit by 1966, repayments will be almost double that amount. If additional replenishments are made which enable IDA to continue committing $300 million a year, then repayments will be greatly increased. Thus, it is possible that with grants from the Bank and with its own repayments coming in that IDA might be self-financing by the end of the twentieth century. For many years to come, however, it is going to have to look to the rich countries for funds. What will be the response of those countries?

The President of IDA proposed that negotiations for replenishment be re-opened in his speech to the 1964 meeting of the Board of Governors. The success of these negotiations depends in large part upon the attitude of the United States. And the United States attitude will be determined in large part by the United States balance of payments position. Although IDA funds are a minute portion of the total U. S. aid program, Congress has attacked IDA on its balance of payments impact. Unless equilibrium can be attained in the U. S. balance of payments it is not likely that a position of leadership will be taken in the negotiations.

When we compare the figures on disbursements in Table 10 with the figures on contributions in Table 7 we find that Japan contributed 4.5 per cent of IDA's original resources, 5.5 per cent of the replenishment, and received 31.4 per cent of IDA disbursements. The United Kingdom contributed 17.6 per cent of original resources, 12.8 per cent of the replenishment, and received 16.6 per cent of IDA's disbursements. Belgium contributed nothing originally, contributed 2.2 per cent of the replenishment, and received 3.5 per cent of IDA's disbursements. Canada contributed 5.09 per cent originally, 5.5 per cent of the replenishment, and received 6.2 per cent of IDA's disbursements. The share of IDA disbursements going to Italy, the Netherlands, and Sweden was also higher than their share in funding IDA. The other member countries, France, Germany, Australia, Austria, Finland, Kuwait, Norway, South Africa, and the United States all received lower shares in the disbursements than their share in the funding of IDA.

The balance of payments question raises the possibility of tying contributions to IDA. The United States has generally received approximately 30 per cent of World Bank purchases of

TABLE 10. --Source of supply by country for all International Development Association disbursements as of June 30, 1964
(millions of U. S. dollars)

Country	Amount	Percent of Total
Belgium	4.4	3.5
Canada	7.7	6.2
France	5.2	4.2
Germany	8.1	6.5
Italy	4.3	3.4
Japan	39.1	31.4
Netherlands	4.8	3.8
Sweden	3.6	2.9
Switzerland	2.2	1.8
United Kingdom	20.7	16.6
United States	18.4	14.8
All other countries	6.1	4.9
Total*	124.6	100.0

*In addition some $67.8 million was expended in local-other disbursements.

Source: Treasurer's Office, International Bank for Reconstruction and Development.

goods and services. But, IDA had made only 15 per cent of its identifiable disbursements in the United States through June 30, 1964. When it is remembered that the United States contributed 40 per cent of IDA's funds, this indicates that only $4 out of every $10 contributed have been returned to the United States. Could part of the United States contribution to IDA be tied in some way? Could IDA award contracts on the basis of international competition and then require the country that won the contract to put up the funds for the project? Such a scheme would appeal to the countries that have received a very small part of IDA expenditures but it would make administration of IDA funds an enormously complicated task. These facts will, no doubt, be taken into consideration when apportioning new shares for IDA but whether a tying arrangement will be possible or not is unclear. It is clear, however, that the underdeveloped countries realize the necessity to arrange aid on such a basis that it has the minimum adverse impact on the rich countries' balance of payments. Several of the Governors from the poor nations made this the point of their speeches in the annual meetings that followed the balance of payments crisis in the United States.

A second source of Congressional irritation concerning IDA's replenishment was the feeling that the United States share was too large. It will be remembered that the United States had contributed 43.12 per cent of IDA's initial convertible currency resources and 41.6 per cent of the replenishment. Judging from the Congressional debate on IDA the objection was not so much to the fact that the United States was contributing $312 million to IDA, but that this was over 40 per cent of the total replenishment! This is a ridiculous attitude. It is hoped that in the next round of negotiations the Administration will seek tentative agreement with the leadership of Congress on the total size of the United States contribution to IDA and will contribute that amount no matter what share of the total it is. It seems absurd to get so bogged down on what is a fair share that the total funds available to IDA get reduced.

It will be remembered that one of the original proposals for raising money for SUNFED included raising funds through voluntary contributions. This proposal has never been tried but it ought to be. The World Bank has always thought of itself as primarily a business institution and has discounted and minimized any aspects of do-goodism about its operations. Thus, it would never have considered the idea of conducting fund-raising campaigns among the masses of the developed countries. It could raise all the money it needed from the capital markets of the rich countries by selling bonds of large denomination. But, with IDA the Bank has begun to lose some of its austere air. It might as well lose the rest of it and admit that IDA is essentially a do-good institution. IDA should seek voluntary contributions from the citizens of the rich countries. These contributions could take the form of non-interest bearing bonds or could be gifts. Such contributions should be made tax-deductible by the governments of the rich nations. What would this accomplish? First, it would raise a lot of money. Properly conceived and executed such campaigns could be enormously successful. Secondly, it would get the citizens of the rich countries personally involved in the process of economic development in the poor countries. This would be no small achievement. It would be an ennobling experience if they could feel that they had some part in lifting the grinding poverty in Asia, in Africa, in South America. The great success of the Peace Corps in the United States has proven that there is idealism waiting to be tapped. IDA should become a vehicle for channeling this idealism into this area of such great need.

CHANGES IN POLICY

Some indications of more flexible policies were given by the new President of the Association, George D. Woods, in his first address to the Board of Governors in September, 1963. Further indications were given in his 1964 address to the Governors.

Mr. Woods started his term as President on a note of optimism. In his 1963 address, he pointed out that over the last fifteen years the industrial production of the underdeveloped countries had risen 2 1/2 times and that agricultural production had risen by almost 40 per cent. Compared with any period in history this was a notable accomplishment.[3] In his address in 1964, Woods' outlook was less rosy. In this address he stated that although a few of the developing countries were making remarkable headway, in most of them population increases had meant that there had not been any improvement in living standards.[4] Despite the change in tone from 1963 to 1964, one aspect of Woods' approach remained unchanged, and that was his willingness to experiment.

In 1963, he proposed that the Bank move into the field of agriculture. Agriculture employs the great bulk of the population in underdeveloped countries. It provides materials and generates demands for goods which are basic to industrialization. Thus, the Bank staff had decided to help finance storage facilities and farm-to-market roads, and to strengthen agricultural organizations to extend credit and technical assistance to farmers. In line with this decision, the Bank and IDA entered into an agreement with the Food and Agriculture Organization (FAO) during 1964. Under these arrangements the organizations will work together to identify and prepare projects for financing. If the Bank or IDA finances agricultural projects, FAO will cooperate in supervising them and in arranging technical assistance. By the time of the annual meetings in 1964, 21 agricultural projects were under consideration.

Woods indicated that he wanted to make industrial financing available on a considerably more flexible basis than it had been in the past. One goal of this change would be to help countries diversify their economies so as to overcome their terrible dependence on one or two commodities for foreign exchange. One result of this changed policy has been mentioned earlier--the shift from complete reliance on projects. The first example of this change was an IDA loan to India to finance the importation of capital equipment, raw materials, and components which were necessary to utilize fully existing industrial plants. Another example of changed policy was the decision to seek approval of a change in the Bank's charter to enable it to loan money to its subsidiary, the International Finance Corporation, so that the IFC could make more loans for industrial concerns without the necessity for a country guarantee of the loan. The third change was a decision to finance local currency expenditures in connection with projects. The new criterion in selection of projects will be the extent of their contribution to the economic development of the country concerned, regardless of whether the costs involve foreign exchange or local currency.

The third area to receive new attention was education. Woods announced in 1963 that the Bank itself would lend for school facilities. Primary attention would be directed toward technical education, but some loans for general secondary education would be approved. To implement this decision an agreement was reached with the United Nations Educational, Scientific and Cultural Organization (UNESCO) in June, 1964. UNESCO will provide experts to help choose projects for financing and will assist countries in the preparation of projects for submission to the Bank and IDA. UNESCO will also help in supervising projects financed and will provide technical assistance. By September, 1964, some 9 educational projects were being actively considered.

The most dramatic changes in policy did not come about in the types of projects to be financed, however. The really exciting aspects of the 1963-1964 meetings involved what the Canadian Governor called "an interesting raising of the Bank's hemline of bankability." The Bank agreed in 1963 to explore changing the terms of its loans and to explore the question of turning over some of its reserves to IDA. In 1964 the decisions were announced. Some $50 million of the Bank's earnings in fiscal year 1963-64 were turned over to IDA. And, the Bank agreed to extended grace periods in some cases and to lengthened terms for its loans in other cases. Liberia received the first extended grace period (8 years) loan in January, 1964, and Colombia got a 35 year loan in February, 1964. Thus, precedents had been shattered and the old order had truly passed.

Some lines along which other changes might occur were suggested at recent meetings of the Board of Governors. Not only were the types of projects undergoing change, but the Bank's clientele has also been changing. Several countries that have received enormous Bank loans, France, Japan, Belgium, have passed the point of needing to rely on Bank financing. But, as some nations leave, others have been added. Spain, New Zealand, and Portugal have all received their first Bank loans recently. But, many of the new nations are not going to be able to afford Bank terms for some time and it is to IDA that they will have to turn. The African nations, in particular, have asked the Bank and IDA to alter their policies to suit African needs. They have suggested that the Bank should establish a regional office in Africa. They have asked for and gotten a new seat on the Board of Executive Directors to represent Africa. They have asked the Bank to reduce the size of the projects financed so that the small nations can take advantage of Bank and IDA financing. They have asked for cooperation in financing the African Development Bank.

The Bank's relationships with the United Nations were undergoing changes, also. Although the Bank is a related institution, it has always enjoyed independence from the United Nations. During the early years of its life the Bank eyed the U. N. with suspicion and saw SUNFED and other proposals as attempts to eliminate the Bank and substitute United Nations control over the financing of economic development. Recently relations have become more cordial between the institutions. IDA entered into an agreement with the U. N. establishing a liaison committee consisting of the Secretary General of the United Nations, the Managing Director of the United Nations Special Fund, the Executive Director of the United Nations Technical Assistance Board, and the President of the International Development Association. There has been a growing amount of cooperation between IDA and the Special Fund in the field of technical assistance and in drawing up projects. There have been numerous cases where the Special Fund has contracted for the services of the Bank staff to make project appraisals.

At the United Nations Conference on Trade and Development (UNCTAD) held in Geneva in early 1964, the Bank took a bold and enterprising approach to the problems of the underdeveloped countries. There was an obvious sense of rapport between the delegates from the poor nations and the representatives of the Bank. There was little evidence of such rapport between the poor nations and the International Monetary Fund. Thus, the two international economic organizations seem to have chosen their roles. The IMF will support the interests of the rich nations and endeavor to fight inflation, barter agreements, and unorthodoxies of all kinds. The Bank is willing to experiment and innovate in the interest of the poor nations. The Conference asked the Bank staff to undertake several studies to which the Bank agreed. First, the Bank agreed to study a plan to raise funds in the private capital markets which will be loaned to the developing countries at long term and low interest, with the rich governments guaranteeing the borrowing operations and subsidizing the interest costs. This is the Horowitz Plan which has been discussed earlier. Another study would look into the feasibility of establishing a system for assisting countries with declining export earnings due to long-term factors beyond their control. A third study would look into the use and terms of suppliers' credits and into schemes for financing exports from developing countries. A multilateral investment insurance scheme will also be investigated. This willingness to experiment raises interesting questions about the long-run role of the Bank and IDA.

THE SIGNIFICANCE OF THE INTERNATIONAL DEVELOPMENT ASSOCIATION

Perhaps we can gain some insight into the future role of IDA if we place it in its historical context. In one sense, the history of mankind has been a history of institution-building. The earliest cave men had very rudimentary social institutions which provided no solutions for many problems men had in living together. Social order was maintained by club and fang. In neolithic societies the social order had been improved. More people were able to survive. Life was less subject to violence. Some codes of behavior had been drawn up which were binding on members of the tribe. With the development of urban civilization we see these codes made applicable to greater and greater numbers of people. Institutions had been developed for dealing with problems of violence, crime, and other social disorders. The history of the last 500 years is a history of extending these institutions to wider and wider areas: the growth of nation-states to replace the old city-states, the extension of laws and rules to wider and wider aspects of behavior, the increase in productivity which made it possible for more and more people to live to maturity, the development of techniques which could make it possible for all members of society to have adequate food, clothing and shelter. In the twentieth century we have seen the development of the concept of universal institutions. The advent of world wide depressions, world wars, nuclear weapons, missiles, etc. has made the nation-state an unworkable political institution. Just as earlier technological developments made the manor an indefensible political unit, so today we have seen the nation-state outmoded.

New institutions were called for. The League of Nations was established when it had become obvious that existing institutions could not deal with international problems. The League had little economic significance and was made politically impotent by the failure to recognize its necessity. After a world-wide depression and another world war had demonstrated the complete inability of existing institutions to cope with contemporary problems, a second attempt at constructing international institutions was made. This time, with the establishment of the United Nations, the economic factors in international life were not ignored. No longer would the world trust the impersonal mechanism of the international gold standard. An international institution, the International Monetary Fund, was created to organize the world payments mechanism. And no reliance was placed on profit-seeking privately-owned capital to reconstruct and develop a war-torn and weary world. No, an international institution, the International Bank for Reconstruction and Development was created to allocate capital. But even this was not the end of innovation. In 1960, another international institution was created, the International Development Association. And, in some ways, this was the most radical and revolutionary step of all. For, this organization was designed to re-distribute wealth from the rich to the poor on a world-wide scale. The implications were enormous. Taxpayers in Europe and the United States agreed to contribute funds to an international agency which would then turn around and distribute them to the nations living in poverty. A truly revolutionary departure!

How will it work? Is there a precedent for such a thing? A useful analogy can be made to developments in the domestic economies of Western Europe and the United States in the past half-century. Marx had predicted that the rich would grow richer and the poor poorer in capitalistic economies. Why didn't his prediction come true? For one simple reason. The capitalists learned that in order to sell goods to the poor and make profits, the poor had to be able to buy the goods. Henry Ford is the prime example of this type thinking. He realized that by paying higher wages he would be able to sell more cars and make more profits. Governmental mechanisms were brought into play, also. The income tax was designed to take more from the rich than the poor--in effect, to redistribute income. Especially with the innovation of the welfare state do we find wealth being transferred through governmental actions. And what was the result of all this? The rich got even richer! The poor improved their lot, true enough, but the rich improved their lot, also.

The International Development Association is an attempt to apply this lesson on the international scene. For it is designed to do nothing if not to transfer wealth from rich to poor. And the rich are contributing to it in the belief that the domestic analogy will hold true internationally. They believe that by improving the lot of the poor, the rich will become even richer.

The proposals made at the United Nations Conference on Trade and Development to pay the underdeveloped countries more for their products are the other half of the story. One could almost hear the ghost of Henry Ford echoing through the Conference--"if you pay them more, you'll be able to sell them more."

In this context it can be seen that IDA is not an insignificant act taken in a fit of absence of mind. No, it represents another step in the long struggle to develop institutions which will enable people to live lives which are not nasty, brutish, and short. The question before the world today is whether the rich nations have the wit and the will to bring peaceful progress to all mankind. Will the Marxian prediction come true on the international scene? Certainly the current trend is in that direction. The hope for a change in direction lies in such institutions as the International Development Association.

CHAPTER 1

1. Estimates of per capita incomes (GDP) and annual rates of growth came from Yearbook of National Accounts Statistics, (United Nations, New York, 1964), pp. 322, 323, and 318, 319. Indian growth rate was computed using the years 1953-60, and U.S. rate was based on 1953-61.

2. The estimates of Soviet output as a percentage of U.S. output came from: U.S., Congress, Joint Economic Committee, Hearings, Comparisons of the United States and Soviet Economies, 86th Cong., 1st Sess., 1959, p. 4, and U.S., Congress, Joint Economic Committee, Annual Economic Indicators for the U.S.S.R., 88th Cong., 2nd Sess., 1964, p. 92.

3. James Morris, The Road to Huddersfield: A Journey to Five Continents (New York: Pantheon Books, 1963), p. 22.

4. Edward Bellamy was one exception to this statement.

5. For further discussion on this point see Robert Heilbroner, The Future as History, and Gerard Piel, "For the Living Generation," Nature, Vol. 202 (April 11, 1964), pp. 120-124.

6. James A. Robinson, The Monroney Resolution: Congressional Initiative in Foreign Policy Making (Eagleton Institute Cases in Practical Politics, Case 8; McGraw-Hill, 1960).

7. Andrew Shonfield, The Attack on World Poverty (New York: Vintage Books, 1960), p. 156.

8. The studies referred to are as follows:

Dragoslav Avramovic, Debt Servicing Capacity and Postwar Growth in International Indebtedness (Baltimore: The Johns Hopkins Press, 1958).

Dragoslav Avramovic and Ravi Gulhati, Debt Servicing Problems of Low-Income Countries, 1956-1958 (Baltimore: The Johns Hopkins Press, 1960).

Dragoslav Avramovic *et al*, *Economic Growth and External Debt* (to be published by Johns Hopkins Press, 1965).

9. Eugene R. Black, *The Diplomacy of Economic Development* (Cambridge: Harvard University Press, 1960) and Morris, *The Road to Huddersfield*.

CHAPTER 2

1. Background information for this chapter has been obtained from two sources not otherwise mentioned. The first, B. E. Matecki, Establishment of the International Finance Corporation and United States Policy (New York: Frederick A. Praeger, 1957), describes the establishment of a sister organization of the International Development Association, within the World Bank group. This study also contains a discussion of proposals for IDA within the United Nations. The second, John G. Hadwen and Johan Kaufmann, How United Nations Decisions are Made (Leyden: A. W. Sythoff, 1961), discusses proposals for SUNFED and the United Nations Special Fund.

2. United Nations, Economic and Social Council, Sub-Commission on Economic Development, Report of the Third Session of the Sub-Commission on Economic Development (E/CN.1/65, April 12, 1949) (New York, 1949), p. 18.

3. Ibid., p. 22.

4. Ibid.

5. Ibid., p. 14.

6. Ibid.

7. United Nations, Department of Economic Affairs, Methods of Financing Economic Development in Under-Developed Countries (1949.II.B.4) (Lake Success, 1949), pp. 78-79.

8. Ibid., p. 80.

9. Ibid., p. 141.

10. Ibid., p. 143.

11. Ibid., p. 99.

12. United Nations, Department of Economic Affairs, _Measures for the Economic Development of Under-Developed Countries_ (E/1986/ST/ECA/10, 3 May 1951) (New York, 1951).

13. _Ibid._, p. 84.

14. _Ibid._,

15. _Ibid._, pp. 85-86.

16. _Ibid._, p. 87.

17. _Summary Proceedings of the 1951 Meeting of the Board of Governors of the International Bank for Reconstruction and Development_ (Washington: IBRD, 1951), p. 6.

18. _Summary Proceedings of the 1952 Meeting of the Board of Governors of the International Bank for Reconstruction and Development_ (Washington: IBRD, 1952), p. 9.

19. _Summary Proceedings of the 1951 Meeting. . ._, pp. 7-10.

20. _Ibid._, p. 10.

21. United Nations, Department of Economic Affairs, _Report on a Special United Nations Fund for Economic Development--Submitted by a Committee Appointed by the Secretary-General_ (E/2381, 18 March 1953) (New York, 1953), p. 12.

22. _Ibid._, p. 10.

23. Interview with Shirley Boskey, Development Services Staff, IBRD, January 24, 1963.

24. _United Nations Report on a Special United Nations Fund for Economic Development_, p. 20.

25. United Nations, General Assembly, _Special United Nations Fund for Economic Development_ (A/2728, August 10, 1954) (New York, 1954).

26. _Ibid._, p. 10.

27. _Ibid._, pp. 15-16.

28. United Nations, General Assembly, Special United Nations Fund for Economic Development (A/2906, May 23, 1955) (New York, 1955), p. 4.

29. Interview with an official of the U. S. Treasury Department, January 17, 1963.

30. Interview with Eugene R. Black, March 13, 1963.

31. Shonfield, p. 100.

32. Harlan Cleveland in an Introduction to Commander Sir Robert G. A. Jackson, The Case for an International Development Authority (Syracuse: Syracuse University Press, 1959), p. 11.

33. Ibid.

34. Shonfield, p. 101.

35. Frederic Benham, Economic Aid to Underdeveloped Countries (London: Oxford University Press, 1961), pp. 106-107.

36. Interview, March 13, 1963.

37. Benjamin Higgins, United Nations and U. S. Foreign Economic Policy (Homewood, Illinois: Richard D. Irwin, Inc., 1962), pp. 89-90.

38. United Nations, Conference on Trade and Development, Final Act of the United Nations Conference on Trade and Development (E/CONF. 46/L. 28, 16 June 1964) (Geneva, 1964), p. 94.

39. Ibid., p. 96.

CHAPTER 3

1. Gordon Gray, Report to the President on Foreign Economic Policies (Washington: U. S. Government Printing Office, November 10, 1950), p. 17.

2. Harlan Cleveland in an Introduction to Commander Sir Robert G. A. Jackson, The Case for an International Development Authority, p. 7.

3. Partners in Progress--A Report to the President by the International Development Advisory Board (Washington: U. S. Government Printing Office, March, 1951), p. 71.

4. Ibid., p. 72.

5. Ibid., pp. 72-75.

6. Ibid., p. 74.

7. Ibid., p. 75.

8. Letter from Stacy May, May 14, 1963.

9. (Garden City, New York: Doubleday & Company, Inc.)

10. Ibid., p. 61.

11. Ibid., p. 146.

12. Interview with an official of the U. S. Treasury Department, January 17, 1963.

13. Ibid.,

14. Ibid.,

15. Interview with U. S. Senator A. S. Mike Monroney, January 25, 1963.

16. Manila Daily Bulletin, November 24, 1956, p. 1.

17. Interview with U. S. Senator A. S. Mike Monroney, January 25, 1963.

18. Information on the sequence of events leading up to the passage of the Monroney Resolution comes from James A. Robinson, The Monroney Resolution: Congressional Initiative in Foreign Policy Making (Eagleton Institute: Cases in Practical Politics, Case 8; McGraw-Hill Book Company, 1960).

19. U. S., Congress, Senate, Subcommittee of the Committee on Banking and Currency, Hearings on S. Res. 264 (International Development Association), 85th Cong., 2d Sess., 1958, p. 167.

20. Interview with an official of the U. S. Treasury Department, March 12, 1963.

21. Senate Subcommittee on Banking and Currency, Hearings on S. Res. 264, 1958, p. 1.

22. Ibid., pp. 5-6.

23. Congressional Record, February 24, 1958, pp. 2261-7 as quoted in Senate Subcommittee on Banking and Currency, Hearings on S. Res. 264, 1958, p. 13.

24. Senate Subcommittee on Banking and Currency, Hearings on S. Res. 264, 1958, p. 176.

25. Ibid., p. 4.

26. Congressional Record, February 24, 1958, pp. 2261-7 as quoted in Senate Subcommittee on Banking and Currency, Hearings on S. Res. 264, 1958, p. 8.

27. Senate Subcommittee on Banking and Currency, Hearings on S. Res. 264, 1958, p. 78.

28. Ibid., p. 81.

29. Congressional Record, February 24, 1958, pp. 2261-7 as quoted in Senate Subcommittee on Banking and Currency, Hearings on S. Res. 264, 1958, p. 11.

30. Ibid.

31. Senate Subcommittee on Banking and Currency, Hearings on S. Res. 264, 1958, p. 87.

32. Ibid., p. 137.

33. Ibid.

34. Ibid., p. 177.

35. Ibid., p. 76.

36. Ibid., p. 77.

37. Ibid., pp. 80-81.

38. Ibid., p. 145.

39. Ibid., p. 82.

CHAPTER 4

1. Avramovic, Debt-Servicing Capacity and Postwar Growth in International Indebtedness.
Avramovic and Gulhati, Debt Servicing Problems of Low-Income Countries.
Avramovic et al., Economic Growth and External Debt.

2. Avramovic, p. 17.

3. Ibid., p. 20.

4. Ibid., p. 147.

5. Ibid., p. 58.

6. Ibid., pp. 61-62.

7. Ibid., p. 79.

8. Ibid., p. 95.

9. Ibid.

10. Avramovic and Gulhati, p. 10.

11. Ibid., p. 28.

12. Ibid., pp. 40-44.

13. Ibid., pp. 18-20.

14. Avramovic and Gulhati, Table III and Appendix Table XXI, p. 19 and p. 73.

15. Ibid., p. 54.

16. Ibid., p. 59.

17. Ibid.

18. *Ibid.*

19. Leonard Rist, "The Capacity to Service Foreign Debts"-A lecture presented to the Economic Development Institute of the International Bank for Reconstruction and Development (IBRD) July 9, 1962 (Washington: IBRD, 1962) p. 10. (Mimeographed.)

20. Shonfield, p. 97.

21. *Ibid.*, p. 30

22. S. J. Patel, "Export Prospects and Economic Growth: India," *The Economic Journal,* LXIX (September, 1959), 501.

23. Shonfield, p. 30.

24. *Ibid.*

25. Robert E. Asher, *Grants, Loans, and Local Currencies* (Washington: The Brookings Institution, 1961), p. 97.

26. IBRD Board of Governors Press Release No. 5, September 19, 1961, pp. 2-3.

27. IBRD Board of Governors Press Release No. 16, September 18, 1962, p. 2.

28. Asher, p. 97.

29. V. K. R. V. Rao, *International Aid for Economic Development--Possibilities and Limitations* (The University of Leeds Eighteenth Montague Burton Lecture on International Relations, 1960), pp. 15-16.

30. Interview with Eugene Black, March 13, 1963.

31. Richard H. Demuth, "Statement on Behalf of the International Bank for Reconstruction and Development Before the Economic, Employment and Development Commission" (Washington IBRD, 1951), p. 10. (Mimeographed.)

32. *Summary Proceedings of the 1959 Meeting of the Board of Governors of the International Bank for Reconstruction and Development* (Washington: IBRD, 1959), p. 10.

33. Eugene R. Black, The Diplomacy of Economic Development, pp. 44-45.

34. Ibid., p. 55.

35. Ibid., pp. 55-56.

36. Ibid., p. 56.

37. United Nations, General Assembly, Special United Nations Fund for Economic Development (A/2906, May 23, 1955) (New York, 1955), p. 18.

38. Interview with an official of the International Bank for Reconstruction and Development, March 8, 1963.

39. Report of the Executive Directors of the International Bank for Reconstruction and Development on the Articles of Agreement of the International Development Association (Washington: IBRD, 1960), p. 7.

40. Interview with Eugene R. Black, March 13, 1963.

41. Ibid.

42. Interview with an official of the IBRD, March 15, 1963.

43. Shonfield, p. 99.

44. (Washington: IBRD, 1958), p. 6.

45. Summary Proceedings of the 1958 Annual Meeting of the Board of Governors of the International Bank for Reconstruction and Development (Washington: IBRD, 1958), p. 13.

46. Ibid., p. 14.

47. Senate Subcommittee on Banking and Currency, Hearings on S. Res. 264, 1958, p. 141.

48. U.S., Congress, House, Subcommittee of the Committee on Appropriations, Hearings, Foreign Operations Appropriations for 1962, 87th Cong., 1st Sess., 1961, p. 97.

49. *Ibid.*, pp. 98-99.

50. Alan D. Neale, *The Flow of Resources from Rich to Poor* (Harvard University Center for International Affairs Occasional Papers in International Affairs Number 2; Cambridge: Harvard University, 1961), pp. 98-99.

51. Organization for Economic Co-operation and Development (OECD) *Development Assistance Efforts and Policies in 1961* (Paris: OECD), September, 1962), p. 23.

52. Commander Sir Robert G. A. Jackson, *The Case for an International Development Authority* (Syracuse: Syracuse University Press, 1959), pp. 41-42.

53. Barbara Ward, "Imagination in Development," *Restless Nations* (New York: Dodd, Mead & Company, 1962), pp. 197-198.

54. Barbara Ward, "New Perspectives," *Restless Nations*, p. 67.

CHAPTER 5

1. *Semiannual Report of the National Advisory Council on International Monetary and Financial Problems for the Period January 1 through June 30, 1960* (Washington: U.S. Government Printing Office, 1961), Table C-9, p. 73.

2. Interview with an official of the U. S. Treasury Department, January 17, 1963.

3. Interview with an official of the IBRD, January 22, 1963.

4. *Dayton Daily News,* March 1, 1958 as quoted in Senate Subcommittee on Banking and Currency, *Hearings on S. Res. 264,* 1958, p. 35.

5. *Des Moines Register,* March 24, 1958 as quoted in Senate Subcommittee on Banking and Currency, *Hearings on S. Res. 264,* 1958, p. 44.

6. Peter B. Kenen, *Giant Among Nations* (Chicago: Rand McNally & Company, 1963), pp. 175-176.

7. *Congressional Record,* February 24, 1958, pp. 2261-7 as quoted in Senate Subcommittee on Banking and Currency, *Hearings on S. Res. 264,* 1958, p. 11.

8. Senate Subcommittee on Banking and Currency, *Hearings on S. Res. 264,* 1958, pp. 58-59.

9. *Ibid.*, p. 59.

10. *Ibid.*, p. 60.

11. *Ibid.*, p. 143.

12. *Ibid.*, p. 175.

13. *Ibid.*, p. 123.

14. _Ibid._, p. 124.

15. _Ibid._, p. 136.

16. IBRD Board of Governors Press Release No. 10, September 30, 1959, p. 3.

17. Shonfield, pp. 39-40.

18. IBRD Board of Governors Press Release No. 60, September 30, 1959, p. 4.

19. IBRD Board of Governors Press Release No. 68, September 30, 1959, pp. 2-3.

20. IBRD Board of Governors Press Release No. 47, September 30, 1959, p. 2.

21. IBRD Board of Governors Press Release No. 65, September 30, 1959, pp. 4-5.

22. _Articles of Agreement of the International Development Association_ (Washington: IDA, 1960), p. 7.

23. Interview, January 22, 1963.

24. Personal letter from J. Burke Knapp, June 25, 1963.

CHAPTER 6

1. Alec Cairncross, The International Bank for Reconstruction and Development (Princeton University Essays in International Finance No. 33, March, 1959), p. 27.

2. IDA Board of Governors Press Release No. 32, September 19, 1961, p. 2.

3. Leonard Rist, "International Cooperation in Development Aid," Address to the fourth SEANZA Meeting (Washington: IBRD, 1962), pp. 16-17. (Mimeographed.)

4. Geoffrey M. Wilson, World Bank Operations (Address before the Economic Commission of the Council of Europe, Paris, December 16, 1963) (Washington: IBRD, 1963), pp. 9-10.

5. U. S., Senate, Committee on Foreign Relations, United States Foreign Policy--Compilation of Studies, "The Operational Aspects of United States Foreign Policy" by Maxwell Graduate School of Citizenship and Public Affairs, Syracuse University (Washington: U. S. Government Printing Office, March 15, 1961), p. 565.

6. Ibid., pp. 598-599.

7. Herbert Feis, Foreign Aid and Foreign Policy (New York: St. Martin's Press, 1964), p. 216.

8. Paul G. Hoffman, "Priorities of Economic Development," Restless Nations, p. 96.

9. Raymond F. Mikesell, "Problems and Policies in Public Lending for Economic Development," U. S. Private and Government Investment Abroad, ed. Raymond F. Mikesell (Eugene, Oregon: University of Oregon Books, 1962), p. 350.

10. Organization for Economic Co-Operation and Development, Development Assistance Efforts and Policies 1963 Review (Paris: OECD, 1963), pp. 79-81.

11. Interview, January 17, 1963.

12. Mikesell, "Problems and Policies in Public Lending for Economic Development," U. S. Private and Government Investment Abroad, pp. 351-352.

13. U. S., Congress, Senate, Special Committee to Study the Foreign Aid Program, Foreign Aid Program, "Administrative Aspects of United States Foreign Assistance Programs," by the Brookings Institution, 85th Cong., 1st Sess., 1957, p. 501.

14. C. Wright Mills, The Power Elite, (New York: Oxford University Press, 1959), p. 290.

15. Morris, p. 59.

16. Roscoe Drummond, "Partnership for Peace," Restless Nations, pp. 10-11.

17. From remarks made by the late Secretary General of the United Nations as quoted in Benjamin Higgins, United Nations and U. S. Foreign Economic Policy, p. 179.

18. Barbara Ward, "Imagination in Development," Restless Nations, pp. 182-183.

19. Senate Subcommittee on Banking and Currency, Hearings on S. Res. 264, 1958, pp. 170-171.

20. Ibid., p. 173.

21. U. S. Congress, Senate, Committee on Banking and Currency, Report on the International Development Association, 85th Cong., 2nd Sess., 1958, p. 6.

22. Ibid., p. 7.

23. Ibid.

24. Ibid.

25. Ibid., p. 9.

26. Ibid., p. 11.

27. Interview with an official of the U. S. Treasury Department, January 17, 1963.

28. Interview with U. S. Senator A. S. Mike Monroney, January 25, 1963.

CHAPTER 7

1. Interview with an official of the U. S. Treasury Department, March 12, 1963.

2. IBRD Board of Governors Press Release No. 4, October 6, 1958, p. 3.

3. National Advisory Council on International Monetary and Financial Problems, _Report on the Proposed International Development Association_ (Washington: U. S. Government Printing Office, 1959).

4. _Ibid._, p. 3.

5. _Ibid._, p. 8.

6. _Ibid._

7. _Ibid._, pp. 8-9.

8. _Ibid._

9. _Ibid._, p. 11.

10. _Ibid._, pp. 5-6.

11. _Summary Proceedings of the 1959 Meeting of the Board of Governors of the International Bank for Reconstruction and Development_, (Washington: IBRD, 1959), p. 2.

12. IBRD Board of Governors Press Release No. 10, September 30, 1959, pp. 1-3.

13. IBRD Board of Governors Press Release No. 44, September 30, 1959, p. 2.

14. IBRD Board of Governors Press Release No. 60, September 30, 1959, p. 3.

15. _Ibid._

16. IBRD Board of Governors Press Release No. 68, September 30, 1959, p. 2.

17. IBRD Board of Governors Press Release No. 69, September 30, 1959, p. 3.

18. IBRD Board of Governors Press Release No. 59, September 30, 1959, p. 3.

19. IBRD Board of Governors Press Release No. 42, September 30, 1959, p. 3.

20. IBRD Board of Governors Press Release No. 45, September 30, 1959, pp. 1-2.

21. IBRD Board of Governors Press Release No. 47, September 30, 1959, p. 2.

22. IBRD Board of Governors Press Release No. 65, September 30, 1959, p. 4.

23. IBRD Board of Governors Press Release No. 71, September 30, 1959, p. 3.

24. IBRD Board of Governors Press Release No. 51, September 30, 1959, p. 3.

25. _Summary Proceedings of the 1959 Meeting. . ._, p. 30.

26. Interview, March 13, 1963.

27. Shonfield, p. 156.

28. Interview, January 22, 1963.

29. Interview, March 13, 1963.

30. _Summary Proceedings of the 1959 Meeting. . ._, p. 11.

31. _Summary Proceedings of the 1960 Meeting of the Board of Governors of the International Bank for Reconstruction and Development_ (Washington: IBRD, 1960), p. 11.

32. Asher, p. 54.

33. *Articles of Agreement of the International Development Association*, pp. 3-4.

34. *Ibid.*, p. 11.

35. *Ibid.*

36. IDA Board of Governors Press Release No. 7, September 19, 1961, p. 2.

37. *Articles of Agreement of the International Development Association*, p. 12.

38. P. N. Rosenstein-Rodan, "International Aid for Underdeveloped Countries," *The Review of Economics and Statistics*, XLIII (May, 1961), p. 111.

39. U. S., Senate, Committee on Foreign Relations, *Hearings on S. 3074*, 86th Cong., 2nd Sess., 1960, pp. 22-23.

40. IDA Board of Governors Press Release No. 57, September 19, 1961, p. 5.

41. National Advisory Council on International Monetary and Financial Problems, *Special Report to the President and to the Congress on the Proposed International Development Association* (Washington: U. S. Government Printing Office, 1960).

42. *Ibid.*, p. IV.

43. *Ibid.*, p. 2.

44. *Ibid.*, p. 9.

45 *Ibid.*, p. IV.

46. *Hearings on H. R. 11001*, 86th Cong., 2nd Sess., 1960, p. 3.

47. *Ibid.*, p. 10.

48. *New York Times*, May 19, 1959, p. 10.

49. House Subcommittee 1 of the Committee on Banking and Currency, Hearings on H. R. 1101, 1960, p. 36.

50. Ibid.

51. Research and Policy Committee of the Committee for Economic Development, Economic Development Abroad and the Role of American Foreign Investment (New York: CED, 1956), p. 29.

52. House Subcommittee No. 1 of the Committee on Banking and Currency, Hearings on H. R. 1101, 1960, p. 102.

53. Ibid., p. 55.

54. Ibid., p. 56.

55. "Statement of the National Foreign Trade Council Concerning U. S. Participation in the International Development Association" (New York: National Foreign Trade Council, 1960), pp. 2-3. (Mimeographed.)

CHAPTER 8

1. _Summary Proceedings of the 1951 Meeting . . ._, p. 8.

2. _Ibid._

3. Eugene R. Black, "The Age of Economic Development," _The Economic Journal_, LXX (June, 1960), p. 269.

4. Leonard Rist, "International Cooperation in Development Aid," Address to the Fourth SEANZA Meeting, p. 2.

5. Black, "The Age of Economic Development," p. 269.

6. Black, _The Diplomacy of Economic Development_, p. 27.

7. _Summary Proceedings of the 1961 Meeting of the Board of Governors of the International Bank for Reconstruction and Development_ (Washington: IBRD, 1961), pp. 14-15.

8. Black, "The Age of Economic Development," p. 271.

9. _Annual Report of the International Development Association 1961-62_ (Washington: IDA, 1962), p. 6.

10. _First Annual Report of the International Development Association 1960-1961_ (Washington: IDA, 1961), pp. 4-5.

11. IBRD Board of Governors Press Release No. 4, September 19, 1961, pp. 5-6

12. _Ibid._

13. Interview with J. P. Hayes, Economic Staff, IBRD, January 21, 1963.

14. _Ibid._

15. IBRD Board of Governors Press Release No. 4, September 19, 1961, pp. 5-6.

16. Interview with J. P. Hayes, January 21, 1963.

17. Avramovic et al., *Economic Growth . . .*, p. 40.

18. Interview with J. P. Hayes, January 21, 1963.

19. John C. de Wilde, "Research in the International Bank for Reconstruction and Development," a paper presented to the Annual Meeting of the American Economic Association, December 29, 1962 (Washington: IBRD, 1962), p. 6. (Mimeographed.)

20. *Ibid.*, pp. 6-8.

21. *Ibid.*, pp. 8-9.

22. Eugene R. Black, *Tales of Two Continents* (University of Georgia Ferdinand Phinizy Lectures, 1961), p. 33.

23. *Ibid.*, pp. 33-34.

24. *Ibid.*, p. 34.

25. Shonfield, pp. 84-85.

26. IDA Board of Governors Press Release No. 4, September 19, 1961, pp. 6-7.

27. IDA Board of Governors Press Release No. 3, September 18, 1962, p. 8.

28. IDA Board of Governors Press Release No. 32, September 18, 1962, p. 2.

29. Organization for Economic Co-Operation and Development, *Development Assistance Efforts and Policies: 1963 Review* (Paris: OECD, 1963), p. 13.

30. Shonfield, pp. 116-117.

31. Personal letter from a member of the staff, IBRD, June 24, 1963.

32. Morris, p. 46.

CHAPTER 9

1. Cairncross, p. 18.

2. *Ibid.*, p. 17.

3. Asher, p. 67.

4. *Articles of Agreement of the International Development Association*, p. 10.

5. Cairncross, p. 6.

6. IBRD, *Trade, Development and the World Bank Group* (Washington: IBRD, 1964), pp. 2-3. (Mimeographed.)

7. International Bank for Reconstruction and Development, "A Note on the World Bank," in Black, *The Diplomacy of Economic Development,* p. 63.

8. Leonard Rist, "The Economic Use of International Resources in Financing Development Projects" (Washington: IBRD, 1961). (Mimeographed.)

9. International Bank for Reconstruction and Development, *The World Bank, IFC and IDA Policies and Operations* (Washington: IBRD, 1962), pp. 31-35.

10. Paul N. Rosenstein-Rodan, "International Aid for Underdeveloped Countries," *The Review of Economics and Statistics*, XLIII (May, 1961), p. 107.

11. *Fifth Annual Report of the International Bank for Reconstruction and Development* (Washington: IBRD, 1950), p. 10.

12. Cairncross, p. 27.

13. IDA Board of Governors Press Release No. 13, September 19, 1961, pp. 2-6.

14. IDA Board of Governors Press Release No. 30, September 19, 1961, p. 3.

15. Report of the Executive Directors of the International Bank for Reconstruction and Development on the Articles of Agreement of the International Development Association, p. 7.

16. Hugh B. Ripman, "Statement on Educational Projects and Problems," (Washington: International Development Association, 1962), p. 5. (Mimeographed.)

17. Ibid., p. 8.

18. Ibid., pp. 9-10.

19. Ibid., p. 10.

20. de Wilde, pp. 13-14.

21. Ibid., pp. 15-16.

22. IDA Board of Governors Press Release No. 23, September 18, 1962, p. 2.

23. Ibid.

24. IDA Board of Governors Press Release No. 72, September 20, 1962, p. 4.

25. These three criticisms were made by Governor A. M. Margai of Sierra Leone at the meeting of the International Monetary Fund in September, 1962. See IMF Board of Governors Press Release No. 62, September 19, 1962, p. 2.

26. IMF Board of Governors Press Release No. 68, September 19, 1962, p. 2.

27. IDA Board of Governors Press Release No. 36, September 18, 1962, p. 2.

28. Ibid., p. 3.

29. Ibid.

CHAPTER 10

1. IDA Board of Governors Press Release No. 3, September 18, 1962, p. 6.

2. _Ibid._, p. 7.

3. _Ibid._, p. 8.

4. _Ibid._, pp. 8-9.

5. _Ibid._, p. 9.

6. _Ibid._

7. _Summary Proceedings of the 1962 Annual Meetings of the Board of Governors_ (Washington: IBRD, 1962), p. 73.

8. IDA Board of Governors Press Release No. 40, September 19, 1961, p. 9.

9. OECD, _Development Assistance . . . 1963 Review_, p. 3.

10. "The Need for an Increased 'Soft Credit' Component in Development Aid" (report prepared by the Staff of IDA) (No date). (Mimeographed.)

11. IDA Board of Governors Press Release No.40, September 19, 1961, p. 10.

12. Reference is made to the previously cited study "The Need for an Increased 'Soft Credit' Component in Development Aid" and to the study entitled _Economic Growth and External Debt_ which was circulated among the participants in the United Nations Conference on Trade and Development in 1964 and will be published by Johns Hopkins Press in 1965.

13. International Bank for Reconstruction and Development, _Trade, Development, and the World Bank Group_ (A report submitted to the United Nations Conference on Trade and Development, April 10, 1964), p. 1.

14. Avramovic et al., _Economic Growth and External Debt_, Vol. I, p. 13.

15. IBRD, _The Commodity Problem_ (A report prepared by the Economic Department and circulated to the participants at the United Nations Conference on Trade and Development, May 12, 1964), p. 30.

16. Avramovic et al., _Economic Growth and External Debt_, Vol. I, pp. 46-48.

17. _Ibid._, pp. 53-55.

18. _Ibid._, p. 44.

19. _Ibid._, pp. 58-67.

20. IBRD _Report on Cuba_ (Baltimore: The Johns Hopkins Press, 1951), p. 13.

CHAPTER 11

1. Letter from Charles P. Kindleberger, March 13, 1963.

2. Shonfield, p. 158.

3. Ibid.

4. Interview, March 13, 1963.

5. Letter from Max F. Millikan, April 10, 1963.

6. Ibid.

7. Letter from Barbara Ward, April 13, 1963.

8. Asher, p. 130.

9. Letter from Paul N. Rosenstein-Rodan, May 8, 1963.

10. International Bank for Reconstruction and Development Press Release No. 63/14, May 16, 1963.

11. Ibid.

12. Rao, p. 17.

13. Letter from Jan Tinbergen, (no date).

14. Jan Tinbergen, Shaping the World Economy (New York: The Twentieth Century Fund, 1962), p. 113.

15. Letter from Jan Tinbergen, (no date).

16. Shonfield, p. 156.

17. Tinbergen, p. 114.

18. Higgins, p. 181.

19. Ibid., pp. 181-182.

20. Interview, May 29, 1963.

21. Interview, May 28, 1963.

22. Interview, May 28, 1963.

23. Interview, May 28, 1963.

24. Interview, May 29, 1963.

25. Ibid.

26. Interview, May 29, 1963.

27. Interview, May 28, 1963.

28. Ibid.

29. Annual Report of the International Development Association 1961-62, p. 7.

30. IDA Board of Governors Press Release No. 20, September 18, 1962.

31. Avramovic and Gulhati, Table III and Appendix Table XXI, p. 19 and p. 73.

32. Organization for European Economic Co-operation, The Flow of Financial Resources to Countries in Course of Economic Development 1956-1959, Table I, p. 10.

33. IDA Board of Governors Press Release No. 20, September 18, 1962, p. 4.

34. IDA Board of Governors Press Release No. 5, September 19, 1961, p. 3.

35. Neale, pp. 15-16.

36. Rao, p. 19.

CHAPTER 12

1. Interview with S. R. Cope, August 13, 1964.

2. Interview, May 27, 1963.

3. _Ibid._

4. _Ibid._

5. _Ibid._

6. Interview, May 29, 1963.

7. _Ibid._

8. _Ibid._

9. _Ibid._

10. _Ibid._

11. _Ibid._

12. IDA Board of Governors Press Release No. 31, September 18, 1962, pp. 1-2.

13. IDA Board of Governors Press Release No. 9, September 19, 1961, p. 5.

14. IDA Board of Governors Press Release No. 15, September 18, 1962, p. 2.

15. IDA Board of Governors Press Release No. 19, September 18, 1962, p. 2.

16. See the _Washington Post_ for August 13, 1964, p. C11.

17. IDA Board of Governors Press Release No. 75, September 20, 1962, p. 1.

18. U. S., Congress, House, Subcommittee of the Committee on Appropriations, Hearings on Foreign Operations Appropriations for 1963, 87th Cong., 2nd Sess., 1962, p. 300.

19. Ibid.

20. Ibid.

21. House Subcommittee of the Committee on Appropriations, Hearings, Foreign Operations Appropriations for 1963, 1962, p. 317.

CHAPTER 13

1. U. S., Congress, Senate, Committee on Foreign Relations, *Foreign Assistance Act of 1963*, 88th Cong., 1st Sess., 1963, pp. 8-9.

2. U. S., Congress, Senate, Committee on Foreign Relations, *Hearings on Amendments to Inter-American Development Bank and International Development Association Acts*, 88th Cong., 1st Sess., 1963.

3. *Congressional Record*, January 20, 1964, pp. 625-647.

4. *Ibid.*, p. 637.

5. U. S., Congress, House of Representatives, Subcommittee on International Finance, *Hearings on Expanding the Resources of the International Development Association*, 88th Cong., 1st Sess., 1963.

6. U. S., Congress, House of Representatives, Committee on Banking and Currency, *Hearings on Expanding the Resources of the International Development Association*, 88th Cong., 2nd Sess., 1964.

7. *Congressional Record*, February 25, 1964, pp. 3462-3469, and *Congressional Record*, February 26, 1964, pp. 3500-3514.

8. *Congressional Record*, February 26, 1964, p. 3505.

9. *The Economist*, March 7, 1964, p. 887.

10. U. S., Congress, House of Representatives, Committee on Banking and Currency, *Hearings on the International Development Association Act Amendment*, 88th Cong., 2nd Sess., March 23 and 24, 1964.

11. *Ibid.*, pp. 9-10.

12. *Ibid.*, p. 64.

13. *Congressional Record*, May 13, 1964, pp. 10360-10385.

CHAPTER 14

1. OECD, Development Assistance . . . 1963 Review, pp. 23-24.

2. IDA Board of Governors Press Release No. 50, October 2, 1963, p. 2.

3. IDA Board of Governors Press Release No. 2, September 30, 1963.

4. IDA Board of Governors Press Release, September 7, 1964.

BIBLIOGRAPHY

PUBLIC DOCUMENTS

Gray, Gordon. _Report to the President on Foreign Economic Policies_. Washington, 1950.

Partners in Progress. A Report to the President by the International Development Advisory Board. Washington, 1951.

U. S. _Congressional Record_. 1958-1964.

U. S. Congress, Joint Economic Committee. _Annual Economic Indicators for the U. S. S. R._ 88th Cong., 2nd Sess., 1964.

______. _Economic Policies Toward Less Developed Countries._ 87th Cong., 1st Sess., 1961.

______. _Hearings, Comparisons of the United States and Soviet Economies._ 86th Cong., 1st Sess., 1960.

U. S. House of Representatives, Committee on Banking and Currency. _Hearings, International Development Association Act Amendment._ 88th Cong., 2nd Sess., 1964.

______. _Hearings on Expanding the Resources of the International Development Association_. 88th Cong., 2nd Sess., 1964.

U. S. House of Representatives, Subcommittee No. 1 of the Committee on Banking and Currency. _Hearings on H. R. 11001_. 86th Cong., 2nd Sess., 1960.

U. S. House of Representatives, Subcommittee of the Committee on Appropriations. _Hearings, Foreign Operations Appropriations for 1962._ 87th Cong., 1st Sess., 1961.

______. _Hearings, Foreign Operations Appropriations for 1963._ 87th Cong., 2nd Sess., 1962.

______. Hearings, Foreign Operations Appropriations for 1965. 88th Cong., 2nd Sess., 1964.

U. S. House of Representatives, Subcommittee on International Finance of the Committee on Banking and Currency. Hearings, Expanding the Resources of the International Development Association. 88th Cong., 1st Sess., 1963.

U. S. Senate, Committee on Banking and Currency. Report on the International Development Association. 85th Cong., 2nd Sess., 1958.

U. S. Senate, Committee on Foreign Relations, Hearings on Amendments to Inter-American Development Bank and International Development Association Acts. 88th Cong., 1st Sess., 1963.

______. Hearings on S. 2214. 88th Cong., 1st Sess., 1963.

______. Hearings on S. 3074. 86th Cong., 2nd Sess., 1960.

______. Report on H. R. 7885 To Amend Further The Foreign Assistance Act of 1961, As Amended, and For Other Purposes. 88th Cong., 1st Sess., 1963.

______. United States Foreign Policy--Compilation of Studies. 87th Cong., 1st Sess., 1961.

U. S. Senate, Special Committee to Study the Foreign Aid Program. Foreign Aid Program. 85th Cong., 1st Sess., 1957.

U. S. Senate, Subcommittee of the Committee on Banking and Currency. Hearings on S. Res. 264 (International Development Association). 85th Cong., 2nd Sess., 1958.

BOOKS

Asher, Robert E. Grants, Loans and Local Currencies. Washington: The Brookings Institution, 1961.

Avramovic, Dragoslav. Debt Servicing Capacity and Postwar Growth in International Indebtedness. Baltimore: The Johns Hopkins Press, 1960.

Avramovic, Dragoslav, and Gulhati, Ravi. Debt Servicing Problems of Low-Income Countries, 1956-1958. Baltimore; The Johns Hopkins Press, 1960.

Avramovic, Dragoslav, et al. Economic Growth and External Debt. To be published by John Hopkins Press, 1965.

Barr, Stringfellow. Citizens of the World. Garden City, New York: Doubleday & Company, Inc., 1952.

Benham, Frederic. Economic Aid to Underdeveloped Countries. London: Oxford University Press, 1961.

Black, Eugene R. The Diplomacy of Economic Development. Cambridge: Harvard University Press, 1960.

______. Tales of Two Continents. University of Georgia, Ferdinand Phinizy Lectures, 1961.

Cairncross, Alec. The International Bank for Reconstruction and Development. Princeton University Essays in International Finance No. 33. Princeton: Princeton University, 1959.

Cleveland, Harlan. Introduction to Commander Sir Robert G. A. Jackson. The Case for an International Development Authority. Syracuse: Syracuse University Press, 1959.

Feis, Herbert. Foreign Aid and Foreign Policy. New York: St. Martin's Press, 1964.

Hadwen, John G. and Kaufmann, Johan. How United Nations Decisions Are Made. Leyden: A. W. Sythoff, 1961.

Higgins, Benjamin. United Nations and U. S. Foreign Economic Policy. Homewood, Illinois: Richard D. Irwin, Inc., 1962.

Hoffman, Paul G. One Hundred Countries: One and One Quarter Billion People. Washington: Albert D. and Mary Lasker Foundation, 1960.

International Bank for Reconstruction and Development. Some Techniques of Development Lending. Washington: IBRD, 1960.

______. The World Bank, IFC and IDA: Policies and Operations. Washington: IBRD, 1962.

Jackson, Commander Sir Robert G. A. The Case for an International Development Authority. Syracuse: Syracuse University Press, 1959.

Kenen, Peter B. Giant Among Nations. Chicago: Rand McNally & Company, 1963.

Matecki, B. E. Establishment of the International Finance Corporation and United States Policy. New York: Frederick A. Praeger, 1957.

Mikesell, Raymond F. (ed.). U. S. Private and Government Investment Abroad. Eugene: University of Oregon Books, 1962.

Millikan, Max F. and Rostow, W. W. A Proposal: Key to an Effective Foreign Policy. New York: Harper, 1957.

Morris, James. The Road to Huddersfield: A Journey to Five Continents. New York: Pantheon Books, 1963.

Neale, Alan D. The Flow of Resources from Rich to Poor. Harvard University Center for International Affairs Occasional Papers in International Affairs Number 2. Cambridge: Harvard University, 1961.

Rao, V. K. R. V. International Aid for Economic Development--Possibilities and Limitations. The University of Leeds Eighteenth Montague Burton Lecture on International Relations, 1960.

Restless Nations. New York: Dodd, Mead & Company, 1962.

Robinson, James A. The Monroney Resolution: Congressional Initiative in Foreign Policy Making. Eagleton Institute Cases in Practical Politics, Case 8; McGraw-Hill, 1960.

Shonfield, Andrew. The Attack on World Poverty. New York: Vintage Books, 1962.

Tinbergen, Jan. Shaping the World Economy. New York: The Twentieth Century Fund, 1962.

ARTICLES AND PERIODICALS

Black, Eugene R. "The Age of Economic Development," The Economic Journal, LXX (June, 1960), 266-276.

Dayton Daily News. 1958.

Des Moines Register. 1958.

The Economist. 1958-1964.

Manila Daily Bulletin. November 24, 1956.

New York Times. 1958-1964.

Patel, S. J. "Export Prospects and Economic Growth: India," The Economic Journal, LXIX (September, 1959), 490-506.

Rosenstein-Rodan, Paul N. "International Aid for Underdeveloped Countries," The Review of Economics and Statistics, XLIII (May, 1961), 107-138.

St. Louis Post-Dispatch. 1958.

Washington Post. 1958-1964.

REPORTS

Annual Reports of the International Bank for Reconstruction and Development. Washington: IBRD, 1949-1964.

Annual Reports of the International Development Association. Washington: IDA, 1961-1964.

International Bank for Reconstruction and Development. Report on Cuba. Baltimore: The Johns Hopkins Press, 1951.

______. Economic Growth and External Debt, Vol. I. Washington: IBRD, IDA, 1964.

______. The Commodity Problem. Washington: IBRD, 1964.

______. Trade, Development, and the World Bank Group. A report submitted by the President of the Bank to the United Nations Conference on Trade and Development and to the United Nations Commission on International Commodity Trade. Washington: IBRD, 1964.

National Advisory Council on International Monetary and Financial Problems. Report on the Proposed International Development Association. Washington: U. S. Government Printing Office, 1959.

______. Semiannual Reports. Washington: U. S. Government Printing Office, 1958-1963.

______. Special Report to the President and to the Congress on the Proposed International Development Association. Washington: U. S. Government Printing Office, 1960.

Organization for Economic Co-operation and Development. Development Assistance Efforts and Policies in 1961. Paris: OECD, 1962.

______. Development Assistance Efforts and Policies, 1963 Review. Paris: OECD, 1963.

Organization for European Economic Co-operation. The Flow of Financial Resources to Countries in Course of Economic Development 1956-1959. Paris: OEEC, 1961.

Report of the Executive Directors of the International Bank for Reconstruction and Development on the Articles of Agreement of the International Development Association. Washington: IBRD, 1960.

Research and Policy Committee of the Committee for Economic Development. Economic Development Abroad and the Role of American Foreign Investment. New York: Committee for Economic Development, 1956.

United Nations Conference on Trade and Development. Final Act of the United Nations Conference on Trade and Development. New York, 1964. E/CONF.46/L.28

______. Department of Economic Affairs. Measures for the Economic Development of Under-Developed Countries. New York, 1951. E/1986/ST/ECA/10.

______. Methods of Financing Economic Development in Under-Developed Countries. Lake Success, 1949. Sales No: 1949. II. B.4.

______. Report on a Special United Nations Fund for Economic Development--Submitted by a Committee Appointed by the Secretary-General. New York, 1953. E/2381.

______. Department of Economic and Social Affairs. International Economic Assistance to the Less Developed Countries. New York, 1961. E/3395/Rev. 1.

______. Economic and Social Council, Sub-Commission on Economic Development. Report of the Third Session of the Sub-Commission on Economic Development. New York, 1949. E/CN.1/165.

______. General Assembly. Special United Nations Fund for Economic Development. New York, 1954. A/2728.

______. Special United Nations Fund for Economic Development. New York, 1955. A/2906.

UNPUBLISHED MATERIAL

Demuth, Richard H. "Statement on Behalf of the International Bank for Reconstruction and Development Before the Economic, Employment and Development Commission." Washington: IBRD, 1951. (Mimeographed.)

de Wilde, John C. "Research in the International Bank for Reconstruction and Development." Washington: IBRD, 1962. (Mimeographed.)

Ripman, Hugh B. "Statement on Educational Projects and Problems." Washington: IDA, 1962. (Mimeographed.)

Rist, Leonard. "International Assistance to Underdeveloped Countries." Address before the Conference of Business Economists. February 21, 1964.

______. "International Cooperation in Development Aid." Washington: IBRD, 1962. (Mimeographed.)

______. "The Capacity to Service Foreign Debts." Washington: IBRD, 1962. (Mimeographed.)

______. "The Economic Use of International Resources in Financing Development Projects." Washington: IBRD, 1961. (Mimeographed.)

"Statement of the National Foreign Trade Council Concerning U. S. Participation in the International Development Association." New York: National Foreign Trade Council, 1960. (Mimeographed.)

"The Need for an Increased 'Soft Credit' Component in Development Aid." A report prepared by the staff of the International Development Association. (no date) (Mimeographed.)

Wilson, Geoffrey M. "World Bank Operations." Address to Economic Commission of the Council of Europe, Paris, December 16, 1963.

______. "Technical Assistance Activities of the World Bank." Address to the Institute of Banking and Financial Studies, Paris, June 4, 1964.

______. "The World Bank's Role in Development Assistance." Speech before the Federation of Swedish Industries, Stockholm, April 15, 1964.

Woods, George D. "Activities of the World Bank and Its Affiliates." Address to the United Nations Economic and Social Council, United Nations, N. Y., April 5, 1963.

______. Address to the Economic and Social Council of the United Nations, United Nations, N. Y., December 18, 1963.

______. Address to the Investment Bankers Association, Hollywood, Florida. December 5, 1963.

OTHER SOURCES

Articles of Agreement of the International Development Association. Washington: IDA, 1960.

International Bank for Reconstruction and Development. Board of Governors Press Releases, 1958-1964.

______. Personal interview with Dragoslav Avramovic, Assistant Director - Economic Department (in charge), August 10, 1964.

______. Personal interview with Eugene R. Black. March 13, 1963

______. Personal interview with J. Burke Knapp, Vice President, IBRD. January 22, 1963.

______. Personal interviews with J. P. Hayes, Economic Staff, IBRD. January, 1963; March, 1963; May, 1963.

______. Personal interview with K. S. Sundara Rajan, Executive Director for India, IBRD. August 10, 1964.

______. Personal interview with Michael L. Hoffman. January 22, 1963.

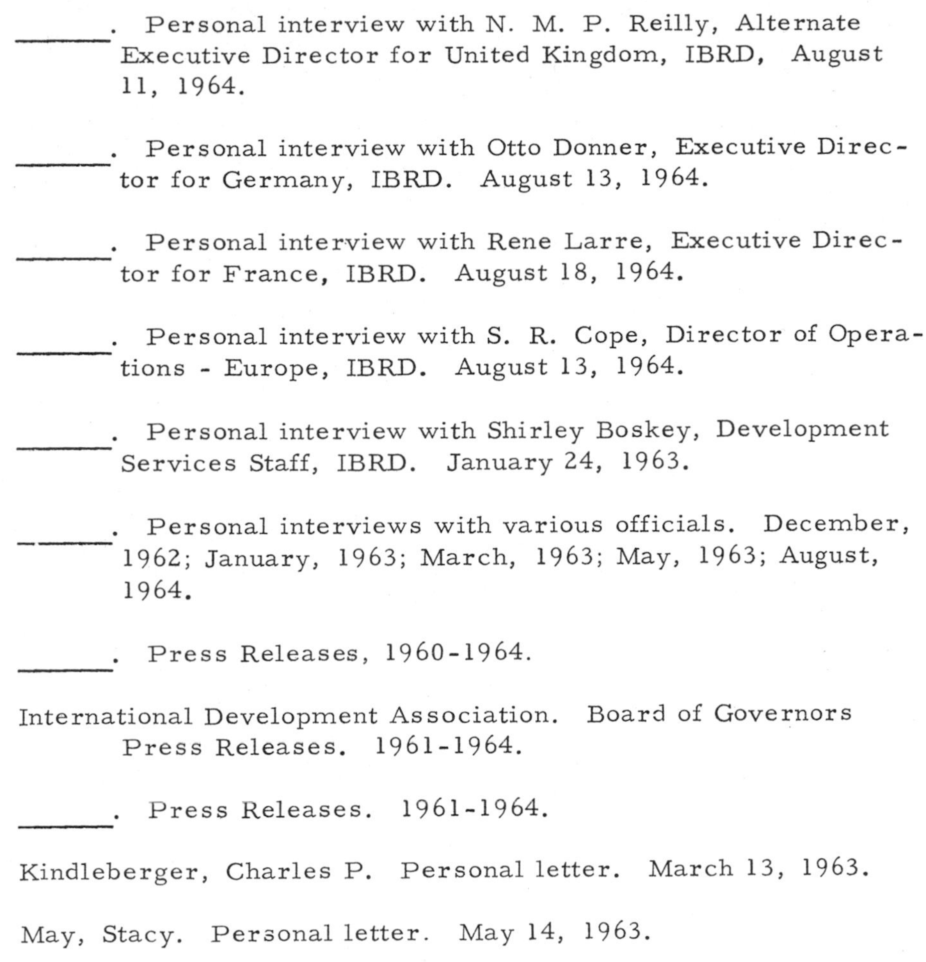

______. Personal interview with N. M. P. Reilly, Alternate Executive Director for United Kingdom, IBRD, August 11, 1964.

______. Personal interview with Otto Donner, Executive Director for Germany, IBRD. August 13, 1964.

______. Personal interview with Rene Larre, Executive Director for France, IBRD. August 18, 1964.

______. Personal interview with S. R. Cope, Director of Operations - Europe, IBRD. August 13, 1964.

______. Personal interview with Shirley Boskey, Development Services Staff, IBRD. January 24, 1963.

______. Personal interviews with various officials. December, 1962; January, 1963; March, 1963; May, 1963; August, 1964.

______. Press Releases, 1960-1964.

International Development Association. Board of Governors Press Releases. 1961-1964.

______. Press Releases. 1961-1964.

Kindleberger, Charles P. Personal letter. March 13, 1963.

May, Stacy. Personal letter. May 14, 1963.

Millikan, Max F. Personal letter. April 10, 1963.

Piel, Gerard. "For the Living Generation." Address delivered in New Delhi, published in Nature, Vol. 202. April 11, 1964.

Rosenstein-Rodan, Paul N. Personal letter. May 8, 1963.

Summary Proceedings of the Meetings of the Board of Governors of the International Bank for Reconstruction and Development. Washington: IBRD, 1949-1964.

Tinbergen, Jan. Personal letter. (no date).

U. S. Senate. Personal interview with Senator A. S. Mike Monroney. January 25, 1963.

U. S. Treasury Department. Personal interviews with various officials. January, 1963; March, 1963; August, 1964.

Ward, Barbara. Personal letter. April 13, 1963.